THE
HILLARY EFFECT:
POLITICS, SEXISM AND THE DESTINY OF LOSS

"The ones who call themselves 'Marshans' read her posts every day...legions of Hillary Clinton fans who have made Marsh their de facto leader."

The Washington Post

The Hillary Effect:

Politics, Sexism and the Destiny of Loss

By Taylor Marsh

For my blue-collar husband,

who bet it all.

Hillary Clinton sculpture by Karen Caldicott

Premier Digital Publishing
www.PremierDigitalPublishing.com
Follow us on Twitter @PDigitalPub
Follow us on Facebook: Premier Digital Publishing

Taylor Marsh
www.taylormarsh.com
Follow Taylor on Twitter @TaylorMarsh
Follow Taylor on Facebook: Taylor Marsh

Note: *Certain minor changes have been made in quoted material for purposes of style only.*

To be involved in politics you have to grow skin as thick as a rhinoceros.

—Eleanor Roosevelt

There are three sides to every story: your side, my side and the truth. And no one is lying...

— Robert Evans, *The Kid Stays in the Picture*, 1994

CONTENTS

Introduction

Some consider Hillary Rodham Clinton a lightning rod; some consider her a heroine. One thing is certain: Not even a decade into our twenty-first century, Hillary became the human conductor through which our country's political sexism was forever changed, if not exorcised. Her presidential campaign was ugly, exhilarating and historic, and because of it (thankfully), the new generation of women rising up won't have to face the same kinds of assaults. The sheer onslaught of sexism directed at her ended the effectiveness of these types of smears.

Hillary was the first female presidential candidate to come out of the modern feminist movement. Her candidacy is also the last of its kind.

> My mother was born before women could vote. My daughter got to vote for her mother for president....
>
> — Hillary Rodham Clinton (Democratic convention, 2008)

It was Hillary who finally convinced me to join her fight. I didn't start out to be a "die-hard Clintonite." Far from it. Yet that's the tag I earned in a *Washington Post* profile back in June 2008.

It all began with a silly public spat when the Clinton team advertised on right-wing websites like Townhall, Power Line and Captain's Quarters at the kickoff of the Democratic primary battle. I called out this strategy on the Huffington Post, as well as in my new-media blog, and the *National Journal*'s Hotline On Call blog picked up my critique, asking Clinton's national spokesperson Phil Singer for a response. "We're on some conservative sites because we're not ceding any territory," he said. "We take nothing for granted."

Well, that in a nutshell described the Clinton team problem out of the gate. They were running a general election campaign before they'd won the nomination. A shock was on its way that would rock the political world.

Clinton's political potential lit up the right long before she ran for president. Her adversaries sensed when she was first lady that they'd better take care of her, hoping to stop her before she got started. When she ran for president, the right was joined by adversaries on the left, with the media piling on and playing along.

Since Hillary Rodham Clinton ran for president women have made even more progress. We had Ladies' Night in the 2010 elections, with women on the right rising and Sarah Palin leading their way. Then in 2011, Rep. Michele Bachmann became the Tea Party presidential hopeful, raising more money in the first quarter of the year than all the other GOP wannabes, including Mitt Romney, the fragile front-runner at the time.

I was well into contemplating this book when the 2010 Ladies' Night happened. It was remarkable for many reasons, especially since the women who won didn't have to fight the gender war. In fact, gender wasn't even an issue. With some help from Sarah Palin, the first woman to benefit from the Hillary Effect, conservative women ruled, and none of them had to wage the old politics-of-sex battle.

But let's not get carried away. As of 2011, the United States is around seventieth on the list of world nations when it comes to female representation, according to renowned feminist and journalist, Gloria Steinem. We've got seventy-six women in the House of Representatives, seventeen senators and six governors.

Their successes, however limited, were made possible by a lot of women who came before. Shirley Chisholm was the first to take the white-male-only sign off the White House door, to paraphrase Steinem. But no woman was more responsible for the 2010 Ladies' Night than Hillary Rodham Clinton, who rose above the she's-only-running-because-of-her-husband stereotype to become the only first lady ever elected to the U.S. Senate and also the first woman to run the presidential gauntlet in every primary and caucus across the country.

Her campaign for president in 2008 was the first and last political sexism battle of its kind, and I was on the front lines covering it, eventually taking Hillary's side. I knew she couldn't fight what was coming at her alone.

If I weren't completely sure the political gender battles had turned the corner before then, all doubt vanished on Ladies' Night, 2010, when I realized even career Clinton-hater Chris Matthews saw the Hillary Effect.

Hillary Clinton would not have been such a strong contender for the Presidency in 2008 if she had not had the courage to run for the Senate in 2000. That took her to the highest level of political competition. It could well be that her strong showing is what's inspired these other women to test their mettle in the ring this year.

— Chris Matthews, *Hardball*, June 8, 2010

It was a body-snatcher moment and a far cry from the Chris Matthews who had pilloried Hillary for a living for close to two decades.

Hillary Clinton's rise, defeat and comeback to record popularity represents a coming-of-age journey for this country. After nearly twenty years in the national spotlight, her fight against the smears and sexist assaults by traditional and new media, and the obsessive and pointless attention to her hair, cleavage and pantsuits were all coming to an end. The Republican attacks, the mindless misogyny, the endless sexism that had followed Hillary from the time she became first lady to the day she endorsed Barack Obama and then became his secretary of state — none of it could make a dent anymore.

Nostalgia set in at *National Review* Online in January 2008 via a post by Lisa Schiffren:

> I am having a tiny little pang of missing Hillary. Not her, but hating her. Hating Hillary has been such a central political impulse for so long now — fifteen years — and I have had to work so hard to keep it up as she became more appealing looking, less shrill, more human — I don't really know what I will do with that newly freed strand of energy.

Hillary had to happen. It was her destiny to take the heat and lead the way for other women. Sarah Palin was the first to benefit from Hillary's courageous path; it was her celebrity that helped put the Tea Party on the map. And even if her power would begin to recede as it did after the 2010 midterms, Palin helped pave the path for Michele Bachmann.

This book is about the heartbreaking journey we all made with Hillary. Many hope it isn't over, though no one can argue she hasn't already made her mark on history.

By the time Hillary lost the nomination to Barack Obama, all vestiges of inevitability, the Clinton-machine myth and the ironclad advantage of insider status would be flipped on their heads.

Out of defeat, Fighting Hillary would emerge, rallying women, the middle class and blue-collar workers, just as her husband had done before her, in a campaign style that lifted our hearts and brought praise from unlikely quarters.

How Hillary's campaign team missed that a female candidate at the top of the Democratic ticket was change-on-steroids is beyond me. Hillary's campaign was founded at a moment in political history when experience was equated with the nightmare in Iraq, and yet the campaign went with "experience on day one."

I was hearing a different theme song: "I learned a lot from my husband, but this is not his campaign," she would say, with her mother and daughter Chelsea standing beside her. This theme had its roots in a signature Hillary speech from September 1995, when, as first lady, she addressed the U.N. Fourth World Conference on Women in Beijing, China, confronting the Chinese and the world about the treatment of women. Her talk lit up the international press and solidified the cause of her political life: "Human rights are women's rights, and women's rights are human rights.

"It is a violation of human rights when babies are denied food, or drowned, or suffocated, or their spines broken, simply because they are born girls," she told the conference.

> It is a violation of human rights when women and girls are sold into the slavery of prostitution for human greed — and the kinds of reasons that are used to justify this practice should no longer be tolerated.
>
> It is a violation of human rights when women are doused with gasoline, set on fire and burned to death because their marriage dowries are deemed too small.
>
> It is a violation of human rights when individual women are raped in their own communities and when thousands of women are subjected to rape as a tactic or prize of war.
>
> It is a violation of human rights when a leading cause of death worldwide among women ages 14 to 44 is

the violence they are subjected to in their own homes by their own relatives.

It is a violation of human rights when young girls are brutalized by the painful and degrading practice of genital mutilation.

It is a violation of human rights when women are denied the right to plan their own families, and that includes being forced to have abortions or being sterilized against their will.

It was arguably the most significant public moment of her life to date and revealed Hillary as a fighter and international feminist. It wasn't a presidential platform, but it was a starting point for a presidential campaign in a country where women were becoming the majority in our nation's workplaces, at a time when the "man-cession" was hitting.

Perhaps it was watching what happened to Hillary that makes me one of the fairest people on the left writing about Sarah Palin and Michele Bachmann, taking both women on through issues and leaving the personal insults to the partisans, media hacks and comedians. As with Palin, Bachmann's gaffes and fact-challenged statements too often provide the perfect set-up for her critics, except when her husband Marcus becomes the issue.

We're in the twenty-first century mega-new-media world, where everything is faster and more complicated, with missteps more costly because everyone has become a witness.

President Bill Clinton learned this the hard way. He's a political genius adept at scorched-earth tactics, but when he found himself campaigning for his candidate wife, who was up against the most gifted African American politician in U.S. history, things quickly careened out of his control. Serious health issues exacerbated by stress only made matters worse. It was a tough turn for the most gifted politician of the modern era, once thought of as the "first black president." But the Comeback Kid proved his resilience yet again, his popularity back and intact, even if his secretary of state wife bests him (and President Obama) in that category today.

Nobody has written this story. But if you're looking for a 2008 primary season rehash, you're out of luck. This is much broader, because the politics of sexism didn't start in 2008, though it was Hillary's presidential run that brought the issue to a head. Now 2012 is upon us, and President Obama is looking much different than he did in 2008, admitting he's a bit "grayer and a little dinged-up."

Clearly, the new political landscape is uncertain and volatile for everyone.

By the time the debt ceiling debacle was finished, just before President Obama's fiftieth birthday, "hope and change" had been reduced to a stale mirage.

I may have ended up being tagged the "online team captain" for Clinton by the *Washington Post*, becoming one of her most vocal advocates in a media landscape that extended from MSNBC to CNN and C-SPAN to Al Jazeera English and beyond, but it's not where I began. I never expected to get profiled in the *Washington Post* and the *New Republic*, but with my site (www.taylormarsh.com) becoming the go-to place on the web for a lot of Hillary fans, as I took on the media spin that piled up against her, it put me on the front lines as well as the firing line. Obama fans hated me (some still do), and when Obama won the nomination and I backed him, which was never in doubt, Hillary fans started hating me too (some still do). Meanwhile, I've returned back to an independent state. Though still a big lib, I've fought my last hyper-partisan war.

What I learned on the front lines of the campaign of the first female candidate to win a presidential primary in American history, while watching the first Republican female vice president burst onto the scene unprepared, is part of a larger tale about the politics of sex at the dawn of the twenty-first century, which includes the media's role in shaping the story. This is a political tale, but it's also personal. Electing the first female president slipped through our fingers, and how it happened is deeply troubling to me.

Team Clinton's failures were monumental, and I saw them from as close as you can get without being inside. For most, that would be too close to write about; for others, it's just too painful to relive. It's as honest an account as I can render, which likely won't make everyone happy. Candor is never kind.

Hillary Rodham Clinton's presidential run is the most important political event for women in modern American history, regardless of your politics.

But I guess if you want to complete the terrain of play in American politics today, the story of Scott Brown is as good as any. As the Massachusetts special election for the late Ted Kennedy's Senate seat heated up, Brown's story provided a cruel, ironic twist for the family who'd written many chapters in the politics-of-sex book. A nude, *Cosmopolitan* centerfold spread of Brown, one he'd posed for when he was in college, was splashed across the Internet during his campaign. Voters didn't flinch and didn't care. They elected him senator anyway.

What would have been the outcome if Scott Brown had been a woman and the magazine had been *Playboy*?

We haven't come that far, baby.

Chapter 1: **What If?**

Hillary deserved a lot better than what she got from her campaign team.

What if the numbskulls in her campaign had kept their mouths shut and kept their internal bickering private?

The girlie-type gossip coming out of Hillaryland was galactically self-defeating, and nothing was more frustrating than reading this drivel splashed across the web. The orgasmic gloating that ensued because Ms. Inevitable couldn't control her campaign was as predictable as it was nauseating.

What if the national news media hadn't become part of the primary story?

What if the elite Democrats who inhabited the upper echelons of Camp Clinton hadn't been so self-destructive?

How could the '90s Dem dinosaurs not "get" online fundraising, causing Hillary Rodham Clinton to end up writing herself a whopping multimillion-dollar check at the height of the primaries? Had campaign chairman Terry McAuliffe been asleep during Howard Dean's rise? This embarrassing nightmare of a fundraising fiasco galvanized Hillary's fan base, but it also freaked the hell out of everyone. (Since my site was the safe haven for many Hillary fans at the time, I witnessed this first hand.)

What if Hillaryland hadn't bought into pollster and analyst Mark Penn's assumption that the race would be over by February 5, as Clinton herself said off-camera to George Stephanopoulos in December, 2007? It hardly matters that her respected veteran political strategist Harold Ickes believed it too, but it sure does explain the caucus-states clusterfuck that ensued.

What if Maggie Williams, Mandy Grunwald and Howard Wolfson, with Peter Daou's expertise showing the team the way on the web, had been on point from the start?

What if Hillary had known and understood what it meant that Iowa was as backward as Mississippi when it came to electing women?

I know this what-if stuff is insufferable, but I've got to get it out of my system, because it's not just that Hillary lost the nomination due to sexism, compounded by media malpractice and general American misogyny alone. The campaign's own unforced errors ensured political panic and general mayhem. After all, we're talking about a front-runner who blew a thirty-point lead. A male would have been inducted into the political collapse hall of fame for such an epic cave-in. On the other hand, if a male had a thirty-point lead, it's just as likely everyone else would have respectfully folded.

And don't get upset at me for leveling a little Trumanesque truth. Anyone following Hillary in the '90s knew she was going to have a formidable force opposing her nomination from the right. While Democratic primary voters wanted her to choke on her Iraq war vote, so she couldn't afford self-induced mistakes.

What if Hillary hadn't placed loyalty above her own candidacy?

What were Patti Solis Doyle and Mark Penn doing at the top of her campaign pyramid? As campaign mistakes go, we're talking the dumb and dumber of decision making.

What if Hillaryland had remembered Obama's 2004 convention speech and understood he was a formidable — aw, hell, no one believed Obama would be a presidential threat in 2008, a point in time when paying political dues was wiped off the map. (See Sarah Palin.)

Sarah's not a focus of this story, but she weaves through it, her headline role on the right a first, as she followed Hillary's lead, lending her support for other women like Rep. Michele Bachmann, South Carolina's Nikki Haley, who became governor, as well as New Hampshire's Kelly Ayotte, who bailed on being attorney general to run for Senate in 2010, which got her pegged as "the next Sarah Palin." The last laugh was Ayotte's, however, because she's now sitting in the Senate.

The Hillary Effect phenomenon occurred the moment Fighting Hillary of the late 2008 primary season left the political stage, and the one-time candidate began campaigning for Barack Obama, leaving women and many other Americans with the feeling that a great opportunity had passed us by.

Don't get me wrong. In the Drexel University debate in October 2007, when Hillary was still the front-runner, she talked about her "record of thirty-five years fighting for women and children and people who feel invisible and left out in this country," as well as her efforts in Arkansas in expanding education and health care in that state. But Fighting Hillary wasn't the carrier of her campaign's message, which seesawed from one theme to another, from "In to Win" and "Renew the Promise of America," to "Working for Change, Working for You."

The what-ifs for Hillary began with her Iraq war vote in 2002. No, wait, what was the rationale again? Her vote was simply to authorize George W. Bush to have the power he needed as commander in chief to do what he felt was necessary.

Really?

What if Hillary had read the ninety-page classified version of the National Intelligence Estimate? Clinton never said she read the classified NIE, saying instead she'd been "briefed" on it. That story originally broke in the book *Her Way*, co-written by Whitewater fiction writer Jeff Gerth and Don Van Natta Jr. Philippe Reines, Hillary's Senate aide at the time (who later followed her to the State Department), confirmed this in a widely reported email, saying Senator Clinton was "briefed multiple times by several members of the administration on their intelligence regarding Iraq, including being briefed on the NIE." Now, only six or so senators read the classified version, which is unconscionable, but one of them, Senator Bob Graham, chairman of the Intelligence committee, urged his colleagues on the Senate floor to do so. Graham voted no on authorization, because of what he'd read in the classified NIE.

I don't know exactly when it became cool to advocate that the founders wanted the executive branch to have unfettered war powers without congressional approval or a declaration of war, but it was cemented somewhere around the time of Vietnam. That legacy continued in 2011, when President Obama decided to attack Libya.

Hillary trying to sell Democratic primary voters that she didn't vote for war was like listening to John Kerry say he voted for the $87 billion in supplemental military funding before he voted against it. It was a nightmare. But it's not like Hillary was alone. All potential presidential candidates who were in the Senate did the same thing. No doubt she believed it, because you can't be the first female vying for commander in chief in America and vote against a war in the age of the war on terror. That was the conventional wisdom for good reason: Against Republicans you need your hawk status secured. Chicks must channel toughness. It was general election strategy thinking.

Hillary's Iraq war vote was the beginning of an offensive crouch that would eventually put her presidential campaign on the defensive for the duration. Considering that it also led to Bill Clinton's ill-received "fairy tale" line about Obama's voting record, it's an understatement to say that an apology would have been a hell of a lot cheaper.

But her Iraq war vote didn't take her down.

Timing is everything.

What if Hillary had run in 2004? George W. Bush was the perfect Democratic target, with no clear-cut candidate considered a shoo-in to take him on.

It was an open contest. So began the political "three bears" conversation for Democrats in 2004. Howard Dean had a lot of people behind him, but the Democratic establishment had no intention of letting that happen, even though no one could have predicted how he'd fall. John Edwards was too new. Or was he too slick? John Kerry was possible, but anyone could see the challenges his candidacy raised. From the start there was no clear answer to who could beat Bush, the war president.

So, why didn't Hillary run in 2004? The only thing blocking her was that she'd promised New Yorkers she'd serve out her first full Senate term. If watching Clinton in the 1990s didn't convince you she is a woman of commitments, well, you probably won't get this part of her story either. Even with the field filled with men nobody knew for sure could make it all the way, Clinton's eyes remained on the Senate.

Contrast that to Barack Obama in 2008. He didn't have the pledge problem, or at least, there is no evidence he felt encumbered by it. He likely saw it as an arbitrary line set by someone in the media asking a question he was under no obligation to honor. Even though he'd told Tim Russert on *Meet the Press* (November 7, 2004) that he'd serve out his full term as senator, Obama didn't miss a beat when he changed his mind. The people would either get over it or not, but he was running. Something told Barack Obama the people wouldn't care about some pledge, and he was right. Besides, he was getting all sorts of encouragement from the Democratic Party establishment under the radar that he'd have their covert support. His instincts took it from there.

Sarah Palin was the same. Sarah Palin got her chance after Hillary exited the scene by riding the Hillary Effect to become the first Republican female on a national ticket. Her galvanizing popularity also gave her the chutzpah to bail on being governor, which was based not on a calling of purpose so much as on an opportunity to cash in. And why shouldn't she? Oh, and it was also based on the media swarm, which she admitted to Tucker Carlson's conservative Daily Caller website in late July 2010: "By her own admission, Palin let the press play a key role in her decision to pull the plug on her governorship."

Sarah Palin was the anti-Hillary.

While Hillary remained committed to the Senate, it doesn't change the fact that a Clinton against a Bush in 2004 would have been quite a battle, perhaps the perfect contest. Two dynasties fighting it out once again, two heirs in different ways, but similarly suited in the game of political warfare. The hard-boiled fighting of Karl Rove versus the famous Clinton do-whatever-it-takes-to-win machine, with even Mark Penn fitting perfectly in this battle of the establishments. She could also have taken her Iraq vote and stuffed it down George W. Bush's throat, using it as an impeachment of Bush's judgment, as the Democratic primary voter was itching for. Getting even for being deceived would have been her sweet revenge. The people would likely have signed on and learned to love it, and she wouldn't have felt forced to say she was sorry for her Iraq vote, which was always a non-starter. The passion she would reveal in standing up against Bush, once commonly judged as shrill or un-ladylike anger, would have come through as tough commitment to a cause and would easily have converted into commander in chief stuff. One is left to wonder if anything could have stopped Clinton.

By the time 2008 came around, everyone was tired of anything tied to the past, which went double for a Bush or a Clinton. Hillary was also tethered to the Clinton '90s, some parts of which people still hadn't come to terms with (and many never will). This would play out in the 2008 primaries, when Clinton's campaign didn't have a solid answer to the "change" cry, which is likely why there was never a consistent message coming out of Hillaryland. Instead, they decided that even after the Keystone Cops routine of

Bush, Cheney, Rumsfeld, et al., Hillary's presence inside Bill Clinton's presidency amounted to right-stuff experience. Because the experience pitch had turned out so bloody well during the Bush-Cheney era.

Hillary's adversaries only remembered years of Clinton drama and the failures of "Hillarycare" at a moment when health care was one of the main issues. Movement progressives, a major political force after Howard Dean's incendiary presidential bid and very successful Democratic National Committee (DNC) chairman tour, were skeptical of Hillary over Iraq. But the abysmal outcome on health care made them doubly doubtful, though there were other issues too, starting with her husband's Third Way strategy, NAFTA and Wall Street coziness.

People had also started dreaming about the post-Bush era very early. We couldn't wait to put the torturous nightmare behind us.

Hillary was tied to George W. Bush through her Iraq war vote, which Democratic primary voters intended to make her pay for or at the very least explain away. It was a challenge from the start, but by October 2007 she was thirty points ahead. Her lead would be wiped out by the time voting started in Iowa, January 2008.

What if Hillary had begun her campaign understanding what it meant that Iowa had never elected a female governor or member of Congress?

Senator Clinton told a *Des Moines Register* columnist that she was "shocked" to hear of Iowa's failure to elect a female governor or member of Congress and said it posed a "special burden" for her. "I have to maybe reassure people here maybe more than I do in New Hampshire, which has had a woman governor," she told the *Christian Science Monitor* on October 26, 2007.

A special burden — was she kidding? Try an insurmountable obstacle, unless met directly. Especially since, according to the Associated Press, as early as June 2007 deputy campaign manager Mike Henry wrote in a campaign memo that Iowa was "our consistently weakest state." Iowa came smack up against the Clinton campaign's inevitability mantra, turning it into a cow pie of presumption.

The traditional and rural nature of Iowa was stacked against her unless she did something to turn it upside down. What if she'd campaigned with her daughter and mother by her side from the start in this state? The quote she would later use about her mother being born before women had the right to vote, as her daughter Chelsea stood next to her representing an empowered new generation, hangs as the mother of all what-ifs. Iowa had been a place where "standing by her man" had polled well during the '90s impeachment hearings, giving her the highest approval of her public life, 67% according to Gallup, which obviously helped her with Iowans. Playing the traditional generational card for all its corn-pone worth was a natural.

Before Hillary finally freed herself of Mark Penn, her political survival instincts seemed to be in the deep freeze. By the time Penn went back to polling patrol, it was too late. No one had figured out what it would take to mount a campaign in an environment where she had to change public perception about who she was.

It wasn't until she'd lost the numbers game that Hillary was freed from the fear of failure, with her loyal supporters pushing her on because they still believed. That's when Fighting Hillary surfaced, an integral part of her persona once again up front, and she started taking it to Obama across blue-collar America. Late in the primary race, Fighting Hillary mesmerized crowds, for a moment making Barack Obama recede from view. Hillary now appeared as the heroine of the middle class in a way that had Clinton supporters wondering what if?

By the time the debt ceiling deal was reached, blogs like Talking Points Memo, the front line in Obama support during the primaries, ran a post with a "Buyer's Remorse?" headline. Thomas Lane wrote, after quoting an email that expressed real anger over supporting Obama over Clinton, "To judge from TPM's inbox that fury is not isolated."

But the power of fan politics ruled in '08.

What if Fighting Hillary had shown up from the start? What if the inevitable Hillary had never been launched? What if?

There are moments you learn about when you're lying in a heap of exhaustion, tears and frustration, when the genesis of things you once ranted about comes to light and pushes you to line up tequila shots.

Take a Clinton campaign anecdote that surfaced in the *New York Observer* on February 27, 2008. In response to an aide suggesting that Hillary show a little bit of humanity, Mark Penn responded, "Oh, come on, being human is overrated." Yeah, because poll-driven politics is so freaking inspiring.

Emotion is the most powerful force in American politics, and 2008 was the political tsunami of emotion. Nothing beats it. Right-wing radio exists because of it. Talk radio hosts have been rubbing Democratic noses in it for two decades. Far right institutions have been using emotion to drive elections since before Ronald Reagan. Emotion drove John F. Kennedy to make his speech on Catholicism. Karl Rove didn't pull anti-gay marriage referendums in 2004 out of his ass; they came out of emotion, proving the adage that the most committed wins. Emotions drive people to get out and vote and often to make the difference.

When a politician captures the emotions of a moment in time, it's like bottling lightning. It created Barack Obama's voter connection, which Clinton mined as Fighting Hillary.

There is nothing more personal for people who vote and pay attention to politics than their choice for president. The president comes into our living room every single day for at least four years. How people feel about him or her matters. It's not a rational aspect of politics. Emotions fuel fan politics, which attaches voters to a particular politician, rather than the issues. They turn politics personal. The connection can happen in an instant, and facts have little to do with it.

Hillary Clinton's win in New Hampshire, after getting her hubris handed to her in Iowa, taught that lesson. Not just through Hillary's transparent moment of vulnerability, but also through the reaction of the media watching and reporting it. In Portsmouth, New Hampshire, all it took was an innocuous slice of girl-talk, but it re-ignited a candidate and changed the course of the campaign.

"How did you get out the door every day? I mean, as a woman, I know how hard it is to get out of the house and get ready. Who does your hair?"

When Hillary began her response to the voter's questions you had no idea where she was going, and neither did she. But anyone who saw the moment replayed over the hours before the vote knew that something powerful had happened.

"I just don't want to see us fall backward as a nation. I mean, this is very personal for me. Not just political. I see what's happening. We have to reverse it. Some people think elections are a game: Who's up or who's down. It's about our country. It's about our kids' future. It's about all of us together. Some of us put ourselves out there and do this against some difficult odds...."

Media reaction was immediate. *Newsweek* (January 6, 2008) asked, "A Muskie moment, or a helpful glimpse of 'the real Hillary'?"

Senator Edmund Muskie, of course, was the man who, in an emotional moment of defending his wife during the 1972 campaign, scuttled his presidential chances by tearing up. (See John Wayne's America before it became Jack Bauer's, and long before Speaker John Boehner made high-profile crying a common occurrence.)

America had never seen this side of Hillary Rodham Clinton. What happened in New Hampshire was the sticky stuff of emotional connection. However, no one knew what would be the reaction, let alone the outcome. It may have been just one moment in front of sixteen New Hampshire primary voters, but it was a campaign event that broke wide.

Sure, some people felt it was contrived, but whoever thought Hillary would take such an emotions-laid-bare gamble didn't account for voters' unpredictability over this type of display. Some things you just don't plan, and sometimes you just get lucky.

The uncharacteristically emotional Clinton revealed a kinship. Who the hell doesn't feel overwhelmed by it all sometimes? The women got it. The networks played it and debated it over and over again just hours before voters went to the polls.

In New Hampshire, we all saw Hillary's inner anxiety about where the campaign was headed, which was far off course from where she began. The Clintons had lost control. After Iowa she was behind, though if we weren't talking about Hillary there wouldn't be a conversation about a woman front-runner in the first place. After coming in third in Iowa after all that work, Hillary just didn't give a damn anymore and couldn't contain her deep disappointment any longer. Or maybe she was just worn out and let her guard down.

Thank the gods, because what if Hillary hadn't let it all out? She'd have been just another presidential wannabe female footnote.

John Edwards attacked her: "I think what we need in a commander in chief is strength and resolve, and presidential campaigns are tough business, but being president of the United States is also tough business."

After her New Hampshire win, the press asked whether it was her tears that put her over the top. Coming after a very tough debate, the coffee shop vulnerability was seen as a "humanizing" moment, Clinton campaign chairman Terry McAuliffe told MSNBC. So much for Penn's assessment that being human is "overrated."

The *New York Daily News* ran this headline after she'd won: "Who's Crying Now?" The *New York Post* blared: "Back From the Dead."

"I had this incredible moment of connection with the voters of New Hampshire, and they saw it and they heard it. And they gave me this incredible victory last night." That's how Hillary put it in a CBS interview after the New Hampshire primary.

An "incredible moment of connection" is the whole ballgame, and whoever gets more of them wins.

From her acceptance speech: "I want especially to thank New Hampshire. Over the last week I listened to you, and in the process, I found my own voice."

Hillary had found her own voice. What if she'd had that voice from the start?

It brought me to tears, as it did others working in the trenches for Hillary, but even as I wanted to believe, I knew the Clinton camp had pulled off an upset that had only kept Hillary alive. It was unlikely Obama would ever again mistake the people standing in line to see him as surefire votes.

The irony that it wasn't a moment of toughness that made Hillary resonate with voters should have hit the Clinton camp like lightning.

After Ken Starr's hair-raising political porn of the '90s, who didn't think Hillary Rodham Clinton was tough enough? Besides, portraying her as some American Margaret Thatcher was wrought with obvious problems in the primary season. Democratic primary voters were sick to death of everything Bush-Cheney, especially the war on terror, and were looking for a way out of the language of wars and endless escalation instead searching for something else.

After one term of George H.W. Bush, two terms of Bill Clinton, then two terms of another Bush, Hillary's run for the presidency in 2008 could only be seen as a return of dynasty. How could they make Hillary Rodham Clinton look new? She needed a re-branding, a re-introduction that showed her on her own, of course, but surely there was something about Hillary for President that was new. Given her years in the public spotlight it would take a heavy lift unless the campaign went with the obvious.

There had never been a haberdasher as president either, but Harry Truman turned out tough enough to drop the bomb. But Truman, of course, was a man. If electing a woman to be commander in chief wouldn't be change enough, what the hell would?

What if Clinton hadn't decided to run a general election and primary campaign all in one?

The conundrum of what Democratic primary voters wanted as opposed to the general election voter could tie anyone in knots, especially if you're looking through Clinton's prism. How can a woman who is looking ahead to be the first female commander in chief vote against preemptive war in Iraq after 9/11, with the public buying the Bush administration's case? That goes double for a senator from New York, ground zero for the most devastating attack since Pearl Harbor, but also someone who came from a place of knowledge through her husband's presidency. Missing was the practical reality that Hillary had to win the nomination first and Democratic primary voters didn't want experience, they wanted change. It was as if she were destined to come so close, because she was a product of the feminist generation, but there was no way to break free from the traditionalism that kept her bound.

It also ignored the times we were entering, which Barack Obama also missed once elected president. It can now be seen clearly in retrospect that people are weary of war and that America's own economic standing depends on our ability to retool our national mission and how we navigate our role in the world.

It seems unmistakable that Hillary Rodham Clinton's instincts about how to build her own campaign were confused. But even finding her own voice couldn't negate her lack of a clear plan for the caucus states. When the time came, team Clinton was totally unprepared. Obama won eleven contests in eleven days after Super Tuesday, which was supposed to be Hillary's knockout punch. There were many excruciating moments in the primary season but none as bad as these.

Miscalculations abounded. Presumptions reigned.

It was presumed because Hillary was a woman she had to work to reach the tough-enough bar. But Hillary's problem was the American obsession with the who-would-you-rather-have-a-beer-with presidential question. She could come off like the second coming of Golda Meir, but if the press reported the American people didn't relate to her, it would be over before it started.

That's likely why the strategy of team Clinton began as it did. They first presented her on a chintz-covered couch from the Clintons' home in Chappaqua, looking beautiful and regal, which would remain an odd memory once Fighting Hillary appeared. Crystal Patterson took questions from people submitting them over the web, then read them to Clinton. The web event was billed as a "conversation" with the American people.

The first question was from a woman in Massachusetts: What can I say to people who say America won't elect a woman?

"We won't know until we try," Hillary responded.

Not exactly inspiring campaign rhetoric. "We don't know until we try" sounded like she was throwing a dart at a board, but came off worse, like false modesty. It also didn't sound very Hillary. This was a woman known for her fight, her never-giving-in relentlessness and her frankness. If it hadn't been for Hillary back during impeachment, Bill Clinton's presidency would have collapsed.

What if the Hillary Clinton who gave the speech in Beijing on behalf of women's rights everywhere had shown up at this moment? Hillary's book, *It Takes a Village*, didn't come out of equivocation. It came from heart. Same goes for her speech as first lady when she said, "Human rights are women's rights."

How about something a little gutsier? Like, I don't know about you, but we rock the cradle, so why can't we run the world?

It was a damn good question in a country that prides itself on women's rights but still hasn't elected a female president. Asserting doubt about why America won't elect a female president also said out loud what all women striving to break glass ceilings know. For all the talk of feminism, women still don't run boardrooms or the media. It was a question that should have led Clinton to say why she was running for president. Did she not hear those same calls of destiny? If not, why run? What was her reason for running?

It sounded like the campaign hadn't decided, or worse, that she didn't know.

What about answering with equanimity that women can do anything a man can? Countries around the world have already elected female leaders, why can't we? That's still the question today.

The second question of the campaign-launch conversation was equally predictable: Did she regret her Iraq war vote? Her answer became a long and winding ramble focusing on what was known at the time of her vote, before the WMDs went missing. She also threw in a lob on Iran's influence and our mandate to prevent it from getting a nuclear weapon. Again with the general election campaigning. She obviously didn't know her audience, or more likely, the strategy of inevitability took for granted that before she was the nominee she'd have to convince Democrats to vote for her.

Let's-have-a-conversation quickly morphed into canned commander in chief lines we'd been hearing for years from men. All I could imagine was anti-war primary voters keeling over as the words came out of Clinton's mouth. Anyone who thought saber-rattling toughness would make the difference in the post-Bush era was taking a leap of faith into a dry pool.

It didn't take long for the incoming to begin.

The late Elizabeth Edwards got in a sexist shot in an interview with *Salon*'s Joan Walsh, in a story picked up by Matt

Drudge, who blasted it under the headline, "Gender Bender: Wife Edwards Says Hillary 'Behaving Like a Man.'"

> Look, I'm sympathetic, because when I worked as a lawyer, I was the only woman in these rooms, too, and you want to reassure them you're as good as a man. And sometimes you feel you have to behave as a man and not talk about women's issues. I'm sympathetic — she wants to be commander in chief. But she's just not as vocal a women's advocate as I want to see. John is. And then she says, or maybe her supporters say, "Support me because I'm a woman," and I want to say and I want to say to her, "Well, then support me because I'm a woman." The question is not so much how she campaigns — that's theater.

> — Joan Walsh, Salon, July 17, 2008

Shorter Elizabeth: Don't feel obligated to vote for Hillary, because my Johnnie loves women more.

Oh, the irony. By insinuating Hillary's campaign expected females to support her based on their shared gender was just cynical. However, we are talking about Elizabeth Edwards, whose convenient amnesia on Clinton's life of activism for women was spiteful, coming as it did from the spouse of an adulterous fraud whose campaign centered on the perfect family. Besides, there was simply no evidence females would automatically side with a female presidential candidate just because she showed up. Quite the opposite, in fact, with a little extra convince-me attitude more likely.

Going back to the 2004 election, *USA Today* and the *Los Angeles Times* both reported that twenty-one million single women didn't even bother to vote. Since Al Gore's loss in 2000 and these numbers became known, women became the most coveted and sought-after voting bloc, with no one yet having the magic touch or answers on how to drive them to the polls.

Hillary also had what some called the "Bill problem," with a segment of modern women never understanding why she hadn't dumped her philandering husband a long time ago.

She could talk about women's issues in a way that no one else could. With Chelsea and her mother next to her, there were three generations of women who could bear witness and testify.

However, young women are manifesting what they want and living lives well beyond what their mothers dreamed. Many of their rights are secure, which some feel has rendered the women's movement irrelevant as a force or as anything to which modern women should feel attached. Issues and challenges remain, but laws now protect women more than ever before, though what's happened with women's reproductive freedom since the Tea Party's rise should give all women pause. So Clinton would have to earn their vote, with older women needing less convincing of Hillary's historic candidacy because they lived it too, with the dream of a female president still unfulfilled and time running out for them. This tied many women to Clinton on a very personal level, which continues even today.

It's true the 1970s sisterhood, if it ever existed, is no longer active, with women feeling less tied to other women, too busy trying to survive to worry about anything else. Ironically, there is evidence the right has resurrected sisterhood in its own image through Sarah Palin, Michele Bachmann and other Tea Party femmes, even as the party's platform includes gutting women's individual freedoms.

Another issue is that equality has arrived for many in the younger generation. Even with Chelsea's privilege, she had to know this fact. The women who pay attention to politics, if only on a cursory level, let alone the activist types, expect a female candidate to have the same leadership capabilities as a man without it being an issue.

Hillary had to make her case bridging the generation gap, while convincing men to give her a chance.

The subject few like to broach is how the sex appeal that draws voters to candidates, especially presidential candidates, crosses the line into sexism when it becomes the overwhelming reason for such voter support. Take a look at the men who back Sarah Palin. Many clearly get off on the babe factor. It's objectification, plain and simple. Never mind that she's shaky on her facts; her physical attractiveness makes some men feel comfortable. Her sex appeal is a turn-on that hits them between the legs. See, sexism works both ways.

Marketing whiz Donny Deutsch weighed in on CNBC's *Squawk Box* after Palin's Republican convention speech, back in September 2008.

> Number one, you'd have supermom in there, no question about it. ...Second, she's sexy. Men want a sexy woman. Women want to idealize about a sexy woman. She's the perfect age: 44. She's certainly got experience, life gravitas experience, but she's still young enough to have that physical appeal.... She's a lioness.... Who wouldn't want a lioness protecting their cubs? She's funny, she's real, she's rock solid, she's feisty, she's smart. If I need to sell woman-in-power to the American public, that's what I'm putting in my cereal. Hillary Clinton's cereal maybe only has two or three of those ingredients.

Palin has been all marketing, but it's not near enough. In 2010, Deutsch's lioness-protecting-her cubs surfaced via Sarah's famous "mama grizzlies" line. However, Mrs. Palin quitting the governorship was not a rock solid move that should be lauded, regardless of whether it has served Sarah's purposes. Physical appeal is the ultimate sexist judgment for a job that includes being commander in chief. Dumb down Deutsch's theory and it amounts to getting a candidate that men want to sleep with, and women want to be. But Sarah's also got the emotional connection, which Hillary learned to mine, with loyal followers for both women who won't accept the dream is over.

By the end of 2010, Mr. Deutsch's 2008 marketing pitch for Palin had been relegated to, "There's no there there.... Once you peel back the layer, not only was there nothing there, it was frightening what was there." His new verdict became a constant refrain on MSNBC's *Morning Joe*, except when Patrick J. Buchanan is around.

Clinton chose to wear the tough role in a way that her team felt men would approve, with the natural female warrior role of fierce fighter for the underdog jettisoned. Unlike a female defending the single citizen against a marauding corporation, for instance, Clinton instead utilized marketing sound bites we've already heard before from men. This was counterproductive and unnecessary, because no one had Clinton's lifetime of advocacy fighting for women, families and children.

She'd always been Fighting Hillary, long before her campaign slammed up against it, and at the end of the campaign, way too late, she remembered this and naturally returned to these roots. With the added experience of a long campaign that had honed her public speaking skills so that her speeches became a rallying cry for the underdog once again, her words touched every woman trying to make her way in a world still run by men.

> My mother was born before women could vote. My daughter got to vote for her mother for president. This is the story of America. Of women and men who defy the odds and never give up.

> — Hillary Rodham Clinton (Democratic convention, 2008)

What if her fight for "women and men who defy the odds and never give up" had been front and center from the start? It was what Hillary had that no other candidate had, something that made her a fighter for the underdog, for people who just keep going, undaunted by life's challenges. It had been her life's work. It came from her own life. She had co-founded Arkansas Advocates for Children and Families, helped establish the State Children's Health Insurance Program, the Adoption and Safe Families Act, and the Foster Care Independence Act, helped lead the fight for the Children's Health Insurance Program as first lady, and along with Janet Reno, created the Office on Violence Against Women, and on and on.

Why did it take until there was nothing left to lose because it was already lost before Hillary found her foundation? What steered Clinton off the organic path of who she is and what made her a political candidate like no other, opting instead for a canned political campaign straight out of Presidents R Us? After all, it was Hillary Clinton's campaign, so it was up to her how to run it.

No politician can delegate the core message of why he or she is running for office, especially not on the wings of a rhyme. "In to win" was chirpy political mush that didn't measure up to Hillary, the woman; "Working for Change, Working for You" was worse. There is also no man who can tell a woman how to run a race, because no one in politics has ever had the opportunity to test how a woman runs a winning race for president.

When the man running your campaign is causing havoc, it doesn't help. And when some duplicitous schmuck inside your campaign is telling the press, "They all want to kill each other," it also tends to dampen the notion you can do the job, because you can't even control your own campaign drama.

I didn't need the dishy political blockbuster (and later HBO movie) *Game Change* to tell me that the third-place finish in Iowa boggled the mind of the once-inevitable candidate:

> He had beaten her among Democrats and independents, among rich and poor. He'd even carried the women's vote. ...Twenty-four hours earlier and all the previous year, she'd been the front-runner, the unstoppable, inevitable nominee. Now Obama stood as the most likely next president of the United States.
>
> — Mark Halperin and John Heilemann, *Game Change*, 2010

After it was all over, why were people who had been inside the room with Hillary leaking anonymous anecdotes to Halperin and Heilemann, indicating that after seeing her reaction to coming in third in Iowa, they felt she shouldn't be president?

Inevitability quickly dissolved into a manic game of catch-up. Scrutiny on caucus preparation, which was in play in Iowa, hadn't surfaced yet. An anonymous source inside Camp Clinton was quoted in *Time* magazine saying, "Caucus states were not really their thing." But it was actually worse than that, which Obama's team didn't miss.

> Some articles even speculated that Penn did not properly understand how the delegate system worked and that late in 2007 he still thought delegates were awarded winner-take-all, not proportionally. I found accusations of such ignorance hard to believe, but it was the first explanation I saw of how they might have developed their flawed strategy for Super Tuesday.
>
> — David Plouffe, *The Audacity to Win*, 2009

It was all just so unfathomable.

> How can it possibly be that the much-vaunted chief strategist doesn't understand proportional allocation?
>
> — Harold Ickes, *Time*, May 8, 2008

In his above-cited book, Mr. Plouffe recalled the moment when Patti Solis Doyle departed as Hillary's campaign manager but Penn stayed put: "Thankfully the real culprit behind their underperformance (in our view), Mark Penn, was left in place."

Penn's wife, Nancy Jacobson, is a boffo Democratic fundraiser who is well liked and has been a partner with former George W. Bush and John McCain adviser Mark McKinnon in the centrist No Labels political movement from its inception, so the niceties of establishment politics were obviously complicated. But no matter how well connected or deeply embedded in a campaign, a woman who had fucked up as badly as Mark Penn would have been fired in a heartbeat.

Regardless of rumors of Bill "yelling at Mark Penn a lot," as reported in the *New York Daily News*, this kind of atmosphere reveals management chaos and does not help a winner rise.

By the time it was all over, the what-ifs had multiplied times ten, most of them directed at Clinton's team. None of them, however, applied to candidate Hillary, who just kept turning out one superlative performance after another. In spite of her campaign, Hillary made history. In her wake, the Hillary Effect would solidify a national readiness for a female president and set the scene for more women to succeed. She also slogged through boatloads of incoming crap that no other woman will have to endure. It was a first, which made Hillary the biggest target in the political game, something she'd had to endure since she and her husband walked into Washington.

It took the wife of a former president to be the first viable female candidate and the first to win a presidential primary. The equation, no matter that Hillary was an accomplished lawyer, civil rights activist, children's advocate, women's civil rights fighter and wife and mother, was the most complex in American history. She got her shot through her education and earlier life, but also through the help from her husband's network of people and financing.

That the first Republican female to be on the national ticket came right after Hillary's defeat was not an accident. She was a total unknown, with Sarah Palin's vice presidential candidacy a beneficiary of perfect timing for Republicans and a big fat target zone for her adversaries, which remains in place today because of Palin's show-horse style.

What if Sarah had come on the scene as prepared as Clinton, or at the very least, what if she had known what she didn't know? Nothing could have saved McCain, but if Palin had been one-quarter of the policy-wonk Hillary Clinton was at the time she ran for president, the stage might have been set for the first female presidential conservative candidate.

Palin's unscripted screw-ups, such as her "refudiate" Twitter belch, conjured up images and sound bites of George W. Bush, but her self-inflicted PR disaster after Tucson was something else entirely. After days of silence and heat over her campaign crosshairs poster in the wake of Jared Lee Loughner's alleged assassination attempt of Rep. Gabrielle Giffords that left six others dead and fourteen wounded, Palin released a video response on the same day of the memorial service where President Obama would speak so eloquently. Invoking "blood-libel" and characterizing herself as a victim, Palin looked petty and small at a time of national tragedy, and required yet a second damage control offensive, this time with the help of Fox News wing-nut and radio bloviator Sean Hannity. Bad news for Palin stretched across the political spectrum.

At one point, conservative journalist and former George W. Bush speechwriter David Frum begged Palin to "stop talking now."

From Public Policy Polling, ten days after the shooting:

> While Americans seem to mostly absolve Palin of blame and at least somewhat sympathize with her news coverage, they do not think she handled her video statement well. Forty percent think her eight-minute speech, released the same day as the president's memorial address in Tucson, was inappropriate. Only 27% think it appropriate, and a third, including a bare plurality of Republicans, are unsure. The GOP only breaks 41-17 in support of her tack, but Democrats side 13-60, and independents 28-42, against it.

It turned out Palin had even ignored the advice of Roger Ailes, one of the most successful Republican media strategists in political history and the president of Fox News Channel. From *New York* magazine in March 2011:

Palin told Ailes she wanted to respond, according to a person with knowledge of the call. It wasn't fair the media was making this about her. Ailes told Palin that she should stay quiet. "Lie low," he said. "There's no need to inject yourself into the story."

What if Sarah had listened to Ailes?

Michele Bachmann's ability to do just that, listen to seasoned pols, has turned her representative career into the stuff of dreams.

But Sarah's real weapon is her "it" factor. The GOP's political earth shook when Palin said, "What's the difference between a pit bull and a hockey mom? Lipstick."

The question continually asked of Republicans before the 2010 midterms was still, "Is Sarah Palin qualified to be president?" Her power at an all-time high, the cable crew thought dissecting her every move was great sport. Chris Matthews asked the question again, never getting why if George W. Bush could run for president and win twice, why not Sarah?

What's different about George and Sarah? The biggest difference is pedigree, a.k.a. class. George's father, Bush 41, offered something for his son that Sarah will never have. George W. Bush was part of the good-ol'-boy network, grandfathered in, quite literally.

John King, in late October 2010, asked Jeb Bush a question that came from a viewer: Would he endorse Palin for president if he does not run himself? Jeb said he wasn't running, then added, "If Sarah Palin's the nominee and she's running against Barack Obama, you betcha!" Looking at his brother, how could he say otherwise?

But being her own brand of red meat for the right still hasn't proved enough for Sarah, because to be president you have to appeal to people beyond your own choir. Michele Bachmann has the same problem. Even as Sarah, her "mama grizzlies" and her fan-base have clout that can be wielded inside the Republican Party for 2012, so do Bachmann and her Tea Party supporters, as displayed in Iowa. There is still no proof yet, though, that Palin, Bachmann and their packs have any wider appeal. That's why Tucker Carlson was glad to blast out a hit piece about Bachmann's migraines and pill-popping incapacitations. Even though Palin is not running and Bachmann's road was rough, these women make the Republican establishment very nervous.

Without Sarah and the Tea Party in 2010, the GOP would never have taken the House. Their energy resulted in a historic win, with more House seats gained than at any time since Democrats won seventy-five in 1948, though Christine O'Donnell and Sharron Angle caused Senate defeats that gave establishment Republicans heartburn. Before the midterms, Senator John Cornyn admitted Palin helped re-orient the Republican Party, saying the Tea Party was "constructive and helpful" on CNN with Candy Crowley, but he couldn't bring himself to say Palin's name.

For a woman with no office or title at the time of the 2010 midterms and someone labeled "quitter" to boot, the success Palin had through using her spokesperson celebrity, helped along by the Fox factor, was more than anyone else could claim. She easily could have been named *Time* magazine's Person of the Year, but the media establishment won't give her an inch.

Palin tapped into the midterm energy at its core while Obama and his White House political team were fumbling with their chess pieces. As a result, when not taking her own candidates across the finish line, she roused enough Tea Party voter power to manifest more Republican wins in state legislative houses than in any election since 1928, according to the bipartisan National Conference of State Legislatures. Her energy helped Republicans to unilaterally control more than 190 U.S. House districts on the cusp of redistricting. Their victories in 2010 also ignited a national union debate that started in Wisconsin, something that hadn't been seen in years, as well as a state-by-state campaign to reverse women's freedoms.

What the Tea Party House members did on the budget fight in April 2011 gave Speaker John Boehner his first big win, while reducing President Obama and the Democrats to delivering the "largest annual spending cuts in history" with "programs people rely on... cut back," to quote President Obama. Those are dubious distinctions indeed for any Democratic president to proclaim. The Tea Party caucus took that win and blew it up to mythic proportions in the knock-down debt-ceiling fight that produced all cuts, no revenue and had President Obama ceding economics to Republicans without ever once making the Democratic case.

David Axelrod, a.k.a. Obama's Karl Rove, revealed epic White House midterm hubris when he suggested the only reason Sarah Palin had power, though it certainly isn't predictive of future political success, was because the press gave it to her. Talk about White House bubble blindness.

> Well, she certainly has a following. And she's an interesting personality. So, you know I'm not going to pass judgment on the level of force she represents in her politics. But she has, you know, when she sends out a tweet on Twitter or puts something on her Facebook, you guys cover it. *People* respond to it, and so that makes her a player in our politics.

> — David Axelrod, *Face the Nation*, October 2010

By August 2011, Axelrod and the Obama White House had felt the power of the Tea Party personally, even if Palin's own influence had ebbed. Through the debt ceiling deal and Standard & Poor's politically motivated triple-A to AA+ downgrade of the nation's credit rating, Axelrod was forced into campaign mode, proclaiming it the "Tea Party downgrade" to save face for a debacle so mismanaged by President Obama and his team as to render an unwanted, historic first.

However, the double-edged sword was that internals in a *New York Times* poll in August 2011 also revealed the Tea Party cratering in support, with only 18% of people asked identifying with them and 73% not. So as their power manifested in the debt-ceiling debacle, it was also a moment when they overplayed their hand, as everyone watching saw just how far they'd go to put their own ideological zealotry before the country's fiscal health.

Hillary Rodham Clinton had real advantages going into the presidential race — the vaunted Clinton machine, her husband's expertise and money train, as well as her own credentials.

Only Hillary Rodham Clinton can answer the what-if questions, though I'm sure her closest aides could too, but they weren't talking on the record. With Secretary Clinton working hard at State and new political jobs for others, no one wanted to look back. For some the loss was just too gut-wrenchingly painful.

The what-ifs aren't seen in a vacuum. It's more like a head-on collision between the first viable female candidate for a major party nomination, the odds against her, and her own mistakes. Hillary was the first woman to show up who had a decent chance of winning, but in living out her date with history, she has set the stage so the next woman won't have to face the same forces and wait so long. Or as Hillary's fans still hope, maybe she'll even take a second shot.

What if in 2016 it's Hillary versus Jeb Bush? What a set-up, a date with destiny for them both: one coming so close, yet denied; the other, the smarter brother of a previous two-time winner, finally getting a stab at it after the Tea Party crowd dumbed everything down.

But that assumes Obama wins reelection, which is not a given anymore.

As for 2012, Sarah Palin is not running and has ceded the limelight for now, but considering the way she proved her political prowess in 2010, if she chooses to retool her message and study up, she's young enough to be able to reinvent herself again. Meanwhile, the question now is whether Palin can repeat in 2012 what she did for Republicans in 2010.

Before the midterms, *New York* magazine's John Heilemann spoke to two dozen senior strategists and operatives, many of whom helped to secure the last three GOP nominations. The consensus? Sarah not only could win the nomination, but some considered her at that time "the de facto front-runner" for 2012. Mark McKinnon, media guru for both Bush and McCain, put it this way in John Heilemann's *New York* magazine article, "2012: How Sarah Barracuda Becomes President", from October 2010:

> She cracked the door in Iowa, and once that door's cracked, it's impossible to close, because all the adulators and supporters around her are going to tell her she has to run, that it's her calling, that it's fate, that it's God's will — and once that starts to happen, it's very difficult to say no.

Representing a freaked-out establishment over a Palin possibility, Karl Rove was stirred to go rogue right before the 2010 midterms in an interview with the UK's *Daily Telegraph*:

> Being the vice-presidential nominee on the ticket is different from saying, "I want to be the person at the top of

the ticket." There are high standards that the American people have for [the presidency], and they require a certain level of gravitas, and they want to look at the candidate and say, "That candidate is doing things that gives me confidence that they are up to the most demanding job in the world."

After the candidate Mr. Rove foisted on America, how ironic to hear him doubt anyone else's gravitas.

At the same time, Sarah Palin told *Entertainment Tonight*'s Mary Hart that of course she'd consider running for president, "If there's nobody else to do it...."

By April 2011, Mark McKinnon was touting another female on the Daily Beast, writing:

> Get ready for a conservative firebrand from Minnesota who may make memories of Palin pale quickly. We are talking about Rep. Michele Bachmann who, while Palin hesitates, has aggressively jumped into the fray. And while she's not my cup of tea (party), Bachmann would arguably be a stronger GOP candidate for president than Palin in 2012. She works harder, she's smarter, she has more discipline, more focus and, perhaps most important, she has fire in her belly.

Karl Rove is a personal friend of Michele Bachmann and helped run her first campaign. He told Bill O'Reilly in April 2011, "She's smart, she's tough, she's funny, she's got a lot of personality and all of that will help her if she throws her hat in the ring." But jumping from the House to the presidency is heavy lifting, and what makes Bachmann's national appeal any more viable than Palin's? Bachman's not going to get there by labeling Planned Parenthood "the LensCrafters of big abortion," which caused that company's parent company, Luxottica Retail, to request she stop using their name (she agreed); or by hoisting up a "five thousand years of recorded human history" argument against gay marriage, which made news on CNN and Politico. And what does Michele Bachmann do with her husband, the man who believes a person can "pray the gay away" and has become a punch line for comedians from Jon Stewart to Kathy Griffin? No matter her Tea Party power, can they possibly make the Republican nominee pick her for vice president with this gift waiting to be handed to Obama's reelection team and the press?

It's a daunting challenge to name another ready, name-recognized Democratic female, let alone one on the left or center-left, a progressive who can match what Hillary had when her campaign began. Of course, many underestimated the forces that would line up against Hillary, not to mention forces inside her own campaign that she, for whatever reason, could not control, manage or direct. It was never going to be easy for Hillary. She'd waited her turn, but people have long memories, and many hold grudges.

Chapter 2: **It's the Baggage, Stupid**

The elite Democratic fraternity was queasy over Hillary's baggage, as if she'd created it herself. There was a colossal case of political amnesia, which was easier than turning the blame back on the culprits who helped manufacture the damaging narrative in the first place.

The establishment press and the right wing started working on the Clintons before Bill had even won the presidency. On March 8, 1992, during the run-up to the elections, Jeff Gerth of the *New York Times* broke the Whitewater story. This baggage that hung around Hillary's neck was entirely manufactured. The *Arkansas Democrat-Gazette*'s nationally syndicated columnist Gene Lyons wrote a book about Gerth's and the *Times*' innumerable falsehoods called *Fools for Scandal: How the Media Invented Whitewater* that was so densely packed with corrections on Gerth's original *Times* fiction you wondered if the editors of the once-vaunted newspaper had read it drunk.

Eric Boehlert, for Media Matters, eviscerated the *Times* in 2007 for journalistic malpractice after Jeff Gerth had the unmitigated gall to write an endnote in the book he co-wrote about Hillary, *Her Way*, blaming his editors for his own concoctions. Here's the endnote:

> Jeff Gerth, "Clintons Joined S&L Operator in an Ozark Real Estate Venture," *New York Times*, March 8, 1992, Al. Gerth, who returned to Washington late Friday night, did not see the edited version of the article until it was first published in the Times' bulldog edition late Saturday afternoon. To his dismay, that version had been rewritten by editors to include a number of mistakes. Gerth quickly corrected the mistakes for subsequent editions. He never saw the headline, which was written by editors in New York.

The word chickenshit comes to mind. Gerth's Whitewater article launched what would become a hounding of both Clintons for the duration of Bill Clinton's presidency, costing the taxpayers approximately $47 million, while saddling Hillary with more baggage than she could possibly deflect through any brilliant political sleight of hand. Anyone in the Democratic Party talking about Hillary's baggage should have had their back checked for a spine.

"The Washington battles of the 1990s," to use one of Barack Obama's favorite phrases during the 2008 primaries, weren't a concoction of the Clintons. Dozens of books have been written about the political climate of this period, the definitive one being Ken Gormley's *Death of American Virtue.*

Honestly, one cannot chronicle all of the misogyny directed at Clinton during the '08 primaries, not even in several hundred pages of a book, because it was unending and woven throughout our media, going back almost two decades. There simply will never be a systematic hazing like it of another female in our politics again.

As for the ingrained Washington snobbery, it hit Bill and Hillary Clinton like a two-by-four in the head. The D.C. calm had been disturbed by the Arkansas hicks from the sticks. Gormley's book quotes William Kennedy, part of the Clinton legal team that investigated Whitewater from inside the White House, saying, "Some of this stuff was aimed at [Hillary's] health care task force. Some of it was aimed at, you know, 'How dare they bring Arkansans up here and stick them in the White House.'"

Some of it, though, was just "pure palpable hatred of the Clintons," Kennedy told Gormley. "It started and it never quit."

Harry and Bess Truman could no doubt feel their pain from the hereafter. That Bill and Hillary were displacing twelve years of comfy conservative upper-crust folks like the Reagans and Bushes, complete with first lady traditionalism, for Hillary's policy-related activism, made them even less welcome.

The Clintons came to Washington with no money and not much else of their own. Wealthy they were not. The new president and first lady were in a hostile town where the taxpayers were just renting them a home.

"This beautiful capital is often a place of intrigue and calculation," President Clinton said in his first inaugural address. "Powerful people maneuver for position and worry endlessly about who is in and who is out, who is up and who is down, forgetting those people whose toil and sweat sends us here and pays our way."

The Clintons weren't prepared for the ego, power and concentrated media overload in Washington, D.C., where many of the full-time residents remained skeptical of the new first family, as if their arrival had all occurred by whim instead of as the American voters' choice.

When you start out by dissing the head D.C. diva, it only makes things worse. As Henry Kissinger is quoted as saying in *The Georgetown Ladies' Social Club: Power, Passion, and Politics in the Nation's Capital* by C. David Heymann, "The hand that mixes the Georgetown martini is time and again the hand that guides the destiny of the Western world."

The D.C. doyenne Sally Quinn, wife of the legendary newsman Ben Bradlee, expected to be the incoming new first lady's guide. Hillary demurred. Rumor of this had floated around for years before Dee Dee Myers, President Clinton's first press secretary, confirmed it to *Vanity Fair*'s Evgenia Peretz in 2010. Hillary's snub permanently pissed off Quinn, who firmly rules the D.C. party circuit just as the legendary Perle Mesta did until the Kennedy era before her. As a result, we've seen a classic, one-sided, establishment grudge and revenge match play out over two decades in the *Washington Post* and on cable TV.

Who knew Hillary would spend the rest of her political life paying for the apparently unspeakable crime of not letting Sally Quinn show her around town? Christopher Ogden, author of *Life of the Party*, a biography of Democratic fundraiser Pamela Churchill Harriman, is quoted saying in David Heymann's book that the seven words people feared the most were, "first in a series by Sally Quinn." If Hillary had known Ms. Quinn was referred to as a "social terrorist" because of her brutal portrayals of people on the pages of the *Washington Post*, Hillary might have jumped when Sally said come hither. Long before social media, cable and new media, Washington, D.C. thrived on Quinn's gossip, especially when the notion had already been floated that her subjects were crooks.

To be fully accurate, the real Clinton insult was that the new Democratic president thought the people who sent him to Washington were more important than Sally Quinn's social set.

When you consider the connectedness of the journalistic elite who ruled opinion across the country before the Internet exploded with websites, new media and activist blogs and reader diaries, Sally Quinn was at the very top of the journalistic heap. This was made possible by hubby Ben Bradlee, the legendary pal to JFK and protector of his secrets, who ran the *Washington Post* during Watergate. Quinn met Bradlee and shacked up with him at the moment Watergate hit the fan. Bradlee was still married but separated, which was confirmed by a reporter friend of Sally's in *Vanity Fair*. If only Nixon had known. The rest is your basic tale of hot trophy wife with talent makes money off of carving people up in the *Post*, while her powerful husband plays protector.

In the lightning-speed field of new media, we all make mistakes, and Sally made a whopper at the height of old media's sluggish cresting that provides a clue to her character. It focused on a story about distinguished former National Security Adviser to President Jimmy Carter, Zbigniew Brzezinski, and his zipper.

> Certain select politicians received equally shabby treatment in Sally's writings. Bill Thomas, editor in chief of *Capitol Style* magazine, recalled "an embarrassing story she wrote for the *Post* on Zbigniew Brzezinski, in which she accused him of having left his fly open during the course of an interview, implying that some sort of sexual impropriety had either taken place or was intended. The newspaper had to print a retraction."
>
> — *The Georgetown Ladies' Social Club: Power, Passion, and Politics in the Nation's Capital*, by C. David Heymann, 2003

Time magazine chronicled Sally's *Post* fiction on New Year's Eve 1979, first by quoting the smear:

> As the reporter was leaving, he began to joke around and flirt with her. Suddenly he unzipped his fly.
>
> — *Washington Post*, Dec. 19, 1979

Time continued by reprinting the *Post*'s embarrassing correction:

> In yesterday's story about Zbigniew Brzezinski, it was stated that at the end of an interview with a reporter from a national magazine — as a joke — Brzezinski committed an offensive act, and that a photographer took a picture "of this unusual expression of playfulness." Brzezinski did not commit such an act, and there is no picture of him doing so.
>
> — *Washington Post*, Dec. 20, 1979

Quinn also wrote novels, which hilariously acerbic Christopher Buckley reviewed as "cliterature," and a book about her stab at anchor stardom trying to take down Barbara Walters. But her career move on the wings of the Clintons coming to town was to take over where Jeff Gerth left off in carving them up.

Through her perch at the *Post*, Quinn could spin whatever tales she wanted. She's also very chummy with New York political powerhouses, including the late Tim Russert and his wife, *Vanity Fair* columnist Maureen Orth, to name two. For biz and for play, New York and Washington have always made up their own interconnected world, as can be seen every day on cable TV. Quinn offered sage bits of insider stuff like telling the *New Yorker*, "There's just something about her that pisses people off." Well, Hillary sure as hell had pissed off Quinn.

Harry Jaffe wrote a piece for Salon back in 1998, when there weren't many of us writing online, titled "The (Not So) Mighty Quinn," in which he recalled a *New Yorker* article by Mary Jacoby that questioned what Quinn's motives might be in continually targeting Hillary Clinton. Jacoby, using the same journalistic jugular tactics on Quinn that Quinn so often used on others, wondered if Sally was "bitter because she's no longer on center stage," and also questioned whether her fading looks had her "frightened." Jaffe's piece went on to say that when Mary Jacoby "insinuated Quinn was a witch in the *Observer*, Russert's wife, Maureen Orth, jumped to her defense." It's a minor note, but I use it to illustrate how the elite have each other's backs when even the slightest perceived offense has been committed on one of their own.

Once the Lewinski scandal hit, Sally's social terrorist skills went into hyperdrive. In a self-important stem-winder, published on November 2, 1998, she wrote about how she was devastated by the Clinton years and, with no trace of irony, what the Clinton culture did to Quinn and her elite D.C. friends. The piece, titled "In Washington, That Letdown Feeling," made her case in a self-righteous rambling that quoted all the super-luminaries of establishment D.C. life, including the late David Broder, a quintessential insider and so-called dean of the Washington press corps.

"He came in here and he trashed the place," she quoted Broder as saying, "and it's not his place."

The dean had spoken, though it wasn't David Broder's place either; it was the people's place, to borrow the line Scott Brown spoke in 2010 before ripping Ted Kennedy's Massachusetts Senate seat out of Democratic hands.

During impeachment, when stories started appearing in the *Post* blasting Bill Clinton, it was obvious there was a bias coming from certain reporters. Mollie Dickenson, in her February 1998 Salon article titled "Starr Chamber," reported on one reason why this was possible. She quoted Ben Bradlee, who said on C-SPAN in 1997, "In my book, Ken Starr can do no wrong; he dismissed a $2 million libel suit that had hung over the Post for seven years."

It's nice to have friends in places of power, especially in the establishment press.

Sally Quinn was still ranting about Monica Lewinsky in 2010, but in Sally's world, the reason Bill Clinton was impeached was because the Clintons didn't court the Washingtonians. She shared this view in a *Washington Post* article from January 27, 2010, titled, "Administrations Should Befriend the Locals — They'll Need Them in Hard Times," which read in part, "When the Monica Lewinsky affair turned into a debacle, during his second term, Clinton was impeached partly because of the ill will toward him in the city." See, Sally and the Washington elite could have saved President Clinton, if only he and Hillary had kissed her ring.

It was as if Arkansas Senator Dale Bumpers never came, spoke and conquered.

After Hillary had lost the nomination in June 2010, Sally felt compelled to weigh in again. In an essay called "Retreat, Hillary" posted on her On Faith *Newsweek/Washington Post* blog, she wrote, "When she ran for Senate and won it was largely because of her marriage to Bill Clinton. When she ran for President she had the same problem. It was never just Hillary Clinton."

Earlier in the piece, she had begun her rumination this way: "What does Hillary want? Who is the real Hillary Clinton? What should she do now? What will she do?" The rest of the post went on to address these questions with suggestions like, "Give up the naked ambition, the lust for power." Yeah, because that's exactly what Sally did.

Hillary's baggage, which she would lug around for the duration of her campaign, must have felt particularly heavy when the activist base booed her at the Take Back America Conference in 2006. I saw it first-hand when she spoke about her Iraq war vote.

For all of the specificity in the 2002 speech she made about giving Bush authorization for force, her most jarring statement was about the trust she put in George W. Bush: "Even though the resolution before the Senate is not as strong as I would like in requiring the diplomatic route first and placing highest priority on a simple, clear requirement for unlimited inspections, I take the president at his word that he will try hard to pass a UN resolution and seek to avoid war, if possible."

It's hard to imagine a time when a prominent Democratic leader pledged that kind of trust in George W. Bush, but Clinton's statement as New York senator came in the fall after 9/11.

Her speech also contained this line: "My vote is not, however, a vote for any new doctrine of preemption, or for unilateralism, or for the arrogance of American power or purpose."

Nobody gave a shit about that part.

Eventually, Hillary would go further on *Good Morning America*. "Obviously, if we knew then what we know now," she said, "there wouldn't have been a vote... and I certainly wouldn't have voted that way."

It's as close as primary voters would get to a Clinton apology, followed finally by: "If we in Congress don't end this war before January 2009, as president, I will."

Republicans clearly saw Bill Clinton as baggage. Conservative Kellyanne Conway, president and founder of The Polling Company/WomanTrend, was quoted in *USA Today*, citing an appearance on *Hardball* from 2005, as wondering whether Hillary's marriage disqualified her from being commander in chief: "The fact is that Hillary Clinton could not stand up to a cheating husband, so how in the world would she stand up to North Korea and some of our other enemies around the globe?"

By Conway's standard, Newt Gingrich would be one mean son of a bitch in office. He'd have to be to treat our country's women the way he did Jackie Battley, the first of his multiple wives.

An infamous story reported in the August 2010 *Esquire* described how Newt headed "to the hospital to present her with divorce terms while she was recovering from uterine cancer and then fought the case so hard, Jackie had to get a court order just to pay her utility bills." It's a story that followed him into his half-baked 2012 presidential campaign, which had his current wife Callista running the show to try and overcompensate for his previous misogyny. This backfired terribly, the $500,000 revolving line of credit at Tiffany blowing him out of the water.

There may be nothing more insulting to a modern woman than to imply her husband is propping her up. But considering that the first female to win a presidential primary and get close to the nomination in our country's history is a former first lady, it's not outlandish to ask how any other woman can compete for the top spot without serious juice to pave her way into the establishment boys club. Hillary's connections to Bill's infrastructure and political donor base are part of what it took to get the first female within sniffing range of the White House. But it's not like those connections provided a buttress.

When Hillary ran for the Democratic nomination, she was a woman cracking 60, finally getting her shot after paying her dues. Of course she got hit with the age issue. This was not something American conservatives worried about when talking about Margaret Thatcher or Golda Meir, who never had their looks maligned as a reason to be excluded from leadership. But they governed in England and Israel, not the United Juvenile States of American Double Standards.

Matt Drudge posted a particularly unflattering photo taken on a day when Hillary was clearly worn out, with the headline "The Toll of a Campaign." It revealed wrinkles that naturally come with age unless you're Botoxed up. The picture caused an online explosion about sexism, ageism and double standards between men and women. Rush Limbaugh started it off with the observational acuity of a pubescent teen: "Will Americans want to watch a woman get older before their eyes on a daily basis?"

How many awful photos have you seen of male candidates over the years? We could paper the National Mall with Alfred E. Newmanesque shots of former President George W. Bush. As for John McCain, opportunities abound. What about flunky presidential wannabe Fred Thompson, whose forehead wrinkles and sagging jowl remind you of a basset hound? Then there's Rush himself. I watched his blubber bounce up and down during his speech to the Conservative Political Action Committee in 2009, a case for why most talk radio hosts don't do TV.

Maureen Dowd's *New York Times* column on the photo included the phrase, "Hillary's latest hurdle: the Old Hag routine." Specializing in Clinton hit pieces, Dowd felt for Hillary on this one, sort of:

> First, the Republicans tried to paint Hillary as angry, but that didn't work because she has shown a steady composure and laughed a lot (even if the laughter isn't always connected to people saying anything funny). She has kept her sense of humor — which has a tart side — mostly under wraps, so she won't be accused of being witchy. But some conservative pundits who disagree with a woman on matters of policy jump straight into an attack on the woman's looks or personal life.

The finish is vintage Dowd, her acidic sentiments slithering into the snake pit:

> The public still has no idea of what part of her is stage-managed and focus-grouped, and what part is legit. It's pretty pathetic, at this stage of her career, that she has to wage a major offensive, by helicopter and web testimonials, to make herself appear warm-blooded.

However, when the race for the nomination began, nobody could outperform Hillary, and none of the boys were able to out-detail her on policy in the debates either. Even if at the beginning I was not buying it, her campaign took off from the start and it looked like it was going to be tough for anyone to catch her.

The debate NBC's Tim Russert co-moderated with Brian Williams in October 2007 was a seminal moment. Everyone was wondering if Obama would finally take off the gloves. Hillary was leading at the time 51% to 21% in polls, but had been ahead all of 2007, since the primary race began. This debate would turn the contest upside down.

It's ironic now to look back at John Edwards trying to take down Hillary that night with comments like, "And I think it is crucial for Democratic voters and caucus-goers to determine who they can trust, who's honest, who's sincere, who has integrity." Yeah, no shit. Unfortunately for John, they eventually found out.

During the debate, Hillary got fifty-two questions: Twenty-five had to do with either Hillary or Bill Clinton, including very personal insinuations, with twenty-two of those overtly hostile. Tim Russert asked twenty-six questions: Fourteen were to Clinton, with five directly targeting her personally.

Chris Cillizza of the *Washington Post* wrote that "for the majority of the debate she acquitted herself well, despite having the deck stacked heavily against her." In the debate's first hour, Cillizza pointed out, "nearly every question and response started and ended with Clinton."

The condensed version will give you a picture.

Complete with document-waving drama, Russert went after Hillary's first lady experience by asking about the National Archives documents:

"Senator Clinton, I'd like to follow up because, in terms of your experience as first lady, in order to give the American people an opportunity to make a judgment about your experience, would you allow the National Archives to release the documents about your communications with the president, the advice you gave, because, as you well know, President Clinton has asked the National Archives not to do anything until 2012?"

His other goal was to remind everyone watching that wherever Hillary goes, so goes her former president husband, the ruination of America sure to follow.

After the debate, I talked to knowledgeable sources very familiar with archive procedures, including someone familiar with the procedures President Clinton followed. Once documents start being produced by a president, something has to be decided about what to do with them in case something happens to the president. It's standard for presidents to choose the twelve-year maximum to hold the documents, which are put in categories like national security, senior administration, secret, etc. The highest-level documents often stay secret, and with regards to Bill Clinton specifically, are then run by Bruce Lindsey, who serves as CEO of the William J. Clinton Foundation, to decide whether to make them public.

Former President Clinton pushed back after the debate. From Reuters, November 2, 2007:

> "I signed a routine letter to the archives five years ago to accelerate the release of my records, which five years later in a different context is misrepresented as an attempt to block information on my wife," Clinton told reporters after a speech to Microsoft Corp. employees. "The whole thing was a total canard," he said. "It was breathtakingly misleading." Clinton said the archives already have released more than one million documents from his presidency including many from his wife's failed attempts at health-care reform.

But this was nothing compared to what would unfold later. During the lightning round at the end of a grueling debate, after Williams asked Obama about U.S. air travel, Russert then asked Hillary, "Why does it make a lot of sense to give an illegal immigrant a driver's license?" New York Governor Eliot Spitzer had proposed to do just that. That this question to Hillary was sandwiched amid questions on air travel, Internet safety, UFOs, life beyond earth, and what Barack Obama was going to wear for Halloween (yes, really), was revealing.

Clinton, not willing to throw Spitzer under the bus, split the difference in a series of answers that ended with her on both sides of the issue, making her sound duplicitous, which played right into the Clintonian perception. It was obvious she'd blown it. Senator Chris Dodd was the first to jump on her, which devolved into a very testy exchange. Why Clinton didn't have a prepared answer stating her own views and letting Governor Spitzer worry about himself was a colossal error, because it was a huge issue in the news and she had to know Russert would come in with rhetorical guns blazing as he always did.

Russert, no doubt smelling blood, then went back to ask her again: "Senator Clinton, I just want to make sure of what I heard. Do you, the New York senator, Hillary Clinton, support the New York governor's plan to give illegal immigrants a driver's license? You told the New Hampshire paper that it made a lot of sense. Do you support his plan?"

"You know, Tim, this is where everybody plays gotcha," Clinton began, but it hadn't even started.

A question went to Edwards about the Internet and protecting children, but he broke away from it in order to pick at Clinton again on the driver's license issue. It was one of Edwards' most effective attacks of the night:

"Unless I missed something, Senator Clinton said two different things in the course of about two minutes just a few minutes ago.... What we've had for seven years is double-talk from Bush and from Cheney, and I think America deserves us to be straight."

Brian Williams broke in to ask why Obama was nodding his head. Obama picked up where Edwards left off: "I can't tell whether she was for it or against it...."

Hillary's hedging on the question was her own fault and a train wreck to watch. By the end, with Hillary getting not only the most difficult and politically explosive questions of the night, but the toughest of the lightning round, the moderators were lobbing softballs for the other candidates to knock out of the park. After Russert asked Dennis Kucinich about UFOs, he followed up with this to Barack Obama: "The three astronauts of Apollo 11 who went to the moon back in 1969 all said that they believe there is life beyond Earth. Do you agree?"

The very last question of the night to Obama came from Williams: "Tomorrow, of course, is Halloween. You will go as what?" It was a gift. Obama's answer was pitch-perfect and lighthearted and allowed him to end with a joke, closing out the debate on a high note.

It had been a disaster. In a subsequent debate Clinton tried to do damage control, but it was too late. The bell had rung, with headlines from this debate screaming in deafening cadence.

The *New York Times* said, "Clinton Hears It From Her Rivals"; the *Washington Post*'s Anne E. Kornblut and Dan Balz column ran under the headline, "Clinton's Foes Go On the Attack"; Politico bannered Roger Simon's column with, "Obama, Edwards attack; Clinton bombs debate"; and on and on.

With Hillary sitting on a thirty-point lead, everyone expected she'd be targeted for some tough one-on-ones, but this was something else. What happened that night would never have happened if it was an all-male debate. There would have been some respect paid to the man who had so far kicked everyone else's ass, not to mention polled better in matchups, while building monster fundraising numbers. This was less a debate than a political frat boy hazing of the chick.

Through Tim Russert's journalistic style, picking and choosing which politician to grill and which to charm, he made himself part of the story and did a disservice to viewers. David Gregory didn't need a gotcha question to get Newt Gingrich to dismiss Paul Ryan's budget plan as "right-wing social engineering," simultaneously insulting the conservative economic darling Ryan and gravely wounding Gingrich's own campaign. Nor did Gregory have to pounce unexpectedly to nail Michele Bachmann, fresh from her Ames straw poll win, on her dangerous debt ceiling economics. But unlike Rachel Maddow's illuminating discussion with Rand Paul, Katie Couric's straightforward questions that stumped Sarah Palin on what she reads, or Roger Mudd's historic interview with Edward M. Kennedy in which the senator couldn't convincingly explain why he wanted to be president, Russert seemed more interested in making news about his own take-no-prisoners technique than in eliciting information from his subject.

In another moment from the debate, Russert plumbed the panel for each candidate's views on Iran:

RUSSERT: I want to ask each of you the same question. Senator Clinton, would you pledge to the American people that Iran will not develop a nuclear bomb while you are president?

CLINTON: I intend to do everything I can to prevent Iran from developing a nuclear bomb.

RUSSERT: But you won't pledge?

CLINTON: I am pledging I will do everything I can to prevent Iran from developing a nuclear bomb.

RUSSERT: But they may.

CLINTON: Well, you know, Tim, you asked me if I would pledge, and I have pledged that I will do everything I can to prevent Iran from developing a nuclear bomb.

But you won't *pledge?* As if any American president holds the keys to what another nation can do. That's the thinking, but it is preposterous.

Paul Waldman, writing in *American Prospect*, did a rundown on some interviewers' insistence on demanding answers that didn't reveal anything on issues that actually matter.

> The two parties' nominees will be decided three months from now, and we can be sure that in that time, at least one or two candidates will have their campaigns upended by the answer they gave to an absurd question, delivered by Tim Russert or someone like him, about what their favorite Bible verse is, or whom they want to win the Super Bowl, or what kind of beer they like. "Aha!" the reporters will shout, as though they actually unearthed something revealing on which the race for the presidency of the most powerful nation on earth should be decided. The one whose tiny little mind devised the question will be praised to the stars for his journalistic acumen.

In the fall of 2007, people were still in denial about what was happening to Hillary. People were afraid to say it, to weigh in and openly call sexism for what it was; those daring to call it out would be grilled as if they'd lost their minds.

Bill Moyers interviewed Kathleen Hall Jamieson Director of the Annenberg Public Policy Center on *Bill Moyers Journal* on December 7, 2007, and she addressed the volume and tactics of right-wing attacks, with Hillary Rodham Clinton a favorite target two decades ago.

JAMIESON: One of the things I think that happens with many of these visual depictions is that the people who are producing them are trying to attach what scholars call negative affect to Hillary Clinton. And I know that's an odd concept for non-academics.

BILL MOYERS: Negative...?

JAMIESON: Affect. To the extent that you have negative feelings, have basic affect when you see something. If I can attach that to something, I can make you feel uneasy about it. I can increase the likelihood that you're going to vote against Hillary Clinton. So we know, for example, that if I show you a picture of someone who's smiling and feels comfortable, and it's a pleasant video... you think more positively of the person, even if you don't know who the person is. Then I show you a scary picture, an off-putting picture. You react negatively. You respond negatively. I can increase the likelihood that you'll say you'll vote against that person even if you know nothing about them. So some of this is what we used to call visual vilification. But it's also attaching an emotional response to the picture to...feel uneasy, feel uncomfortable. And as a result, keep that emotional tag tied as you hear her explaining positions on [an] issue. Keep that discomfort. Hold onto it till you go into the voting booth....

A perfect example, though there are innumerable from which to choose, was the May 2008 *New Republic* cover with a large photo illustration of Hillary in a Hitleresque pose, wild-eyed and mouth agape, with cartoon thought bubbles around her screaming, among other things: "Caucuses are elitist!" "I bowl with Jesus!" "Wait, I'm getting verklempt!" "How do you say 'Judas' in Spanish?" and "You'll take away this nomination from my cold, dead hands!" Marginalizing and dehumanizing Clinton had been a sixteen-year task that started back during her husband's presidency. To say traditional media didn't know how to handle Hillary Clinton's presidential campaign, let alone do it fairly, is an understatement. New media was just as hostile.

It's no wonder the public had a question about what part of Hillary was stage-managed and focus-grouped and what part was legit. At the moment in her career when she got the chance to run for president, besides proving she's commander-in-chief tough, Clinton also had to wage a major offensive to prove she was warm-blooded.

The other side of the story is that because of what Hillary Rodham Clinton had endured with the press in the '90s, she wasn't giving them an inch. The trust factor was understandably nonexistent, which made it more difficult for Hillary and her campaign team. There's a reason she finally did interviews with Fox's Bill O'Reilly, which was one of her best of the primary season, and with Greta Van Susteren. Of course, these hardly made up for the smears and lies told by Sean Hannity about Clinton, and for the talking heads invited onto the channel, chief among them disgraced toe-sucker Dick Morris, who were glad to join in. They continue to this day against President Obama, former Fox blowhard Glenn Beck leading the way. A case in point was Beck's unhinged invective after showing a tape of Obama speaking in front of the AFL-CIO on his birthday: "It's like the damned planet of the apes!" No explanation required on that beauty.

On Neil Cavuto's Fox show in April 2008, there was a conversation about Elton John's fundraiser for Hillary where the pop superstar said he was "amazed by the misogynistic attitudes of some of the people in this country." Cavuto's guest, self-proclaimed anti-feminist Marc Rudov, chimed in, "This is a gynocracy.... The reason that Hillary is losing is because people don't like her. That's all it is." Fox legal analyst Lis Wiehl took him to task about the double standard of those who admire aggressive men but think of an aggressive woman as a bitch. Obviously threatened by Ms. Wiehl's assertiveness, Rudov squealed, "The woman is not called a B-word because she's assertive and aggressive; she's called a B-word because she acts like one," proving Ms. Wiehl's point. This stuff went on all the time at Fox.

The unrelenting sexism and non-issue-based critiques, especially when over the top or out of place and with no one pushing back on them, can have an effect opposite to what is intended, triggering support for a targeted candidate, regardless of the odds against her. Take the moment that finally pushed me to take Clinton's side. I'd been covering the election and watching the moves of all the candidates, with no intention of declaring support for any of them. That is, until Robin Givhan wrote her cleavage column in the *Washington Post*, "Hillary Clinton's Tentative Dip Into New Neckline Territory."

> There was cleavage on display Wednesday afternoon on C-SPAN2. It belonged to Senator Hillary Clinton. She was talking on the Senate floor about the burdensome cost of higher education. She was wearing a rose-colored blazer over a black top. The neckline sat low on her chest and had a subtle V-shape. The cleavage registered after only a quick glance. No scrunch-faced scrutiny was necessary. There wasn't an unseemly amount of cleavage showing, but there it was. Undeniable....

Bitch, strap that shit down. Thank the gods Clinton's cleavage moment didn't involve an "unseemly amount," though one can only guess how that's judged, especially for a woman of Clinton's, shall we say, *maturity*.

After Obama won the nomination it was immediately clear the vacuum left by Hillary had to be filled by someone, which could only be a woman. By the time fall came around, Joe Biden had been chosen for vice president, with the Democrats having a solid ticket that would be hard to beat on inspiration, talent and foreign policy gravitas. The huge female excitement Clinton had awakened in many left women salivating for more, which is why her campaigning for Obama was so important to him, as well as to her. Even after a grueling primary there were just so many supporters that didn't want to let her go, or let the moment die. Hillary was still on the political scene campaigning for Obama while soothing her fans' depression. Republicans were waiting for McCain to pull a political rabbit out of his hat.

No woman had written a chapter comparable to the whole book Hillary wrote during her campaign. Hillary's success, but also her ultimate failure to get the nomination, inspired the Republicans to finally turn to a woman for the first time in their history, mainly because they hoped they could capitalize on the Hillary Effect and what she'd stirred up. Republicans had always been notoriously stingy with women, preferring them in supporting roles only, or giving them titles but usurping their responsibility. Their policy prescriptions were decidedly anti-female. However, in the aftermath of Hillary's defeat, Republicans embraced the fantasy of the vagina vote, women voting for women for the sake of gender. This is how hopelessly clueless Republicans were until the Tea Party femmes came on the scene, because all the power and propaganda on the right had resided with the men.

Unlike Clinton, however, the female picked by Republicans was an unprepared national novice who hadn't run the gauntlet of traditional and new-media scrutiny. She came with plenty of negatives too, except hers were all well earned.

John McCain went looking for a running mate after seeing his opponent had star quality he couldn't equal in a million years. He had to try something big, because looking across at Barack Obama, the baggage McCain carried went beyond age. Google and YouTube became the McCain team's initial vetting process. They didn't need national security credentials with McCain at the top of the ticket, but what about some political eye candy with a maverick streak? A good-looking woman with natural political gifts who can perform on cue? Oh, and she's a governor, too. She must have seemed like an aging war horse's dream running-mate.

The worst baggage for Sarah was the general disarray of the Republican Party. When it came to women's issues, the right was AWOL, except on national security where Republicans had been beating Democrats for decades until Bush's misadventure in Iraq. There just weren't any women's issues for Sarah to tout that crossed over. McCain was even against the Lilly Ledbetter Fair Pay Act that would codify into law the principle of equal pay for equal work. I interviewed Carly Fiorina, who at the time was one of McCain's top spokespeople, and she had a hell of a time explaining the reason for his stance on this one, because it made absolutely no sense. But that is the Republican Party when it comes to modern women's issues.

Sarah Palin was also the governor of a state that might as well have been the moon for all its relevance to the American people's mindset. She was an unknown from Alaska, a far off frozen wonderland away from where members of the Washington press corps tread. That meant the media was going to descend with a vengeance. Nobody in the McCain campaign seemed prepared. In an interview for Tucker Carlson's conservative Daily Caller website in mid-2010, Palin recalled the "hordes of Obama's opposition researchers-slash-reporters" that invaded Alaska once she was announced.

The Daily Caller piece accused Journolist, a now-defunct, private web forum for left-leaning journalists founded by *Washington Post* blogger Ezra Klein, of coordinating media "attack lines" on the new VP candidate, a theory Palin heartily endorsed. "It was too obvious to me, my family, my administration and anyone else who knew me (and my record) that we were in a defenseless position the minute I gave my acceptance speech," she said. "To not have had the McCain campaign staff defend my record was an insurmountable challenge, because once a bell is rung, it's impossible to un-ring."

Rick Davis, McCain's campaign manager, who was charged with examining Palin's background for signs of potential trouble, said she went through "the full vetting process," including, among other things, scrutiny over her financials and an FBI background check. This turned out to be false. In fact, the FBI normally only does this type of full background check when security clearances are required, which wasn't the case for Palin. As reported by Sam Stein of the Huffington Post, McCain's team didn't even do a basic search of Sarah Palin's hometown newspaper before selecting her on August 29, 2008. It was Democratic operatives who first requested information on Palin, according to the Huffington Post story.

Sarah Palin initially seemed the perfect Republican counter to the Democratic star who'd just put eighteen million cracks in the ultimate glass ceiling. She was a female politician who had rocketed to stardom and was met by flocks of curious Republicans, wowing many with her persona. Some didn't care that she was naked when it came to policy knowledge, because Sarah immediately made conservative sexy again.

The *Anchorage Daily News* called her a "maverick," who was "running as the outsider breath of fresh air," in 2001, and used the word "skyrocketing" to describe her career trajectory at the time. "People are tired of the rich white guy" image of the Republican Party, the article quotes Palin as saying.

One of Sarah Palin's résumé points was her appointment to Alaska's Oil and Gas Conservation Commission, the value of which conservative Matthew Continetti describes in his book, *The Persecution of Sarah Palin*: "A seat on the obscure and highly technical board required no particular skill set."

But Sarah's pick wasn't about résumé. It was about sizzle. She also gave the Phyllis Schlafly wing of the Republican Party a much need facelift. That she represented their true, pure image of womanhood helped. Staunchly anti-women's-rights and anti-feminist in ideology, but saying it with a smile, her message attracted conservative women and would evolve into her "mama grizzly" pack of die-hard Palin supporters.

Republicans picked Sarah because she was a governor and they assumed she knew what she was doing. How can you run a state if you don't? But Alaska isn't California. It's not even Delaware. Besides, being governor doesn't mean you're ready for the national stage where the scrutiny is in your face 24/7.

It didn't help that Palin came with soap-opera drama. Family messiness, scandals and political intrigue are never a good combination, which went double for a woman, since the gauntlet of political baptism is not particularly friendly to females. Palin's story goes on and on: ethics charges, hypocrisy, rhetorical brawls played out in the press, all as McCain brought her into the womb of Republican presidential politics.

But who could have possibly guessed it would be Katie Couric who would expose Sarah Palin? Couric was the first solo female nightly news anchor, but she'd never quite gotten a handle on her CBS job, and rumors were flying at the time about how much longer she'd last in her role at the network. In fact, Couric and CBS decided to end their partnership after her contract expired in 2011. But she solidified Sarah's political image forever with a question as simple as, "What newspapers and magazines did you regularly read?" Can anyone imagine Hillary Clinton screwing that one up and surviving the day? Could any man survive it? *Fuhgeddaboudit.*

Palin has not only survived her disastrous vice presidential run, but when her governorship became burdensome, and also out of a combination of ego gratification and media frustration, she simply up and quit.

In July 2010, the Daily Caller acquired the emails of Journolist, the liberal, electronic bulletin board. The software application had been subscribed to by a bunch of insiders, journalists like Joe Klein, Democratic establishment types and others. When Palin was picked as McCain's running mate, it was clear from some of the Journolist exchanges that baggage for a female politician was being redefined.

Ryan Donmoyer, at the time a reporter for Bloomberg News, is quoted in one Journolist post, saying, "Her decision to keep the Down's baby is going to be a hugely emotional story that appeals to a vast swath of America, I think." Ben Adler, who was at Politico and then an editor at Newsweek, weighed in that "leaving [said] baby without its mother while she campaigns weakens that family-values argument."

The notion that a mother of five could possibly be vice president was blowing minds all over the country. "It's the Mommy Wars: Special Campaign Edition," the *New York Times* reported on September 1, 2008.

> Ms. Palin was selected by Senator John McCain in part to draw female voters, as Senator Hillary Rodham Clinton and Representative Geraldine A. Ferraro did before her. But Mrs. Clinton and Ms. Ferraro ran for president and

vice president when their children were grown, meaning they were survivors of — not combatants in — the bitter debates over whether and how to combine work with motherhood.

Mrs. Clinton's recent candidacy was a moment of reckoning for women of her generation, who treated her run as a mirror in which to examine their own lives. With Ms. Palin's entry into the field, a younger generation of women have picked up that mirror, using her candidacy to address the question of just how demanding a job a mother with such intense family obligations should tackle.

When people looked at John McCain, the reality of Palin being president also came to mind. How in the world could Sarah Palin handle that job along with the needs of her family? After all, not only was Trig a child with Down syndrome, but Palin's single daughter had just announced she was pregnant at age 17. What a mess! Blogs and message boards were exploding with talk about the conflicts. When you're discussing Sarah Palin, preparedness, motherhood of five *and* the vice presidency, now that's baggage.

It was the first time in American political history the subject had come up. Day care in the vice president's residence took on a whole new meaning. Sally Quinn tackled the subject as a guest on *The O'Reilly Factor* in November 2009, discussing Palin with guest-host Laura Ingraham and Kellyanne Conway:

> I think the irony here is that the criticism, so much of the criticism you're talking about, you know, having the governorship and trying to raise all these children, a Down syndrome baby, those — the people who normally would be anti-that are her base. These are the Christian right, who believe that a woman's place is in the home. And that criticism I've heard for her and sort of taking on this job with all these children and the Down syndrome baby of three months and the pregnant daughter was that maybe she should have stayed home at this particular time.

But women in the workplace know all about the "motherhood penalty." The 2010 Government Accountability Office (GAO) reported that 63% of women in management today are "childless," though someone should tell the government wordsmith geeks that the term is "child-free." Fourteen percent have children under 18 years old, according to the report. The penalty is real, however, because mothers reportedly earn 79% of what fathers in the workplace do. And even though flexible schedules are available for mothers who work, tough economic times and competition for jobs put a chill on any woman hoping to take advantage of that benefit.

Maria Shriver studied the issue in "The Shriver Report," launched in conjunction with the Center for American Progress in 2009, and learned that almost 40% of women are their families' sole breadwinners and 24% are co-breadwinners, with these numbers only going to increase if you use past data as foreshadowing for possible future growth.

> In 2007, 25.9% of wives were earning more than their husbands in households where both spouses work, according to the most recent data available from the Bureau of Labor Statistics. That's up from 17.8% two decades earlier.

> Among all married couples, including those where the husband isn't necessarily working, 33.5% of women were making more than their husbands, according to the 2007 data.

> — Allison Linn, MSNBC, November 2, 2009

In 2009, close to one in eighteen women were making six figures, according to the *Washington Post* (October 7, 2010), which is a jump of 14%, according to U.S. Census figures. Females are still not close to parity among Fortune 500 CEOs, however, numbering only 3%, according to the same report, which also touted "wonderful" Washington, D.C., as a "talent magnet" pool for young professional women.

Considering how stingy Republicans have been toward women, McCain's team was missing the read by a mile. But for all Palin's baggage, her rise wasn't exactly through traditional establishment routes. Sarah had made a name for herself by taking on her own.

A July 2010 Daily Caller article titled, "When McCain Picked Palin, Liberal Journalists Coordinated the Best Line of Attack," quotes a Journolist post from Democratic strategist Ed Kilgore: "Okay, let's get deadly serious, folks. Grating voice or not, 'inexperienced' or not, Sarah Palin's just been introduced to the country as a brave, above-party, oil-company-bashing, pork-hating maverick 'outsider.' What we can do is to expose her ideology."

When the leaking of the Journolist emails hit, it gave Palin an opportunity, or an excuse, to finally come clean about exactly why she quit the governorship.

From "Sarah Palin Strikes Back at Journolist's 'Sick Puppies,'" on The Daily Caller, July 22, 2010:

> When those lawsuits — which Palin said she won, but the media didn't cover — caused legal costs in the hundreds of thousands of dollars, Palin had finally had it, she said. "I said, 'Enough. Political adversaries and their political friends in the media will not destroy my state, my administration, nor my family. Enough.' I knew if I didn't play their game any longer, they could not win. I would not retreat, I would instead reload, and I would fight for what is right from a different plane."

Palin's Alaska governorship became too much baggage.

Palin learned the hard way to mistrust the national establishment, a lesson Hillary was taught during Bill's presidency. Appearing in a one-on-one interview after her 2010 speech at the Tea Party convention, TV cameras caught the words "energy," "tax," and "Lift American spirits" scribbled on her hand. Robert Gibbs, from the White House podium no less, mimicked Mrs. Palin by writing on his own hand. Never mind that she didn't hold public office and was not running for office; the White House couldn't resist making fun of her. Weeks later, appearing during Jay Leno's *Tonight Show* re-launch week, Palin turned the tables on her critics and got in a subtle dig at President Obama as well, when she said her hand was simply "a poor man's teleprompter." The crowd ate it up.

Palin's big problem, if she wants to leap beyond TV celebrity status, is there's still no sign of a gravitas gene anywhere to be found. Still, Palin was turning out to be a much better performer than her competitors until she overexposed herself on Fox News and her reality TV show, then made her gaffe after the Loughner shootings. Meanwhile, Rep. Michele Bachmann was unceremoniously raising buckets of cash and honing her pitch.

Michele Bachmann came on the scene and was able to share Tea Party thunder, because she's not a celebrity but has the job of actually making decisions and governing. Unfortunately, Bachmann's legislative record is not just slim, it's nonexistent. But her day job was never more important than during the budget battle in early April 2011, when Palin was reduced to Twitter bursts, while Bachmann made the media rounds from NBC's *Today Show* and *Daily Rundown* to Bill O'Reilly's *The Factor* on Fox, making the case for budget cuts and leading the push for Speaker Boehner to keep squeezing Democrats.

However, Bachmann also proved the importance of compromise when political principles meet a legislative brick wall. She tweeted at the height of the budget battle, during the last hours of the very last day, "I'm ready for a big fight that will change the arc of history. The current fight in Washington is not that fight." Appearing later with John King on CNN, then on Fox, she said the 2011 budget fight wasn't "the main event," indicating an ability to back down when absolutely necessary. Immediately after giving Boehner the space he needed to avert a government shutdown, Bachmann went back to being Bachmann, writing on the RedState blog that "the deal was not enough." If you want to be a player, you have to learn to maneuver the minefields, which she's done much better than Palin, though both women are fact-challenged.

What's dangerous about Michele Bachmann and other politicians like her is the hypocrisy she displays when her Tea Party marketing slams up against her actions, such as shunning Medicaid while her family business benefits from it; or railing against farm subsidies while taking them; or bitching about "Obamacare," when she enjoys the best health care in the country through her job in Congress; or especially, when she enthusiastically hauls stimulus money back to her own district to create jobs, as she rails against the stimulus.

The Huffington Post's Sam Stein filed a Freedom of Information request and in August 2011 wrote about some interesting tidbits that drive the above point home:

> A Freedom of Information Act request filed by The Huffington Post with three separate federal agencies reveals that on at least sixteen separate occasions, Bachmann petitioned the federal government for direct financial help or aid. A large chunk of those requests were for funds set aside through President Obama's stimulus

program, which Bachmann once labeled "fantasy economics." Bachmann made two more of those requests to the Environmental Protection Agency, an institution that she has suggested she would eliminate if she were in the White House. Taken as a whole, the letters underscore what Bachmann's critics describe as a glaring distance between her campaign oratory and her actual conduct as a lawmaker.

Even Tea Party Republicans know what creates jobs, but they're willing to sell out the working class in their rhetoric while benefiting from Democratic policies. Then they dupe the public into voting against their interests while telling them Republicanism is the way, even though it undermines middle-class wages and security while, at the same time, these politicians enjoy the benefits of progressive economic policies they want to cut for the people.

In the same Huffington Post article, titled "Michele Bachmann Repeatedly Sought Stimulus, EPA, Other Government Funds," Sam Stein quoted John Feehery, a top adviser to former House Speaker Dennis Hastert, saying, "It had been a longstanding tradition in Congress to be fiscally conservative in every other district other than your own. Bachmann apparently is being a traditionalist."

The Hillary Effect made Sarah Palin possible, with Bachmann's run happening because of what was set in motion after '08, but neither Bachmann nor Palin comes close to what Hillary offered. Neither Tea Party candidate could win a national, general election. One reason Clinton's fans won't give up on the possibility, no matter how remote, that she'll try again, is that they believe Hillary can.

Michelle Goldberg captured some of Sarah Palin's star power in her essay "Flirting her way to Victory," in *The Guardian*, which was later included in the book *Going Rouge: Sarah Palin — An American Nightmare,* a compilation of essays by progressives taking aim at their favorite target. "There is indeed something mesmerizing about Palin," Goldberg writes, "with her manic beaming and fulsome confidence in her own charm." Goldberg continues by eviscerating the "emptiness of her answers in the debate" with Joe Biden.

When Sarah Palin announced prior to the debate that "I may not answer the questions that either the moderator or you want to hear, but I'm going to talk straight to the American people," she wasn't kidding. A man would have gotten creamed for this crap, and Hillary would have been pilloried.

But at least Hillary never had to endure assaults on Chelsea's paternity.

Sarah Palin's vice presidential implosion created baggage beyond belief. Obama's birther crazies have a lunatic cousin among the Trig "trutherism" conspiracy theorists, pushing a line of attack that has been championed by the Daily Beast's Andrew Sullivan, who began his ravings while still at the *Atlantic Monthly*. After he got wind of an amateur posting on the influential Daily Kos website that accused Sarah Palin of possibly not being the mother of Trig, Sullivan continued to imply, even as late as December 2009 on HLN's *Joy Behar Show*, that there were questions surrounding Trig Palin's parentage.

The *Los Angeles Times* reported on Sept. 2, 2008, that Palin's daughter was five-months pregnant, which meant that since Trig was born not even five months earlier on April 18, 2008, there was no way he could have been Bristol's baby. Days later, smart funny-man Bill Maher joined Sullivan in the insanity, proclaiming on his HBO show, "I'm not that convinced that that's [Sarah Palin's] baby."

Nicolle Wallace, a former McCain presidential campaign staffer who was much closer to the Palins than Maher or Sullivan, offered brutally blunt and factually informed assessments of Palin from the moment she was picked for vice president. In a conversation with Anne Kornblut posted as a *Washington Post* video in January 2010, Wallace let fly:

> Were we ready for anything? No, we weren't ready.... I remember not knowing who she was.... Mark Salter said, "She sort of believes in creationism; do you think that's a problem?" I don't know, I'll have to Google that. Then Steve Schmidt said, "...and her daughter's pregnant, what do you think of that?" And I said, "I'll be right back." No! We were ready for nothing. Three boys picked her and so they didn't ask girl questions. And so no one was prepared to defend her. If you pick Jesus Christ you have to be able to defend him. If your nominee is perfect, known and

vetted, you have to be able to defend them.... Everyone was Googling her to find out who she was and what she believed in.... Nobody knew anything."

However, it was Katie Couric's easy question on newspapers that laid bare the characteristics that led to Sarah Palin's rise: She was a scrappy fighter with an eye for opportunity but not preparation or self-preservation. Why wait? Why prepare? When opportunity knocks, answer. It's been a scramble for Sarah Palin ever since. After a tough struggle, she rallied impressively to have a strong year in 2010, though by mid-2011 Palin was pure backdrop.

You also can't discount that in the void left by Hillary Rodham Clinton's presidential run, Palin sensed her entry onto the national stage would never get a better send off, regardless of her unpreparedness. The Hillary Effect paved the way for Palin to make Republican Party history. Pretty impressive for a girl from Wasilla.

Hillary and Sarah both carry baggage from media scrutiny into their political past, present and futures. Clinton, however, had much of her baggage concocted, beginning in the '90s, by right-wing power-brokers and enemies made through her husband. Palin's baggage from Alaska was her own creation, exacerbated by the very small political world of Alaska. But while Hillary learned to re-direct the media glare onto issues and policies that matter to her, Sarah always turns it into a political pity party. It was hard to take Palin's beef seriously about what she calls "the lamestream media" and new media landing in Alaska, because it's been proven that not even the Republican establishment knew much about her. McCain hoisting her into history on the Republican national ticket forced serious press scrutiny for the first time. Like Hillary, Sarah's experience with the press the first time out has had its effect.

Speaking on *The O'Reilly Factor,* Glenn Beck called her the most guarded woman he'd ever seen in his life. "I've never met anybody with shields up more than Sarah Palin," Beck said.

Michele Bachmann seemed to have learned from Palin's media mistakes. Bachmann took a page out of Hillary's playbook, staying focused on why she was running and not the noise around her. Tina Brown's *Newsweek* ran a wild-eyed cover photo of Bachmann in August 2011, right before the Ames straw poll, but when asked about it in Iowa the candidate and her team simply brushed it off. They had no intention of getting into a media back-

and-forth. Bachmann was focused on Iowa, her one chance to catapult herself firmly into the presidential race. She not only won the Ames straw poll; she became the first Republican female to win any straw poll, caucus or primary in American history. Matthew Dowd, chief strategist for the Bush-Cheney '04 campaign, was the first and only prominent political person to mention this historic achievement.

The inaugural Tea Party convention offered Sarah Palin her first real platform since her vice presidential catastrophe. By early 2010 she had even begun wowing the likes of David Broder and *Time* magazine's Joe Klein, who compared Palin to Bill Clinton:

> I have a theory about Bill Clinton: His philandering worked in his favor politically, especially with a demographic chunk that usually shies away from liberalism: American working guys. It made him more accessible. Here was a fellow who got it on with faded lounge singers and then celebrated with a Double Quarter Pounder and fries at the local McDonald's. If that ain't pickup-truck nirvana, what is? Democrats haven't produced many such men of the people; they produce law-professor presidents, a theme Palin launched in Nashville that we will be hearing a lot more frequently in the future.
>
> Palin hits the same mystic chords as Clinton. A woman who goes to war against the 19-year-old boy who knocked up her daughter and then posed for *Playgirl* is far more comprehensible to most Americans than deficit spending is.
>
> — Joe Klein, *Time*, February 11, 2010

Klein went further to say, "One might even argue that 'You betcha' is American for 'Yes, we can.'" Really? Based on what, a contraction?

Broder wrote about Sarah Palin's "pitch-perfect populism" in his column, also pronouncing, "She's good."

When Hillary ran for president we were still a frat boy nation. To hear the way Rush, the late Mr. Broder and Joe Klein gushed over Sarah Palin in 2010, with Limbaugh still a devotee today, proves that in some quarters, we still are. However, since Hillary's presidential run, some of the air has gone out of the gasbags, who at least can finally envision a woman at the top. But it's interesting these anti-Hillary males find Sarah so appealing. Let's just say they're more comfortable with Sarah. She's less threatening. They never think too hard about the commander-in-chief question and whether she can lead.

Having two favorite establishment journalists send a strong message to the Republican pooh-bahs — essentially saying, "She's okay in our book, even if you don't take her seriously" — was a godsend for Sarah. Broder and Klein sent a rebuke to a political party dying on the vine at a time when all Americans are ready to chuck both major parties. Palin was golden in 2010, though her Tea Party wing wields a double-edged sword for the Republicans. They have become the heart of what used to be Reagan's GOP, a political party that likely wouldn't even nominate him today.

Palin, Bachmann, Rand Paul, Rick Perry and now perhaps Herman Cain and their Tea Party activists have become not only the heart, but the muscle inside the Republican Party, which looked ready for the grave when Obama was elected. Even after his team's nasty relationship with Palin, John McCain had to bite the bullet and ask her to help him save his Senate seat in 2010.

Whatever her baggage, she's dropped it like a rock and moved on. Palin is also an asset for political writers, new media and magazines, but certainly not for reasons of gravitas. By contrast, the first cover story Tina Brown ran after acquiring *Newsweek* was about Secretary Hillary Clinton, titled, "The Hillary Doctrine." It focused on "her most heartfelt mission: to put women and girls at the forefront of the new world order."

Even after David Weigel got unceremoniously (and undeservedly) shit-canned by the *Washington Post* for a messy email tantrum from a private communication gone public, he felt Sarah's pain and empathized with her plight. He wrote about it for *Esquire*'s Politics Blog in early July 2010, in a post titled, How I Learned to Stop Worrying & Love Sarah Palin (Kinda):

"But damn if I didn't feel sorry for the way every utterance Palin ever makes is taffy-pulled and inspected for lies...."

They tried, but her adversaries couldn't keep Sarah down.

They tried with Hillary too and almost succeeded. No, she's not president, but she made history in spite of those who didn't want her anywhere near President Obama, with the Hillary Effect of her candidacy widely impacting women. But President Obama is no dummy. He knows first-hand what she's made of, and he knows having what she's got a phone call away is good for his presidency and good for the country. Unfortunately, there are many others who aren't nearly as smart.

Chapter 3: **You Can Keep a Good Woman Down**

"Hillary's problem isn't that she's too moderate; it's that she's too inauthentic," said Arianna Huffington, resurrecting an opinion of Hillary that was a pure '90s Republican talking point regurgitated for the 2008 primary season. But coming from a former die-hard Newt Gingrich conservative-turned-liberal, or at least very independent, it wasn't surprising. That's not to say that some Democrats didn't agree. Most people with this opinion had never actually met Clinton or seen her in action, though in the political game of perception it hardly mattered.

Arianna is the web's political Oprah of aggregation and one of the most successful new-media moguls online, a position that was solidified when AOL bought Huffington Post for a reported $315 million in February 2011. Not long before this happened, in late 2010, she ran into headwinds when Peter Daou and James Boyce, both of whom I've worked with, consider friends and trust implicitly, filed a lawsuit alleging Arianna had gotten her model for Huffington Post from them, a story covered in *Vanity Fair*. After the 2008 campaign, Ms. Huffington became a champion of economic reform on behalf of the middle class and against Wall Street greed. So it's ironic that long after collecting a nine-figure payment for her site, Huffington started taking incoming for not paying the bloggers who helped put her on the map, while at the same time hiring traditional media veterans such as Howard Fineman and Peter Goodman. Arianna's enticement, going back to when I started writing for her in early 2006, was all about being a Huffington Post contributor and not money, which everybody knew.

Posting on Huffington Post was always worth it for the visibility and for the quality of the site's readership. When I slammed *The Sopranos* creators for their bomb of a series finale in a 2009 year-end piece that covered the best and the worst of the year and the decade, David Chase sent me the entire box set of the series, along with a charming yet scathing letter. It remains the classiest, concealed "fuck you" I've ever received, and I've gotten quite a few, many of which I display on my own website's "hate mail" page. Even after Huffington Post became Obama central, my political posts were regularly featured there, which continued even after I started writing about Sarah Palin, something that always brought lively comments.

Ms. Huffington tried to deny that her bias for Obama during the 2008 primaries ever impacted the editorial stance on HuffPost, which was laughable to anyone reading or writing on the site. After I became a Hillary supporter, the comments to my HuffPost essays were always harsh, which I expected, because the site was pro-Obama all the way.

HuffPost also became notable for its vigilant stance against the war in Afghanistan, pounding President Obama's policy relentlessly.

In early August 2009, when President Bill Clinton went to North Korea and came back with the two journalists, Laura Ling and Euna Lee, the headline on the front page blared: "BILL UPSTAGES HILLARY... ONCE AGAIN." I was outraged, and so were many HuffPost readers, including some working inside the organization. I weighed in with, "Dear Huffington Post, About That Headline," which included a screen capture of the offensive front-page banner. My essay made it around the web, garnering a lot of attention. Hillary Rodham Clinton sent me a personal note of thanks, not under her secretary of state title. In the piece I wrote that the headline was "petty" and "small," but also that whoever chose it had gone down "Clinton Derangement Highway." Commenters thanked and agreed with me, and emails flooded my inbox.

During the primaries, Arianna Huffington was one of Hillary's most vicious critics. In one sense, her Hillary critiques should have come as no surprise, because as a one-time conservative national columnist, she had also spoken out for President Clinton's resignation back during the Lewinski scandal. In 1998, Huffington had even started a petition site called Resignation.com that offered gag prizes for the best sample President Clinton resignation speech. Her theory was "enough is enough." Second prize was a trip to San Clemente, where former President Richard Nixon made his home. Her rationale was simple: It would be for the good of the nation. She stated there was "something kind of heroic about resignation."

Huffington's disdain for former President Bill Clinton transferred with a vengeance to his wife. Her attacks were personal and malicious, with her venom powerfully descriptive and fearlessly delivered, whenever she weighed in.

The *New York Press*, the recently shut-down alternative weekly, quoted Huffington in October 2006, saying about Hillary, "You can smell the fear on her.... It wafts around her like a cheap perfume: Eau de Don't Let Me Screw Up and Flush My Chances Down the Toilette. As a result of her fear of losing and the soul-sapping tyranny of trying to please and placate everybody, she's become more processed than Velveeta."

I couldn't help thinking of Mark Penn when Arianna delivered some of her analytic zingers.

"You can almost see every word that comes out of her mouth first being marched through the different compartments of her brain — analyzed, evaluated and vetted by each of them.," the *Press* story continued. "What will the consultants think of this? How will it poll? Will working women between 25-35 in eastern Ohio think it's okay? Her fear has caused a complete disconnect from who she really is and what she really thinks (that is, if she even knows anymore)."

Huffington Post delivered an unrelenting attack that pushed Clinton supporters away in droves. I received dozens of emails and comments complaining about it, most correspondents heartbroken over the unfairness because they had loved the site. But they refused to visit anymore because of the one-sided coverage that was all Obama all the time, even though there were plenty of us over there writing about Clinton, including Peter Daou, her campaign's Internet director.

One Arianna Huffington post gave advice to Clinton on what she should say during a planned appearance on the *Late Show with David Letterman*. Some lines were very funny; others were dreadful, because they steered into the stereotype that Hillary was not her own woman. Even ghostwriters sometimes need a rewrite.

DAVE: What was your feud with Barack Obama about?

HILLARY: I just had to set him straight about a few things. He'd make a great addition to the ticket, but I had to let him know that the days of the VP running things are coming to an end.

DAVE: I thought it was about using nuclear weapons against Pakistan or something.

HILLARY: As I said at the time, Dave, a presidential candidate shouldn't discuss foreign policy questions of that nature in a forum like this.

DAVE: Where should they be discussed then?

HILLARY: At home with Bill Clinton.

It was yet another reminder that Bill would never be far away if Hillary were commander in chief. Not very subtle, but it was becoming a theme.

Before the New Hampshire primary, Ms. Huffington wrote a post under the headline, "Portrait in Cynicism: Hillary Attacks Obama from Every Angle." This was not exactly groundbreaking stuff. That's politics, baby, something Huffington, whose former support of Newt Gingrich was detailed exhaustively in *Time* magazine's 1995 piece, "Arianna Huffington: A Woman on the Verge," certainly knew.

Long before Hillary won Senate approval as Obama's secretary of state, Huffington Post helped lead the progressive movement's vilification and demonization of her online. After all, if you can dehumanize a woman, then making her irrelevant is much easier. This can also happen with men, but women start with strikes against us. We're still made to prove we can lead, while men are automatically assumed able to do so, regardless of their history. (See George W. Bush.)

There has been a media bias against women since at least the beginning of TV news, with most of the journalists covering politics men. How are we going to get more women running America, let alone as president, if the people who tell the political stories don't give the most qualified women in politics a fair shake on the airwaves? At the start of the post-Hillary political era, things were changing. Fox News not only signed up Sarah Palin but built her a studio in Alaska. John McCain made her qualified, even if she's now only a political celebrity. Clinton never got close to such a perk, but then again, she's a policy wonk, not a talking head.

Women have never been given equal time on television to help shape ideas or find solutions to far-ranging problems, especially on national security issues, the president's primary job. Katie Couric was the only female nightly news anchor on broadcast television until Diane Sawyer assumed that role for ABC in 2009. It wasn't until after Hillary's presidential run that we saw the first woman anchor appear in the all-important Sunday political show lineup in the past nineteen years, with veteran journalist and reporter Candy Crowley headlining a program for CNN. Crowley had to schlep a lot of miles, file a lot of stories and pay her dues and then some before she got the gig.

The same goes for Christiane Amanpour, who took over *This Week* on ABC in August 2010. The instant Ms. Amanpour was announced for the slot, the right began a campaign against her, which was boosted by Tom Shales of the *Washington Post*, because she covered Islam for CNN and her father was an Iranian with the first name Mohammed. After Amanpour's show premiered, Shales went at her again, only this time he questioned whether she might be a Taliban sympathizer, simply because she said, "We remember all of those who died in war this week" while the names of U.S. soldiers who died flashed on the screen. "All," to Shales, evidently meant Taliban too.

Meanwhile, over at Fox News, Greta Van Susteren not only was respectful of Hillary Clinton during the primary season, but understood the importance of Clinton's presidential campaign to millions of women around the country. While continuing her coverage of Secretary Clinton, Van Susteren has become just about the only female anchor Sarah Palin will talk to.

The ladies of ABC's *The View*, Barbara Walters, Joy Behar, Whoopi Goldberg, Elisabeth Hasselbeck and Sherri Shepherd, made political history in 2010 when President Obama came on their show to talk about everything from Afghanistan to Snooki. It was the first time a sitting president had ever made a solo, daytime talk show appearance.

Mika Brzezinski's co-anchor job on MSNBC's *Morning Joe* is like herding squirrels. That she does it at the crack of frickin' dawn, while talking foreign policy before most people are even awake, is medal-worthy. Keeping crap off the show seems to be her biggest challenge, though it's hard to resist when the boys crack up at trending stories like Charlie Sheen or TSA employees pictured groping travelers. Kudos to Ms. Brzezinski for giving attention to First Lady Michelle Obama's critically important obesity campaign. Joe Scarborough plays the bad boy to Mika's scold on this issue, but let's hope she keeps ignoring him.

The most important female broadcaster on the scene today, as far as I'm concerned, is MSNBC's Rachel Maddow. Taking a page from veteran Andrea Mitchell, the under-appreciated grande dame of the foreign policy beat for NBC News, Maddow unflinchingly forged a path into foreign policy. That's never easy terrain for a woman, especially in the cable world, though the captivating and fast-developing Arab Spring of 2011 helped change that.

Maddow provided the best coverage on any channel during the Egyptian uprising, not counting Al Jazeera English, which if more people could watch might save us from ourselves. One night, Rachel's team was rolling inside Egypt as she interviewed reporter Richard Engel from the studio, and she was there the moment the Egyptian Army intervened for the first time on behalf of the protesters. It was some of the most riveting coverage of the uprising. It wasn't so easy when President Obama chose to bomb Libya and go for regime change, while former Secretary of Defense Gates said it wasn't "in our strategic interest," but Maddow held the debate and her audience was the wiser for it.

The Sunday gold standard is *Meet the Press*, but "If It's Sunday, It's Misogyny" was a regular headline for me throughout Tim Russert's reign. Russert's all-male, talk-fest format was replicated on every other network, which is still the case, with insiders and lots of conservatives the main staple. Anyone watching on Sunday would swear there were no women in Congress or in the political sphere at all. The headliners are mostly male almost all the time, with guests pretty much the same as they were fifteen years ago, though a shakeup has begun due to the rise of new media's prominence. The Sunday political shows kick off the coming week's round of political stories. That they also provide the setup and staging for dispensing conventional wisdom of Republican and Democratic talking points to the public about political issues is obvious. Women's presence is critical on these shows, because this is where foreign policy issues are discussed, so if we're going to have a female president we need leading women's voices to have visibility on matters of national security.

Media Matters for America, the progressive media watchdog group, analyzed the Sunday talk show guests on ABC, CBS and NBC between 1997 and 2005, shedding some light on the conservative history of those news shows. And it's not about what party is in control of Washington either. The right has won a lot of ground, because of its "liberal media" talking point, even if there's not much truth to it.

In both the Clinton and Bush administrations, conservative journalists were far more likely to appear on the Sunday shows than were progressive journalists. In Clinton's second term, 61% of the ideologically identifiable journalists were conservative; in Bush's first term, that figure rose to 69%.

In the summer of 2010, a study from The Green Bag legal journal revealed that of the nine legislators seen most frequently on the Sunday shows the previous year, only one, Senator Dianne Feinstein, was a woman. Even worse, only 13.5% of the guests on the five morning shows were women. At a time when the first female Speaker of the House in U.S. history was in power, women continued to be slighted.

The Republican Party leadership — majority and minority leaders and whips — appeared on these shows a total of forty-three times in 2009, while the Democratic Party leadership, including Speaker of the House Nancy Pelosi, appeared only eleven times, according to the Green Bag analysis.

In 2009, after Hillary's historic presidential candidacy, not to mention Sarah Palin's prominence on the right, the Green Bag study reported CNN's *State of the Union* had 20.2% female guests; next was ABC's *This Week* with 16%; CBS's *Face the Nation* had 10.9% females; *Fox News Sunday* had 8.75%; and bringing up the rear, unsurprisingly, was *Meet the Press* with 5.7% female guests. For those of you counting, that would be two women for an entire year on *Meet the Press*.

On one particular Sunday back in 2004, moderators Tim Russert for *Meet the Press* and George Stephanopoulos for *This Week* both convened all male guests, which is nothing unusual, and both shows were discussing family issues. Stephanopoulos billed his as featuring "four of America's most prominent Christian preachers, thinkers and activists." Russert chose the topics of abortion, life and family values, the last being an all-time favorite for traditional media types. Even with female producers at the time, according to a transcript from the late November 2004 show, the all-male guests Russert chose were Dr. Jerry Falwell, of the Faith and Values

Coalition; Dr. Richard Land, president, Ethics and Religious Liberty Commission, Southern Baptist Convention; Rev. Al Sharpton, National Action Network; and Rev. Jim Wallis, editor, *Sojourners* magazine. This is a regular occurrence, which Christiane Amanpour continued on Easter Sunday 2011, when Rev. Franklin Graham and Pastor Tim Keller were her guests, along with panelists Rev. Al Sharpton and Eboo Patel of the Interfaith Youth Core, and Dr. Richard Land, president of the Ethics & Religious Liberty Commission, with no female religious leaders anywhere in sight.

Someone needs to explain to me how the hell a conversation about abortion, life and family values on what was arguably the most important Sunday show of the week at the time can get away with not have even one female headliner.

In December 2009, David Gregory had a discussion at the height of the health care debate with an all-male panel yet again. The debate had many focal points, but none as combustible as the abortion issue. Politico ran a headline at the time that blared "Health Deal Hinged on Abortion." Yet Gregory's *Meet the Press* discussion was void of any women at all.

Women in media power spots hadn't spanned into cable when Hillary came to Washington with her president husband. She had to combat a boys club that held sway over all political opinion before new media arrived.

Back in 1996, the rhetorical pooh-bah for the *New York Times* for close to thirty-two years, the late Bill Safire, weaver of word webs for Richard M. Nixon and a favorite of Mr. Russert's, began his campaign against Hillary Rodham Clinton by pondering her possible indictment in print. Hillary's "corrupt banking clients and her crooked law firm partner" were subjects of Safire's "Practice to 'Deceive'" *Times* opinion piece, which railed about the Rose Law Firm. Safire's hit-piece library on Hillary was stuffed with columns invoking words like "infamous," "prime suspect," "obstructing justice" and of course "deceit," all of which turned out to be sheer hyperbole with a side of hatred for all things Clinton. In 2000, Safire's column "Habitual Prevaricator" concluded, "She had help in escaping indictment." Facts tend to do that for people.

Ken Gormley shed light on those facts in 2010. The proposed, but never-filed indictment against First Lady Hillary

Rodham Clinton was titled *United States of America v. Hillary Rodham Clinton and Webster Lee Hubbell.* The Office of Independent Council depended on, among other things, Hillary's demeanor when she testified about how Rose Law Firm billing records had appeared on a table, and whether she had the opportunity to make them "reappear." The OIC said the alleged cover-up of Hillary's involvement in these matters "began in earnest" in 1992, during her husband's first presidential campaign. In Gormley's book, Sam Dash, who was the OIC ethics adviser, said the evidence amounted to "a bunch of nothing." Dash would eventually resign over Ken Starr's salacious, pornographic report.

In David Brock's book, *The Republican Noise Machine*, he quotes the late, legendary reporter David Halberstam as saying upon Safire's hiring that he's "not a Conservative...but a paid manipulator. He is not a man of ideas or politics but of tricks."

After the Clintons left the White House, with Hillary setting her eyes on the Senate, one of the punditocracy's favorite sports was to attack her using a '90s bank shot.

After Hillary's stunning win in New Hampshire, Chris Matthews said to Howard Wolfson, "I give her a lot of personal credit. I will never underestimate Hillary Clinton again." Irony exploded the very next morning. For Matthews, "never" didn't even last a day.

"I'll be brutal," Matthews bellowed on *Morning Joe* hours later, on January 9, 2008. "The reason she's a U.S. senator, the reason she's a candidate for president, the reason she may be a front-runner is her husband messed around. That's how she got to be senator from New York. We keep forgetting it. She didn't win there on her merit."

Matthews was wrong about how Hillary won the New York Senate seat, and he was hardly alone among the media elite. The *Washington Post*'s Kathleen Parker, who flunked out of CNN but was a frequent guest on NBC's *Chris Matthews Show*, the un-hardball, thirty-minute, insider-ass-kissing festival, parroted the same talking points in a September 2007 column widely disseminated on the web. "Public sympathy, as well as Hillary's dignified public response to humiliation, trumped her lousy record as a policy-maker and, voilà, she was the junior senator from New

York. Now she's nearly the presumptive Democratic nominee for president," Parker wrote.

In another column, Parker called the Clintons "Mr. Id and Mrs. Superego," and said Hillary "carried the cross of self-discipline and moral vigor" for her husband.

The truth is that Hillary fought hard to win her Senate seat; New Yorkers, besides being notoriously independent-minded, rightfully made her earn their votes. Having lived in New York City for a spell, I know their hard-edged skepticism, and share it. So when Hillary started her Senate listening tour in preparation for seeking a U.S. Senate seat there, a Zogby poll in the summer of 1999 showed New Yorkers in many upstate areas didn't give a flying fig about hearing anything from Clinton, with Utica area voters calling it a publicity stunt and 51% of Oneida County voters saying her tour wouldn't impact how they voted. However, Hillary's favorability factor went from 47% to 53.1% in June, 1999.

Even Whitewater huckster Jeff Gerth had to give her credit for what she accomplished with her tour. In the book, *Her Way: The Hopes and Ambitions of Hillary Rodham Clinton,* Gerth and co-author Don VanNatta Jr. wrote that New Yorkers ended up convinced Clinton "'seems like one of us.'" Taking a page from Bill, Hillary shook as many hands as she could, kept listening and asked questions, and New Yorkers were duly impressed.

Matthews' MSNBC show *Hardball* was once must-see political TV, partly because of his obvious love of politics and history, but it became so contaminated with unhinged Clinton derangement, his prejudices sabotaged his analysis and ultimately made it unwatchable. Matthews continued spewing his vitriol long after it became clear the media was in pile-on mode. He was forced to offer what was billed as an apology for his previous, sexist indictment of her accomplishments on *Morning Joe*, but the comment instead became a long-winded, self-serving monologue about his own "good heart." He babbled on and on about William Faulkner, Obama, McCain, hope and America. He blathered about his TV yacker job and about not having a script, about addressing tricky subjects and being "tough, fearless and blunt," though he neglected to mention anything about honesty, due diligence or fairness. The statement may have masqueraded as "I'm sorry," but in typical Matthews fashion, it was really all about him.

The cringing piggishness of Chris Matthews, the alter ego to his wondrous working-class persona, was caught on tape in an exchange with then-CNBC-anchor Erin Burnett, back in August 2007.

MATTHEWS: Could you get a little closer to the camera?

BURNETT: My — what is it? Is it zooming in strangely?

MATTHEWS: Come on in closer. No, come in — come in further — come in closer. Really close.

BURNETT: What are you — what are you doing?

MATTHEWS: Just kidding! You look great! Anyway, thanks. Erin, it's great to — look at that look. You're great.

BURNETT: I don't even know. I'm going to have to go look at the tape here. I'm in a strange location.

MATTHEWS: No, you're beautiful. I'm just kidding. I'm just kidding. You're a knockout. Anyway, thank you, Erin Burnett.

BURNETT: All right, Chris. See you later.

MATTHEWS: It's all right getting bad news from you, even, OK? Thanks for coming on Hardball.

Ms. Burnett is a professional business analyst, jumping networks to CNN, but for Matthews she's just another good looking woman to be exploited for his amusement, live on camera no less, giving the woman less respect than any man would get who's equally good looking.

But Matthews had finally said out loud what the chattering establishment class had been whispering about for awhile. It didn't matter to them what Hillary Rodham Clinton had done: her sparkling record at Wellesley College and at Yale Law School; her achievements as founder of Arkansas Advocates for Children and Families; or her extended advocacy for children and civil rights work as a board member for several organizations, including the Childrens' Defense fund. They weren't impressed by her public service on numerous caucuses and non-legislative committees, or even by her experience on a variety of Senate committees, including Budget, Armed Services, Environment and Public Works, and on and on. She also chaired the Legal Services Corporation and joined Senate caucuses on the National Guard, rural health, and steel. Her

Senate résumé includes heading the Steering and Coordination Committee, and the Task Force of National Health Care Reform. And that's just a short list of what she's accomplished.

Howard Kurtz finally wrote an article on Clinton and the media in December 2007, quoting über-insider and *Game Change* co-author Mark Halperin saying what many of us had known for months:

> "She's just held to a different standard in every respect," says Mark Halperin, *Time*'s editor at large. "The press rooted for Obama to go negative, and when he did he was applauded. When she does it, it's treated as this huge violation of propriety." While Clinton's mistakes deserve full coverage, Halperin says, "the press' flaws — wild swings, accentuating the negative — are magnified fifty times when it comes to her. It's not a level playing field."
>
> — Howard Kurtz, *Washington Post*, December 19, 2007

Halperin repeated his analysis to Charlie Rose in January 2008, saying "I have no doubt in my mind that the press corps favors Barack Obama; that the coverage is much more optimistic, enthusiastic.... Arianna [Huffington]'s right, it's a great story, but I'm for fairness in the process, and I think the press has an obligation.... I don't think it's close to equal."

When I began reporting on the media bias, a side of the story that wasn't being covered yet because few would admit the sexist nature of Clinton's coverage, the heat coming my way increased, as did the attacks. I didn't care, because the truth told the story. Kurtz quoting Halperin again, from the above-cited *Post* story: "'Your typical reporter has a thinly disguised preference that Barack Obama be the nominee. The narrative of him beating her is better than her beating him, in part because she's a Clinton and in part because he's a young African American.... There's no one rooting for her to come back.'"

Before he couldn't take it anymore and bailed out of his MSNBC anchor job, Keith Olbermann saved my sanity during Clinton impeachment back in the '90s. Olbermann's *Countdown* became an important show during the Bush years and again during Obama's first two years, right up until the Friday in 2011 when cable's most prominent left-leaning media personality walked out, leaving his high-profile gig behind. He and the network said their split was by mutual agreement, which is likely because the whole *Countdown* enterprise had become a pain in everyone's ass.

Olbermann's misogyny burst out while he was covering Hillary during the primary season of 2008, making a lot of people glad he was gone. I was not one of them, because there are far too few effective cable rebels. Now trying to build a similar platform for his show on Al Gore's Current TV, he's just as good and maybe better. But Mr. Olbermann's hyperbole during the '08 primaries turned him into a caricature, morphing him into MSNBC's version of Sean Hannity.

Mr. Olbermann's reaction to the comment Geraldine Ferraro made to California's "Daily Breeze" newspaper, was representative. Ferraro's remark that "If Obama was a white man, he would not be in this position" was clueless, but it didn't require a nuclear response.

Seeing Barack Obama on the campaign trail, for me, was the political equivalent of watching Magic Johnson play basketball in his prime. So, I have no doubt that if Obama had been white he would have bowled over audiences, even if his word salads didn't really manifest change. The truer statement was that if Obama were a *woman* he would not have been in that position. Unfortunately, Ferraro played the race card, and Olbermann took the bait, but instead of going after Ferraro, he chose instead to slam Hillary:

> I'm sorry to sound speechless. It seems remarkable to me that a campaign being run in the twenty-first century or even the second half of the twentieth century would allow itself to be associated in any kind of way and not step back. If it was two African Americans running against each other, and one of them had somebody say this on behalf of their candidate, that the other guy is only in there because he's equal opportunity, or there's been some sort of quota system, or that he's a black man does it not have disaster written all over it, or are we living in South Africa?

> — *Countdown with Keith Olbermann*, March 11, 2009

Leaving aside the silly apartheid slap, it didn't matter to Olbermann that Geraldine Ferraro was freelancing when she made the comment that ultimately caused her to step down from a voluntary finance committee position. Clinton campaign spokesman

Howard Wolfson disavowed the remark. Ms. Ferraro went on to do the cable circuit, speaking regularly on Fox, which gave the story legs Clinton didn't need and neither did Ferraro, because her comment not only demeaned the extraordinary oratory talent of candidate Obama, but made her look like a bigot or worse.

It's not an accident that both Olbermann and Matthews were demoted by MSNBC from anchoring live campaign news events in early September 2008 because of a clear pro-Obama bias that McCain certainly felt was unfair, especially after witnessing what had happened to Hillary from the MSNBC frat club twins during the primaries. The *San Francisco Chronicle* was among the newspapers finally covering MSNBC's ongoing sexism, writing that network commentators were "no strangers to insulting the Clinton women." It must have burned the two bombastic Obama fans to be yanked from headlining programming during the most exciting election in recent memory and having their slots turned over to NBC's David Gregory.

Even veteran newsman Tom Brokaw felt compelled to jump into the fray. Howard Kurtz quoted Brokaw at the time, saying sometimes Olbermann and Matthews went too far. Later, after Clinton won California in February of 2008, Brokaw made a point of telling his MSNBC colleagues on camera that "in all of our conventional and collective wisdom, we were wrong."

When Hillary hit a sour note, invoking the murder of Robert F. Kennedy in an interview with South Dakota's *Argus Leader* editorial board, all hell broke loose. In response to a question about whether she could envision a point at which Democratic leaders would step in and cut short the Obama-Clinton competition, Hillary responded, "No, I really can't. I think people have short memories. Primary contests used to last a lot longer. We all remember the great tragedy of Bobby Kennedy being assassinated in June in L.A. My husband didn't wrap up the nomination in 1992 until June. Having a primary contest go through June is nothing particularly unusual."

There was no reason to be defensive about staying in the race, which any man in the same situation would have done. But there was no reason to invoke Bobby Kennedy's heartbreaking murder either. Howard Wolfson explained what Clinton meant.

"She was talking about the length of the race and using the '68 election as an example of how long the races in the past have gone. She used her husband's race in the same vein."

Whatever. But she most certainly wasn't insinuating an assassination attempt on Mr. Obama, because what politician would think this would benefit her?

Olbermann's head exploded.

> ...We have forgiven you the photos of Osama Bin Ladin in an anti-Obama ad.... We have forgiven you the 3 a.m. phone call commercial.... We have forgiven you the dozen changing metrics and the endless self-contradictions of your insistence that your nomination is mathematically probable rather than a statistical impossibility. We have forgiven you your declaration of some primary states as counting and some as not....We have forgiven you for boasting of your "support among working, hard-working Americans, white Americans...." But Senator, we cannot forgive you this....We cannot forgive you this — not because it is crass and low and unfeeling and brutal. This is unforgivable, because this nation's deepest shame, its most enduring horror, its most terrifying legacy, is political assassination.
>
> — *Countdown with Keith Olbermann*, May 23, 2008

One of the best takedowns of Olbermann-type political coverage came from John F. Harris of Politico on May 25, 2008, in a post titled, "How Small Stories Become Big News," which focused on Clinton's RFK comments:

> The signature defect of modern political journalism is that it has shredded the ideal of proportionality....
>
> The truth about what Clinton said — and any fair-minded appraisal of what she meant — was entirely beside the point. Her comment was news by any standard. But it was only *big news* when wrested from context and set aflame by a news media more concerned with being interesting and provocative than with being relevant or serious....
>
> Perhaps half an hour after the story broke, [colleague Jonathan] Martin called me back over to his desk. It turned out the *Argus Leader* had video of its big interview. I huddled over Martin's computer as we

watched. It was a deflating experience. The RFK remarks were deep in a twenty-minute clip of an otherwise routine conversation. Then, once we actually got to the relevant portion of the video, it was hardly an electric moment....

It was...clear that Clinton's error was not in saying something beyond the pale but in saying something that pulled from context would sound as if it were beyond the pale.

Keith Olbermann's brand of sexism came with a side of mean for selected women. He didn't just punch up to the likes of Hillary Clinton or Sarah Palin, but actually turned the heat on high by humiliating some women, like Carrie Prejean, for sport. Prejean was the former Miss USA contestant whose answer to gossip-monger Perez Hilton's same-sex-marriage question ran notoriously afoul of Hilton and then Olbermann.

When the Daily Caller ran its Journolist trove of email text, Keith Olbermann turned out to be a subject in an exchange entitled "I Hate Keith Olbermann Again." An email from the *Nation*'s Katha Pollitt was quoted: "[Olbermann] and Michael Musto did this whole long riff about beauty contestant Carrie 'opposite marriage' Prejean's breast implants, stupidity, breast implants, tacky clothes, earrings, breast implants. They went on and on about how she was 'part plastic' and pathetic. You'd think they were celibate vegans who spent their lives Zen meditating. It was just a whole TV humiliation of her, and it made me feel sorry for her, which wasn't easy."

Rebecca Traister of Salon wrote about Paris Hilton, including that Keith Olbermann "felt free to call Hilton a slut on air and speculate about whether anyone had ever ejaculated in her face."

Also from the Daily Caller Journolist documents, blogger-reporter Lindsay Beyerstein focused on Olbermann's "misogynist garbage," which was a common feeling among many women.

From Olbermann's frequent pro-Obama guests, his favorite during the primaries was public relations flack, access journalist, pundit poser and let's not forget corporate lobbyist, Richard Wolffe. Wolffe's sycophantic rendering of candidate Obama in 2008 through his book *Renegade: The Making of a President* landed him out on his ass from his previous job at *Newsweek*. According to Ben Smith's reporting at Politico in June 2009, when Wolffe left the magazine he had a "frosty relationship with his employer." One *Newsweek* staffer in Smith's article was blunt about it: "We should have had most of what's in the book." No doubt *Newsweek* would have loved to have Wolffe's scoop that got candidate Obama on the record calling out Bill Clinton on alleged "bald-faced lies." According to *The New Republic*, which, in a piece that August, called Wolffe's book proposal "radioactive," after Wolffe read Smith's Politico piece, he confronted him in a train station whining, "What do you have against me?"

At candidate Obama's prodding, Wolffe seemingly was seduced by the prospect of being cast as a modern-day Theodore White, the legendary journalist who wrote the amazing story of John F. Kennedy's 1960 campaign. What resulted instead turned into a nightmare for Wolffe, as he "lavishly delivered on the heroic-light end of the bargain," as Smith recounted it. Republicans were even less kind. From Smith:

> "Richard Wolffe was doing PR for Barack Obama throughout the campaign," said Michael Goldfarb, a former aide to John McCain and a writer for the conservative *Weekly Standard*. "At least now, with the new book and the new job, he's dropped even the pretense of being a journalist."

Wolffe next found himself inside the smarmy world of corporate public relations, playing the character of PR flack. At the same time, he took a turn at guest-hosting on MSNBC, but that ended up a huge mess when author and Wonkette founder Ana Marie Cox busted him in a tweet: "No problem with R Wolffe earning enough to pay for his nice kitchen, but hosting Countdown without revealing this?" The appearance of a corporate lobbyist playing talking-head without disclosing it, ignoring the possible conflict of interests that could arise from interviewing people he was being trusted to grill, smacked of the worst of what cable offers.

Glenn Greenwald of Salon noted that Richard Wolffe's Public Strategies bio actually touted his NBC/MSNBC access as a plus for their corporate clients. According to Greenwald, one section of Wolffe's bio read, "In addition, Wolffe is an NBC political analyst. He provides political commentary on several MSNBC programs, *Meet The Press* and *Today*." The translation from there seemed like a slick seduction of a guy who has access to large audiences, with a wink and a nod to potential clients that he could have their back on air. There was nothing nefarious ever revealed on Wolffe's side, but not disclosing his lobbying job, while parading his puss on air, reeked of duplicity and this reputation has followed Wolffe forward.

Also a regular guest on Olbermann was Pultizer Prize-winner Eugene Robinson, who carried candidate Obama's talking points every hour on the air, and in his *Washington Post* column, while eviscerating Hillary through personal, often sexist, attacks. Mr. Robinson was giddy to regurgitate the traditional media talking points early on, using the old can-the-wife-control-her-husband theme. It was an insider, establishment favorite among the D.C. elite:

"For now," Robinson wrote in a December 2007 *Post* column, "I'm asking a simpler question: Since the Constitution provides for one president, not two, could he find a way to live in a White House that wasn't all about him?"

No one's doubting former President Clinton's large spousal footprint, but implying that Hillary couldn't be her own woman, or that Bill would rob her of her presidency because she couldn't handle him, is sexism in its purist form. Mr. Robinson's deep concern was transparent.

No, not even Bill Clinton would disrespect the office of the presidency.

Jonathan Alter, in early March 2008 wrote that "Hillary Should Get Out Now," an arrogant analysis by the *Newsweek* guy telling the chick to take a hike. He even floated the governorship of New York as a "consolation prize" for Clinton. When was the last time the media asked a leading male politician running for president to throw in the towel? Alter left *Newsweek* shortly after Tina Brown took over, something that didn't surprise anyone. Brown's respect for Hillary Rodham Clinton goes back to Tina's *Talk* magazine days in 1999, when Hillary was preparing her Senate run. As was recounted in Michael Tomasky's *Hillary's Turn*, Ms. Brown "made her admiration of the Clintons clear in the pages of the *New Yorker*, which she ran before she left to start *Talk*." And who was featured in the very first front-page piece on Newsweek's cover, shortly after Tina arrived? It wasn't Sarah Palin. Brown's "Hillary's War: How She's Shattering Glass Ceilings Everywhere" made a statement that put *Newsweek* under Brown diametrically opposed to where it was in the Jon Meacham era. So it's hardly a stretch to see that having someone afflicted with serious Clinton derangement syndrome, like Alter, on the *Newsweek* payroll wouldn't fly under Brown's banner.

Slate ran "Hillary Deathwatch" articles, with graphics to show the futility of her plight.

The media was one thing, but Hillary Clinton was also up against the most powerful group in America, the United States Boys Club, Senate Branch.

A powerful point of control came through Senator Ted Kennedy before he was diagnosed with terminal brain cancer that would take his life. He was arguably the preeminent Democrat in the Senate and was rumored to have run an under-the-radar campaign to get Barack Obama the nomination from the start. Kennedy likely also thought there was a way to further his own ascendance in an Obama administration, including through facilitating Obama's relationships with other Democratic leaders. But mainly, Kennedy wanted his people inside a possible Obama administration, which would hopefully be a route to even wider power and lasting legacy for the senior statesman.

The rally where Senator Kennedy made his endorsement announcement blanketed the airwaves, as did glory stories for days afterwards. The media loved the tale, filling the atmosphere with heady remembrances of John F. Kennedy, with the torch being passed to another generation yet again, signaling Obama as the chosen one. As someone who studied JFK, writing and producing a one-woman show on his politics and his impact on my life through my older brother, who had gotten me interested in politics in the first place, I knew the excitement Senator Kennedy's endorsement would cause. It was understandable, as the Kennedys are Democratic royalty among the elite, including the media, a twentieth century political dynasty that is hard to imagine today.

All kinds of gossip swirled about the call between former President Clinton and Senator Kennedy, with Bill making the pitch for Hillary. Mark Halperin and John Heilemann, in their book, *Game Change,* have Clinton supposedly saying, "A few years ago, this guy would have been getting us coffee," which allegedly pissed Kennedy off. It was also rumored Kennedy got an uproarious laugh out of causing former President Clinton such angst over his Obama endorsement. When the time came, Kennedy passed the torch to Obama with an in-your-face slap at Hillary, echoing her own campaign theme by saying Obama would be "ready to be president on day one!"

But what was the real reason Senator Kennedy endorsed Obama over Clinton, saying, "Senator Obama is running a dignified and honest campaign," even after the Clintons had gone to bat for him in the '90s? Politico columnist Roger Simon claimed it was all about rebuking Hillary for how she had run her campaign. Senator Kennedy, no stranger to hard-boiled politics, had become just another propaganda-peddler on the Obama clean-campaign-machine myth.

It was "The Sleuth" column by Mary Ann Akers at the *Washington Post* that got the real story, which revolved around this remark from Hillary: "Some people compare one of the other candidates to John F. Kennedy. But he was assassinated. And Lyndon Baines Johnson was the one who actually" signed the Civil Rights Bill into law. From Akers' January 30, 2008, column:

> Sources say Kennedy was privately furious at Clinton for her praise of President Lyndon Baines Johnson for getting the 1964 Civil Rights Act accomplished. Jealously guarding the legacy of the Kennedy family dynasty, Senator Kennedy felt Clinton's LBJ comments were an implicit slight of his brother, President John F. Kennedy, who first proposed the landmark civil rights initiative in a famous televised civil rights address in June 1963. One anonymous source described Kennedy as having a "meltdown" in reaction to Clinton's comments.

Looking back on Obama's nomination win, Senator Kennedy's endorsement in the end didn't perform the magic either of them had hoped, not that it mattered, because it worked on the establishment, particularly the press. But not even Kennedy could stop the Clinton avalanche in Kennedy's home state of Massachusetts, where she beat Obama by fifteen points. Obama also lost in Nevada and California, both heavily Hispanic states where Kennedy's endorsement could not turn the political tide no matter how beloved he was. When Senator Kennedy learned of his tragic illness, his hopes of access to another White House would forever vanish. There will never be anyone like Teddy again.

Senator Kennedy's passing closed out a chapter in my life, too, the one which eventually led me into politics. As a little girl, I spied my big brother and sister in front of the television crying as they watched the funeral of John F. Kennedy, something I recounted in my one-woman show, "Weeping for J.F.K." In fact, in early fall 2011, my sister, brother and I were going through his JFK memorabilia when note cards none of us could remember ever seeing before fell out. Turns out what is on these cards is my very first political reporting, crudely chronicling what I saw as a little kid on those dark November days in 1963. *What kind of president makes people feel like that?* It's a question of inspiration and possibility, which for me began here, and anyone interested in politics attempts to answer every four years.

Senator John Kerry endorsed Barack Obama, with many believing there was a promise of secretary of state in the offing. There would be no cabinet post for Kerry's endorsement, though maybe it will manifest if Obama is reelected. The same proffer was rumored to have been made to New Mexico Governor Bill Richardson for his endorsement. Richardson was officially offered commerce secretary, only to have to beg off because of an untimely investigation. Richardson's endorsement of Obama came very late in the primary season, which was called "an act of betrayal" by Clintonite James Carville, who didn't stop there, telling the *New York Times*, "Mr. Richardson's endorsement came right around the anniversary of the day when Judas sold out for thirty pieces of silver, so I think the timing is appropriate, if ironic." It turned into an all-out media war between Richardson and Carville, with President Clinton simmering on the sidelines.

We now also know Nevada Senator Harry Reid backed Obama early in 2008, even though he said publicly he was not committing to any candidate. Other elite Democrats covertly threw in with Obama in the same way. *Game Change* broke the bombshell. "If you want to be president, you can be president now," Reid admitted telling Obama, because the majority leader didn't see any future in the Senate for Obama. Jim Manley, Reid's spokesman, was forced to confirm in a statement at the time *Game Change* broke that there's "no disputing the fact that he was one of the very first people to encourage Obama to run for president."

Former Senate Majority Leader Tom Daschle played an early role in helping Obama rise in elite Democratic Party circles, too. As former Daschle aides landed administration jobs, there was talk he was shooting for chief of staff before he was dropped to health and human services secretary-designate, then out on his ass after running afoul of the IRS. Daschle had neglected to pay more than $128,000 in taxes plus $11,964 in interest over a three-year period, though Senator Kennedy, New York Senator Charles Schumer and others continued to back Daschle even after his troubles came to light. He'd known about the issue since June 2008, as reported by the *Washington Post*, but didn't know it was such a "jaw-dropping" amount.

How someone as savvy as Tom Daschle got caught in a tax trap remains a mystery — even if it was an accounting error, as many have labeled it. Why wouldn't Daschle clean up a $140,000 tax problem if he knew he was headed for a confirmation hearing? Funny how Tim Geithner's similar tax troubles didn't seem to bother the boss at all. But once Barack Obama took up residence in the White House, Daschle was out, and fellow Chicagoan and former Clintonite, Rahm Emanuel, now mayor of Chicago, was in. And somewhere between Rahmbo and Max Baucus — the man Ron Suskind calls "the vanquisher of Daschle" in *Confidence Men* — real health care reform became a casualty.

Even Greg Craig, who worked as President Clinton's assistant and special counsel, and directed the impeachment team, didn't choose to support Hillary. There was talk Craig was hoping to be named national security adviser. Instead, he got the same job with Obama he had with President Clinton. But when plans to close the U.S. military prison at Guantanamo Bay bogged down, and Craig was out in front on it, he was unceremoniously axed from the White House inner circle. This went over like a lead balloon with many, because Craig is a popular figure in Washington.

John Edwards was promised — well, that hardly matters at this point, but it should be noted that while the Democrats had their sights trained on taking down Hillary, Edwards pulled off one of the biggest cons in modern presidential history, passing off what had developed into a sham marriage as a major asset to his campaign.

A lot of insider Democratic powerhouses supported Obama instead of Hillary, but all along, from Harry Reid on down, nobody was talking publicly. It reminds me of when Hillary Clinton's good friend John McCain came face to face with a woman on the campaign trail asking "How do we beat the bitch?" and just stood there and laughed. The woman had said in public what it seemed establishment Democrats were saying behind closed doors. Hey, no harm in picking a favorite, but the secrecy of the establishment boys club versus the girl running for president was powerful symbolism in a country that's never had a female president.

The presumed insider was the outsider from the start, which makes a mockery of every assumption Mark Penn laid out from day one and points out how out of the loop this man was on what was going on inside the Democratic Party.

Hillary's "bitch" status was always good for a laugh — at least until the *Washington Post*'s Dana Milbank suggested, in an attempt at humor in the *Mouthpiece Theater* feature on the *Post*'s website, that Mad Bitch Beer would be a good brew for her. The indiscretion incited such an uproar that the *Post* had to cancel the site's web series Milbank had co-hosted with Chris Cillizza. Milbank failed upwards, to the paper's influential op-ed pages.

New-media outlets had their embarrassing moments as well. At the height of the 2008 primary season, I got an email from blogger Linda Hirshman saying she'd been "sacked from TPM," referring to Talking Points Memo, the influential political website founded by Josh Marshall. At the time, Hirshman also provided proof of the back-and-forth she'd had with TPM's Andrew Golis, who later moved on to become editor of blogging for Yahoo News and then editor and digital director at PBS' *Frontline*. "TPM Cuts Female Writer Not Making Case for Obama" was the post she did for my website about her firing. Hirshman wanted an explanation why she was no longer needed to write at TPM, and wrote an email to Golis, saying, "I am assuming it's not that you don't want anyone who's not already in the tank for Obama." To which Golis replied:

"I'm not sure the accusation of bias is particularly helpful. For now, like I said, we're focusing on getting our long-standing regulars and folks covering things we don't on the blog. I recognize that you think female voters should be one of those things, we disagree."

In a national contest that included Hillary Clinton running hard for president and would eventually include Sarah Palin as the Republican vice presidential nominee, it's hard to imagine why "female voters" shouldn't be one of the things a major progressive blog would want to cover. Today, we are the voting majority.

It was Josh Marshall's choice, of course; Golis was just following TPM policy, which says something about the tone deafness of even the biggest progressive new-media sites in 2008. At a time when Democrats had their first viable female presidential candidate, and Republicans for the first time in history had put a woman on the national ticket, Marshall's TPM decided female voters shouldn't be a focus.

TPM struck again when David Shuster, who was suspended multiple times before severing his ties with MSNBC, said Chelsea Clinton was being "pimped out" by her mother "in some weird sort of way." As the back-and-forth raged between Clinton's camp and MSNBC, TPM covered it all, making sure to post a photo of a smiling, happy and handsome Shuster on its home page, juxtaposed against Drudgesque Hillary Clinton shots that showed her frowning or worse. It was much like what the right wing did in the '90s, branding images of Hillary to associate her with negative feelings.

The Daily Kos diary section was inundated by overwrought, Clinton-hating screeds, with anyone pro-Hillary blown out by Obama's blog army. Die-hard fans of Obama were allowed to target pro-Clinton diarists with impunity. Under defamatory headlines, their posts were filled with accusations and even lies, while Clinton supporters expressing anti-Obama positions were often greeted with "You've Been Warned" boxes above their posts, requiring them to check off a box stating, "I understand the above warning (posting is no longer allowed until this is acknowledged)."

Markos Moulitsas, the founder of Daily Kos, in a post headlined "The Clinton Civil War," revealed his editorial philosophy on the matter, while opining on a writer strike by pro-Hillary diarists: "Given that candidate Clinton is a member of the [Democratic Leadership Council], voted to authorize the war, accepts federal lobbyist and PAC money, clearly thinks that a lot (if not most) states 'don't matter,' and epitomizes a 1990s style, top-down form of doing politics, it's no surprise that for all of 2007

Clinton never exceeded 11% support in the monthly Daily Kos users straw poll."

These were salient points made by many progressives, though the problem with this analysis is that Barack Obama wasn't any different. Moulitsas missed it, though he had a lot of company. His emotional spleen-venting went deeper, as he concocted Hillary horror stories out of whole cloth, irrationally ranting on and on about some imagined "coup," instead of respecting the process that Hillary and her supporters were entitled to keep going until Obama received the number of delegates he needed for the nomination.

> First of all, the only path to victory for Clinton is via coup by super delegate....
>
> Clinton knows this, it's her only path to victory, and she doesn't care. She is willing — nay, eager to split the party apart in her mad pursuit of power....
>
> It is Clinton, with no reasonable chance of victory, who is fomenting civil war in order to overturn the will of the Democratic electorate. As such, as far as I'm concerned, she doesn't deserve "fairness" on this site. All sexist attacks will be dealt with — those will never be acceptable. But otherwise, Clinton has set an inevitably divisive course and must be dealt with appropriately.
>
> — Daily Kos, March 17, 2008

The Clinton marriage was a continual source of cheap potshots for talking heads on both sides. Susan Estrich, who was campaign manager for Michael Dukakis — she's the one to thank for that unforgettable, picture-in-a-tank debacle — continually whined on Fox's *Hannity & Colmes* that she wished the Clintons would just go away. As early as May 23, 2006, Patrick Healy, writing for the *New York Times*, culled out a special Clinton marriage gossip beat for himself. In a piece called "For Clintons, Delicate Dance of Married and Public Lives," he did some extra digging, counting how many days they spent together.

> Since the start of 2005, the Clintons have been together about fourteen days a month on average, according to aides who reviewed the couple's schedules. Sometimes it is a full day of relaxing at home in Chappaqua; sometimes it is meeting up late at night. At their busiest, they saw each other on a single day, Valentine's Day, in February

2005 — a month when each was traveling a great deal. Last August, they saw each other at some point on twenty-four out of thirty-one days. Out of the last seventy-three weekends, they spent fifty-one together. The aides declined to provide the Clintons' private schedule.

— New York Times, May 23, 2006

This trashy front page tabloid piece on the Clinton marriage didn't have a single news angle or hook, except that Hillary Rodham Clinton might want to run for president. So, hey, let's have a look see at her marriage, shall we?

The only person more interested in the Clinton marriage was Chris Matthews, whose *Hardball* turned into pornball tabloid titillation whenever the subject of the Clinton marriage was in the headlines. In late October 2009 he admitted, "I accept I am obsessed with her husband and everybody in politics." Matthews' obsession with Monica Lewinksi had even caused problems for the late *Meet the Press* moderator Tim Russert, when the Clinton White House threatened to keep guests off his show. With the Healy piece, Matthews was in gossip-rag heaven.

"I love these topics," Matthews said at the top of his show in May 2006, his face red and puffed up, fairly salivating at the chance to delve into the prurient nature of anything surrounding the Clinton marriage. Not surprisingly, Tim Russert was brought in to provide extra gravitas to the importance of exploring the topic. Later in the show, Matthews couldn't get over the dish about what the establishment, you know, the guys making decisions about big campaign investments, were talking about. He actually asked then-DNC chairman Howard Dean if the Democratic power-brokers don't whisper back and forth about the Clinton marriage wondering, "Is everything okay? Are we going to get embarrassed next year by something with regard to that marriage?"

Dean said simply, it was not Topic A on anyone's mind. But, Matthews sputtered, he talks to "a lot of people in politics, in and out of it, journalists and everyone else, and they talk about it. Because they want to know what will be coming next year. People try to figure out what's coming next in American politics." At least that was his observation.

On May 24, 2006, Matthews went at it again, introducing an upcoming segment on his show: "Plus the elephant in the room. Hillary Clinton wants...to be our next president, but how is her marriage to Bill fitting into the master plan?"

This time former *New York Times* columnist Bob Herbert jumped in to help, which was really depressing:

> I can tell you that in my travels, people are really interested in the state of this marriage and, frankly, I think, you know, with Hillary's presumed presidential ambitions, the state of the marriage is going to actually be a factor in her chances of getting the Democratic nomination, and then perhaps, you know, becoming president....
>
> The fact that we're talking about the Clintons' marriage here, I think is just that kind of discussion. The story in *The Times* today is really harmful for Hillary's presidential chances, because I think that there is a real hunger for change in this country politically, and I think if we keep harping on that, and I think it is a legitimate story, but I mean, if the media does keep harping on that, there will be a tendency among the electorate to say, you know, enough already.

None of the elite establishment journalists, not even the esteemed Mr. Herbert, got that it was *their* obsessive voyeurism that drove this crap. This was your liberal media at work.

When, later in the segment, Matthews compared Hillary's national prominence to "putting on the old bad tire that you've gotten fixed a few times on your car," the incessant harping made you want to scream.

Herbert was part of it too. "I mean, the state of their marriage and the Clintons' scandals is sort of lurking there, just beneath the surface, almost all the time," he said on Matthews' show.

All the time Chris Matthews was covering the Clinton marriage, he'd say things like "Let's not get into the particular human details of their relationship (*Hardball*, May 21, 2007)," while acting like a teenage boy caught looking through a keyhole.

Longtime *Washington Post* political correspondent Lois Romano (now at the Daily Beast), wrote about the Clinton marriage and how many days they spent apart, which naturally made Romano a prime guest for *Hardball*. In a conversation with Romano and Daily Beast writer Jonathan Darmon on that same, May 2007 show, Matthews was in his typical state of agitation: "Are they living on the same planet?" he asked Romano. "Do they ever see each other physically? ...Is that what you got, Jonathan, in your reporting, that they're together half the time overnight?"

Romano finally confronted Chris — "What is your obsession with logistics here?" — but Matthews wouldn't give up: "You don't think it's relevant whether Bill Clinton comes back and lives in the White House. You don't think that's relevant."

Keyhole Chris was breathless at the thought.

When Romano said it was "crazy to think he's not going to live in the White House," but implied it was relevant mainly because some people were concerned he'd be controlling the presidency again, Chris was obviously disappointed he didn't get the answer he wanted. He turned to Chris Cillizza of the *Washington Post*.

MATTHEWS: I think this is a bigger issue than you think. Chris Cillizza, will this be an issue in the election?

CHRIS CILLIZZA: Sure. Of course. I mean, her last name is Clinton.

The sitcom storyline dialogue was incessant.

Once Hillary went to the State Department, Matthews calmed down. In the post-Hillary political era, Matthews changed his tone, even getting access to President Bill Clinton for a documentary, *President of the World: The Bill Clinton Phenomenon*. But who wanted to watch Matthews suck up to President Clinton after how he'd covered the Clintons, especially Hillary?

He didn't find much in Sarah Palin to malign, though he used Michele Bachmann like a punching bag until she started gaining in the GOP presidential horse race. Perhaps Sarah's mavericky status, her "mama grizzly" following and the fact she's good for ratings are what make him soft-pedal his sexism toward her. Or maybe it's simply because Sarah's great looking and turns Chris on.

It's interesting that Sally Quinn, who delighted in eviscerating Hillary Clinton, has done the exact opposite when writing on Palin, but in her August 29, 2008, *Washington Post* "On

Faith" column, she did have the audacity to question Palin's values and standards of motherhood.

> And now we learn the 17-year-old daughter, Bristol, is pregnant. She and the father of the child plan to marry. This may be a hard one for the Republican conservative family-values crowd to swallow. Of course, this can happen in any family. But it must certainly raise the question among the evangelical base about whether Sarah Palin has been enough of a hands-on mother.

Holding court from Washington with her foot firmly planted in 1950s America, Mrs. Quinn's language is what has passed for political wisdom in Washington until new media (thankfully) took over.

This Palin shot seemed particularly spiteful, considering Ms. Quinn's own parenting shortcomings. This is a woman who lost her *Post* Style section spot when she poured her wedding family drama into a column titled "No 'Dueling' Bradlee Weddings, Just Scheduling Mistake." Sally's tale of woe revealed how she'd screwed up, which resulted in Ben Bradlee's granddaughter and their son having the same wedding date. The mix-up had the effect of hauling ABC's Martha Raddatz, who is the mother of Bradlee's granddaughter, into Sally's soap opera storyline. Turned out Quinn Bradlee's fiancée was also pregnant, making things even more complicated. Sally blamed the scheduling conflict on her husband, who apparently hadn't made a written note of the first commitment. If the great Katharine Graham were alive today, she truly wouldn't recognize the *Washington Post.*

All of Sally's wedding anxiety pales in comparison to the way she orchestrated the omission of Ben Bradlee's sons, Dino and Ben Jr., from *A Life's Work: Fathers and Sons*, the book Ben wrote with Quinn Bradlee, the only son he had with Sally. The sorry details of that episode were examined in the July 2010 issue of *Vanity Fair.*

The issue of Palin's status as mother of a larger family than many, and one with a young daughter and a child with Down's syndrome, was brought into question by people who doubted she would have the time to be an effective vice president, let alone president. No male candidate is ever asked about family conflicts, and it shouldn't be asked of a woman anymore either. But when Sally Quinn questioned Sarah's mothering skills, she was saying something else from her perch in the twentieth century: The mother must always be in charge of full-time child care, regardless of whether there is a father willing to step in or not. Mrs. Quinn's own difficulty raising her son Quinn, who is learning-disabled, colored her judgment about what is right for Sarah, instead of helping her realize it's none of her fucking business.

The next generation is finally finding itself on female-friendlier terrain. Writing for the *Atlantic* magazine in July/August 2010, Hana Rosin lays out what awaits women in a story titled "The End of Men":

> Earlier this year, for the first time in American history, the balance of the workforce tipped toward women, who now hold a majority of the nation's jobs. The working class, which has long defined our notions of masculinity, is slowly turning into a matriarchy, with men increasingly absent from the home and women making all the decisions. Women dominate today's colleges and professional schools — for every two men who will receive a B.A. this year, three women will do the same. Of the fifteen job categories projected to grow the most in the next decade in the U.S., all but two are occupied primarily by women. Indeed, the U.S. economy is in some ways becoming a kind of traveling sisterhood: Upper-class women leave home and enter the workforce, creating domestic jobs for other women to fill. The post-industrial economy is indifferent to men's size and strength.

Going back to the 2010 GAO report, data showed that only 40% of women hold management positions, with an average salary that is 20% less than that of men in the same positions. This got very little coverage, with MSNBC's Andrea Mitchell one of the few people to pick it up. But as Ms. Rosin's piece suggests, there is real evidence that this is likely to change in the coming decades, with more women graduating from business, law and graduate schools. Lisa Caputo, Hillary Clinton's former press secretary and her chief of staff as first lady, says, "Women are not only the CFO in the household, but they're the chief purchasing officer," which provides a completely new role model for daughters and sons than that of previous generations.

Even in culture, it's women's turn. We've seen it through fictional characters like Cherry Jones, who won an Emmy in 2009 for playing the president in *24*, and through Kathryn Bigelow's historic first female-director Oscar win for *The Hurt Locker,* as well as for the film's win for best picture. Barbra Streisand, bursting with excitement, was a fitting presenter when she announced Bigelow's name. In 2010, along with all the male action stars on America's movie screens, moviegoers now had the choice to see *Salt*, Angelina Jolie's rocking, full-assault, CIA heroine, in the film by the same name.

All of those were cultural breakthroughs, but it's a whole 'nother world in "mama grizzly" land. Sarah Palin's power was drawn out in *Newsweek*'s "Saint Sarah," by Lisa Miller, in July 2010: "With her new faith-based message, Palin gathers up the Christian women that traditional feminism has left behind.... These Christians seek a power that allows them to formally acquiesce to male authority and conservative theology, even as they assume increasingly visible roles in their families, their churches, their communities, and the world."

So even as women rise, Miller writes, the women Sarah Palin represents are longing for power that "allows them to formally acquiesce to male authority." I mean, holy shit. That's the conservative message for the twenty-first century? Presidential candidate Michele Bachmann certainly thinks so:

> Dr. Bachmann's influence on his wife is an article of faith within the family.
>
> "He is her godly husband," said Peter Bachmann, Dr. Bachmann's oldest brother, who lives on the family dairy farm across the eastern border in Wisconsin. "The husband is to be the head of the wife, according to God." It is a philosophy that Michele Bachmann echoed to congregants of the Living Word Christian Center in 2006, when she stated that she pursued her degree in tax law only because her husband had told her to. "The Lord says: Be submissive, wives. You are to be submissive to your husbands," she said.
>
> — Jason Horowitz, *Washington Post*, July 5, 2011

It's ironic, considering that the right is continually talking about freedom. Just not for women.

Chapter 4: **Is Freedom Just for Men?**

The right loves to cry freedom. It began every Sarah Palin rally in 2010. It's in every political speech. Michelle Bachmann talks about "liberty" all the time. The trouble is, the right seems to think freedom is only for men. They don't respect a woman's basic individual freedom, the right to have exactly what a man has, including control over her own body, because you simply aren't free if you don't.

But did you know Hillary wanted to force taxpayers to pay for abortions? Did you know she also believes disabled unborn children should have fewer protections than healthy babies in the womb? She also wanted to socialize abortion through health care. When the right can't get at a liberated woman through the truth, they'll just make shit up. "Abortion on demand" is how right-wingers described Hillary's views on a woman's individual freedoms. The contempt for women drips from these words, which imply that a woman would ever think life is expendable on a whim. It's the vilest charge the right hurls not only at liberals and progressives, but also at conservatives who believe government has no business in our personal lives. As the saying goes, if men could get pregnant, we wouldn't be having this discussion.

I remember having an exchange with a male commenter on this very subject at Huffington Post who said he believed that a woman does have individual rights equal to a man's, but he was also adamantly opposed to abortion. There was no way out, he grudgingly admitted, proving this is where the conversation must begin, especially with conservatives, people who trumpet individual freedom, but want to exempt women from this fundamental human right. We have fought and won this power through the courts, as well as through scientific and pharmacological advances.

So why did Democrats give in?

The Democratic Congress, under Speaker Nancy Pelosi, handed conservatives exactly what they wanted by championing the politics of Rep. Bart Stupak. During the historic health care debate, Speaker Pelosi allowed Catholic bishops to have a presence in the room when the Affordable Health Care for America Act was on the floor. President Obama empowered Rep. Stupak and his conservative contingent further by signing an executive order that amounted to a super-duper promise that abortions wouldn't be paid for at the federal level in the new health care bill, even though that was already assured through the Hyde Amendment, which prohibits federal funds from the Department of Health and Human Services to be used for abortion. By signing the order, Obama actually went further, codifying the Hyde Amendment in the Affordability Care Act, which before only put Hyde in the budget for Congress to authorize yearly. It was the first time Democrats had sold women out and compromised on rights we'd already earned.

It wouldn't be the only time. At the last minute in the 2011 budget battle, President Obama caved to Speaker Boehner, bargaining away the right of poor women in Washington, D.C. In an April 2011 *Washington Post* column, Colby King expressed outrage:

> Congress used the budget negotiations to attach riders that prevent locally raised tax dollars from being used for reproductive services for low-income District women. Another provision forced a federally funded school-voucher program on the city.
>
> If that weren't galling enough, President Obama threw the city under the bus and bought the deal, telling GOP House Speaker John Boehner, "John, I will give you D.C. abortion. I'm not happy about that." Boo-hoo. Like hell.

In the fight for individual freedom, poor women are always left out.

Few would have believed the first female Speaker of the House in U.S. history would invite religious leaders into the room, then allow them to chip away at women's rights. It's not what I thought Speaker Pelosi would do when I proudly watched her be sworn in inside the Capitol on that historic day when she took charge. It's not what the woman who championed progressive liberalism through policy by wielding her power successfully should have ever done, but she did and it is part of her legacy.

During the health care debate I was driving in D.C. and listening to NPR when I heard Speaker Pelosi proudly proclaim she'd made sure Stupak got his vote:

"I was part of recommending that it come to the floor," she said. "Both sides are whipping, the pro-choice side and others who want to support the amendment. But no, that was my recommendation to allow a vote on that amendment."

The *New York Times* reported it in November 2009, but also something else — that the Catholic Church was mobilized against the health care bill, which wasn't exactly surprising:

"The representatives of the nation's bishops made clear they would fight the bill if there were not restrictions on abortion," the *Times* reported. "In an extraordinary effort over the last ten days, the bishops' conference told priests across the country to talk about the legislation in church, mobilizing parishioners to contact Congress and to pray for the success of anti-abortion amendments."

Churches across the country continue to get involved politically on the issue of abortion, though why they continue to enjoy tax-exempt status is beyond me — except that no politician has the courage to challenge the Catholic or evangelical churches who wage political war against women while enjoying a tax-free privilege of doing so. It makes it easier when voters are lazy and don't reject this practice.

In May 2010, Sister Margaret McBride was excommunicated by Bishop Thomas J. Olmsted for saving a woman's life. No, really. Pro-life is only a *selective* policy for some abortion-rights opponents. In November 2009, a 27-year-old woman was admitted to St. Joseph's Hospital and Medical Center in Phoenix for heart failure, according to an NPR report. Her doctors said if she didn't terminate her pregnancy, the likelihood of her dying was "close to a hundred percent." But still, Sister McBride was the one who got punished for saving the woman's life.

Too bad the Catholic Church wasn't this aggressive when it discovered pedophile priests were ruining the lives of children who trusted them. The priests weren't excommunicated; they were hidden, protected and shuttled around.

Politics, sex and faith are a toxic trio, especially when the Speaker of the House invites her religious institution of choice to reverse rights women have won.

I'll take no backseat to anyone where faith is concerned. As a rebel Episcopalian who now relies on daily meditations for solace, guidance and connection, I've been going to church since I was a kid. My mother used to roust me out of bed on Sunday mornings no matter what. When I tried to play hooky, the crap I took for staying home just wasn't worth it. She'd walk around not talking to me all day Sunday. It was hell, which was the point, but I'm grateful that amid our shared torments she gave me this gift, because the journey of faith and spiritual discovery is one of the abiding adventures of my life. But faith is private, with church leaders certainly not meant to be part of the American political process. That's a basic American principle sometimes abused by Republicans and Democrats alike.

After hearing what Speaker Pelosi had orchestrated, Rep. Lynn Woolsey let fly:

In a November 2009 opinion piece posted on Politico, she wrote,

> "I expect political hardball on any legislation as important as the health care bill.
>
> I just didn't expect it from the United States Council of Catholic Bishops USCCB).
>
> Who elected them to Congress?
>
> The role the bishops played in pushing the Stupak amendment, which unfairly restricts access for low-income women to insurance coverage for abortions, was more than mere advocacy....
>
> The IRS is less restrictive about church involvement in efforts to influence legislation than it is about involvement in campaigns and elections.
>
> Given the political behavior of USCCB in this case, maybe it shouldn't be."
>
> — Politico, November 9, 2009

Exactly, who elected the church to Congress? Somewhere Jerry Falwell was laughing.

As for the Hyde Amendment, it came after *Roe v. Wade* and was in response to its passage — a way to begin to diminish *Roe* through legislation, not unlike what the states are doing with their mini-Stupak amendments today. The late Rep. Henry Hyde, a crusading zealot who had no interest in the poor women his amendment would impact, simply wanted to codify his religious beliefs into legislation. Because politicians have always been too cowardly to stand up to the religious right, the Hyde Amendment has become their line in the sand at the federal level. In fact, he said so. From the non-profit Guttmacher Institute:

Poor women have been pawns in the congressional debate over abortion since the procedure became legal nationwide. For opponents of abortion, public funding has been a proxy for overturning *Roe*. As Hyde told his colleagues during a congressional debate over Medicaid funding in 1977, "I certainly would like to prevent, if I could legally, anybody having an abortion, a rich woman, a middle-class woman, or a poor woman. Unfortunately, the only vehicle available is the...Medicaid bill." For pro-choice leaders, on the other hand, public funding was a matter of fundamental fairness and equal protection under the law. "If we now restrict or ban Medicaid funding for abortions, the government will accomplish for poor women indirectly what the 1973 [Supreme Court] opinion expressly forbade it to do directly...a right without access is no right at all," said then-Senator Edward Brooke (R-MA), speaking in opposition to the Hyde Amendment during one of the early congressional debates.

— Heather D. Boonstra, Guttmacher Institute, Winter 2007

If poor women had a lobbying arm, we wouldn't be arguing this issue. Democrats have been allowing Republicans to get away with marginalizing the poor for decades. No one will challenge the Hyde Amendment on behalf of poor women, and as a result, they have fewer freedoms.

Dana Goldstein nailed this betrayal on The Daily Beast in March 2010:

Now, in a Faustian bargain with Rep. Bart Stupak of Michigan and other Democrats who oppose abortion rights, President Obama will issue an executive order enshrining the Hyde Amendment. Language in the bill inserted by Senator Ben Nelson of Nebraska expands Hyde's reach into the new private insurance exchanges in which the uninsured or under-insured will purchase coverage. Because only about 13% of abortions are billed directly to insurers, it is sometimes assumed that abortion is a relatively inelastic good — that women who really want one will get one, come hell or high water. But that assumption is false. A 1999 study of poor women in North Carolina found that about one-third of them had carried pregnancies to term only because Medicaid funding for abortions was unavailable during certain parts of the year.

An abortion can cost between $350 and $1,000 — equal to several months of rent or groceries — so the price can be prohibitive. The result of unaffordable abortion is another mouth a working-class mother cannot afford to feed, house or educate during a time of record unemployment.

— Daily Beast, March 21, 2010

In the post-Hillary political era, "safe, legal and rare" is now gone, because the Democratic majority and President Obama made a deal against women through the health care bill. Women even get the privilege of writing two checks for health care, watching the insurance pool for reproductive services tighten. From Adele M. Stein of Alternet:

"Stupak, for months, held the line on his position, and it was his amendment to the original House bill that inspired the anti-abortion provision in the Senate bill that was negotiated by Senator Ben Nelson of Nebraska. Stupak, backed by the United States Conference of Catholic Bishops, contended that Nelson's provision did not, in the end, actually prevent federal dollars from funding abortions, he said, even though it demands that women receiving federal subsidies for health insurance write a second check to their insurer for policies purchased through the government-administered exchanges for any portion of their policy that covers abortion."

The Center for American Progress named the state efforts at curbing women's individual freedoms, "Mini-Stupak Amendments," after the man Speaker Pelosi and President Obama made famous. The CAP report was released in June 2010, which offered harrowing setbacks to women's freedoms across the country at the time. They reached out to the Guttmacher Institute for some of the statistics they gathered. Here are some low points where women stood at that time, though by the time you read this, who knows where women will stand? Arizona, Idaho, Mississippi, Nebraska, Oklahoma, Tennessee, Utah, Virginia, and West Virginia have passed twenty-three provisions that enact abortion-related restrictions. Fourteen states are moving to enact laws that "limit abortion coverage in private insurance plans — either those purchased in the new health exchanges, in private markets outside of those exchanges, in government employee plans, or some combination thereof," with Arizona, Mississippi, and Tennessee so far succeeding, according to the report.

Oh, and if you're a modern woman and thinking of living in Oklahoma, be warned, the legislators in that state believe freedom is just for men. More from the June 2010 CAP report:

> Eight — The number of bills that Oklahoma passed this year. The governor signed bills outlawing "sex-selective" abortion; allowing employees to refuse to participate in abortions, fetal transplants, procedures involving embryos, and euthanasia; requiring clinics to post signs saying that women cannot be forced to have abortions; and increasing restrictions on RU-486, also known as the "abortion pill." The governor vetoed an insurance coverage ban, mandatory ultrasounds with a detailed description of the fetus, a thirty-eight-question survey about each abortion procedure, and immunity for doctors who omit or provide inaccurate information to women carrying fetuses with abnormalities. The legislature successfully overrode all the vetoes except the insurance ban. The ultrasound law is not in effect yet, pending a court challenge.

Additionally, nine states had introduced TRAP laws — a classic acronym, I know, which stands for Targeted Regulation of Abortion Providers. These laws make it a pain for abortion clinics to help women, having special requirements that other outpatient medical practices don't have to follow. Nebraska and South Carolina legislators introduced several bills that were known to be unconstitutional, because they "banned abortion for almost any reason after twenty weeks gestation based on the unsubstantiated and highly contested claim that fetuses can feel pain at that point." Then there is Utah: One law that defines criminal homicide "to include a 'knowing' act by a pregnant woman that causes a miscarriage or stillbirth. This bill is so broad that it could apply to a woman who smokes cigarettes or takes prescription medication," the report states.

An American Progress report from July 2011, updates the right's war on women:

> More than nine hundred anti-abortion laws have been introduced since the midterm elections last November, and more than sixty have been passed.... Among the most dangerous laws are those that restrict or ban abortion after twenty weeks of pregnancy. So far, six states — Alabama, Idaho, Indiana, Kansas, Nebraska and Oklahoma — have passed twenty- week laws, and more are likely to follow. Only about 1.5% of all abortions occur after twenty weeks

of pregnancy, but those that do are often medically necessary.

The types of reproductive health services Planned Parenthood provides enjoy strong public support. A recent poll by the Public Religion Research Institute shows that a solid majority of Americans support access to contraception, and six in ten believe abortion should be both legal and available. People of faith are among these majorities.

One piece of very good news is that in August 2011, Health and Human Services designated contraception as preventative health care. Private insurers will now join public insurers in offering FDA-approved contraceptives without any fees or co-payments.

Tea Party politicians gaining power see women's rights as a prime target. In April 2011, Politico reported that Rep. Ron Paul, speaking of the "unborn" at an Iowa Family Leader's presidential lecture series, said, "The purpose, if there is to be a purpose, for government is to protect life and liberty." The woman's individual freedoms are never mentioned by this cafeteria Libertarian. Sarah Palin and Michele Bachmann also regularly rail against women's rights, with Palin claiming she represents the "new feminists," an oxymoron if ever there was one. For people squealing about liberty all the time, they're very quick to deny women their own.

There is a bumper sticker that's been around for a long time that states it plainly: "Against Abortion? Then don't have one." Let's remember, it's a legal procedure.

The right's war against women and its inherent disrespect for our intelligence can be seen in the sonogram bill in Texas, which Gov. Rick Perry signed into law in May 2011. The Life News website perfectly encapsulated it: "The bill is meant to give women a chance to get information they may not normally receive from an abortion center before they have an abortion." Hardly. It intrudes at a time when a woman is in a terribly emotional state, where privacy is of the utmost importance and where strangers have no right to tread.

However, a federal injunction two days before Perry's forced sonogram law was to go into effect on September 1, 2011, blocked it, with U.S. District Judge Sam Sparks stating that it "compels physicians to advance an ideological agenda with which they may not agree, regardless of any medical necessity, and irrespective of whether the pregnant women wish to listen." Judge Sparks also took aim at those who'd force women who have been raped or are victims to go public, or make them listen to a doctor discuss a state-compelled sonogram: "The Court need not belabor the obvious by explaining why, for instance, women who are pregnant as a result of sexual assault or incest may not wish to certify that fact in writing, particularly if they are too afraid of retaliation to even report the matter to police."

So called "heartbeat bills" are also being introduced, as abortion rights opponents take their fight to the states in an effort to challenge *Roe v. Wade* surreptitiously. Ohio became a battleground for this fight after right-wing Republicans won sweeping victories in the 2010 midterms, with former Rep. John Kasich now governor. But these "heartbeat bills" are also causing a rift between abortion rights opponents in Ohio and other states, with many believing these types of bills will be seen as unconstitutional and set a tougher precedent, which will make their jobs harder. Dahlia Lithwick of Slate wrote in "The Death of *Roe v. Wade*," *that with the loopholes being exploited at the state level, the landmark ruling may no longer be the law of the land, so while some abortion rights opponents still want to overturn Roe, they don't feel the need to.*

In the same piece, Lithwick quotes Rev. Pat Mahoney, director of the Christian Defense Coalition, speaking in an interview with Christian Broadcasting Network: "'We don't have to see a *Roe v. Wade* overturned in the Supreme Court to end it.... We want to. But if we chip away and chip away, we'll find out that *Roe* really has no impact. And that's what we are doing.'"

From January to April of 2011, quoting Lithwick, "Nine hundred sixteen measures seeking to regulate reproductive health have been introduced in forty-nine states." The Guttmacher Institute reported that by mid-March, fifteen laws had been enacted in seven states. Most of these measures undoubtedly violate *Roe v. Wade*, meaning they are unconstitutional. But abortion rights proponents haven't challenged the laws, because after Sandra Day O'Connor was replaced by Samuel Alito, many feared the Roberts Court could overturn *Roe*. In April 2011, NOW's president Terry O'Neill told Rachel Maddow just that: "We're afraid that the Supreme Court might actually take the opportunity to overturn *Roe v. Wade*."

With legislation making headlines at the end of March 2011 that would ban legal abortions in the state even in the first trimester, the *Columbus Dispatch* reported that "House Bill 125 would give Ohio the most restrictive abortion law in the nation, outlawing the procedure once a fetal heartbeat can be medically detected, generally six or seven weeks into a woman's pregnancy."

ABC News covered the Ohio's law challenge to *Roe v. Wade*, which established that a fetus must be "viable," meaning "potentially able to live outside the mother's womb, albeit with artificial aid." The Ohio law is another flashpoint.

"They are making decisions for women in banning abortion basically before some women even know they are pregnant," Nancy Keenan, president of NARAL Pro Choice, said. "Technology can give us information, but it can't make the decision for us."

As ABC News also reported early in 2011, Indiana's state senate committee endorsed legislation requiring "doctors to tell women who want to have an abortion that human life begins at conception and that a fetus might feel pain at or before twenty weeks." How is this *not* unconstitutional, because it would deny a woman a *legal* abortion of a pre-viable fetus? Gov. Mitch Daniels signed the bill, with Indiana joining Nebraska and North Carolina in having strict anti-female laws, which go much further than just invading a woman's privacy. This law actually demands doctors *lie* to women to comply with an anti-abortion ideology.

From the Fort Wayne, Indiana, *News-Sentinel*'s website in April 2011: "The Indiana proposal includes requiring that women seeking an abortion be told that human life begins at conception and that a fetus might feel pain at or before twenty weeks. The bill also requires written notice that women undergoing abortions face a greater risk of infertility and breast cancer."

This is utter bullshit. The National Cancer Institute, the American Cancer Society, the Susan G. Komen Foundation and the American Congress of Obstetricians and Gynecologists have all stated that there is no link whatsoever between abortion and infertility or breast cancer. From the American Cancer Society website: "The topic of abortion and breast cancer highlights many of the most challenging aspects of studies of people and how those studies do or do not translate into public health guidelines. The issue of abortion generates passionate viewpoints in many people. Breast cancer is the most common cancer, and is the second leading cancer killer in women. Still, the public is not well-served by false alarms. At this time, the scientific evidence does not support the notion that abortion of any kind raises the risk of breast cancer."

As for the wild, greater-risk claims about infertility and abortion, Roger W. Harms, M.D., the editor in chief of the Mayo Clinic website in spring 2011, wrote: "Only rarely would an abortion cause problems in a subsequent pregnancy."

By far the most incendiary move against women's freedoms came when a South Dakota legislator decided to expand the definition of "justifiable homicide" to include anyone who would kill a fetus. So now the Republican war on women includes targeting doctors who perform an abortion, something that is, again, a *legal* procedure in this country. The bill was eventually shelved, but this insanity was mimicked in Nebraska.

Then, in early September 2011, the Eighth Circuit U.S. Court of Appeals thankfully stepped in and overturned an earlier ruling stating that a woman had "an existing relationship with that unborn human being and that the relationship enjoys protection under the United States Constitution and under the laws of South Dakota." Translation: Screw *Griswold*, screw *Roe*, screw women's freedoms.

Buttoning down all the lies and anti-women's rights legislation percolating in the country is impossible, because they continue to multiply. There are also efforts across the country to fight what's happening. After Gov. Sam Brownback of Kansas stripped Planned Parenthood of federal family planning monies, the impact of which was also felt in mid-Missouri, all hell broke loose twice — first, when the decision was called unconstitutional, and second, when Kansas was forced to comply with a court order to fund Planned Parenthood while the state appeals the ruling.

Republicans are in a race to see which state they can make most hostile to women. This has resulted in a war on women, who are being subjected to unconstitutional legislation and invasions of privacy from which we're supposed to be protected under the law.

Women who don't have access to doctors and abortion, in rural Iowa for instance, now have to seek out telemedicine.

From ABC News in July 2011:

A woman seeking an abortion via telemedicine has an ultrasound performed by a trained technician, receives information about medical abortion and signs a standard informed consent for the abortion. Once that is complete, a physician steps in via teleconference. The doctor reviews the woman's medical history and ultrasound images, and once it is determined that she is eligible — up to nine weeks pregnant and not an ectopic pregnancy — she has time to ask questions. Then, the doctor enters a computer pass-code to remotely open a drawer at the clinic containing two pills. She then swallows the mifepristone, under the doctor's supervision, and then is instructed to take four additional tablets of misoprostol within the next twenty-four to forty-eight hours. The actual abortion happens at home.

Republicans and Tea Party activists rail against government, but they want to expand the job of government to enter women's lives down to the most personal levels. It would be ironic if not for their hypocrisy. The extremist views of these people even pertain to preventing pregnancy.

During the budget fight of 2011, House Tea Party members refused to budge until Planned Parenthood funding was pulled and were ready to shut the government down to get it done — even amid facts that the Hyde Amendment prohibits any federal funds to be used for abortion services. Sean Hannity made an ass of himself on his radio show, though that's hardly news, by saying Republicans only want to stop federal funds from being used for abortions, something which is already the case. Mr. Hannity is either dangerously ignorant or lying. I think it's both, as Hannity implies federal funds are being used in order to make Republicans sound righteous, instead of revealing their dangerous plan to block almost four million women from their only means of health care. Senator Jon Kyl, an Arizona Republican, made the mistake of going to the Senate floor to rail against Planned Parenthood, regurgitating Tea Party extremist factoids to make his point.

"Everybody goes to clinics, to doctors, to hospitals, so on. Some people go to Planned Parenthood. But you don't have to go to Planned Parenthood to get your cholesterol or your blood pressure checked. If you want an abortion, you go to Planned Parenthood, and that's well over 90% of what Planned Parenthood does."

Senator Kyl got this exactly backward. Planned Parenthood's services are 90% preventative care, with only 3% going toward abortion services, verified by Politifact. In fact, as Think Progress and a lot of other progressive sites reported after Kyl's blatant lie, because most conservative sites don't offer preventative health care facts for women, Planned Parenthood performs "one million cervical cancer screenings, 830,000 breast exams, and nearly four million exams, treatments and tests involving sexually transmitted diseases." The gaffe was so monumentally stupid that Kyl became an immediate late-night punch line for comedic wordsmiths like Jon Stewart and Stephen Colbert.

But instead of simply saying he screwed up, Senator Kyl doubled down, releasing a statement that was read by CNN anchor TJ Holmes: "'His remark was not intended to be a factual statement, but rather to illustrate that Planned Parenthood, an organization that receives millions of dollars in taxpayer funding, does subsidize abortions.'"

Stephen Colbert pounced, starting a Twitter campaign, complete with a hashtag: "#NotIntendedToBeAFactualStatement." For you non-Twitterites, when someone sends out a missive over Twitter, a.k.a. a tweet, a hashtag can be utilized to categorize what the tweet is about so it can be easily found in a search. They are often used as pure snark. Colbert's tweets caught fire. I've been on Twitter for years, so I couldn't resist writing about Kyl's idiocy with my blog post, "Senator Kirsten Gillibrand Disembowels Jon Kyl," utilizing Colbert's hashtag. Because when schadenfreude broke out in the Senate, Senator Kirsten Gillibrand, who now holds Hillary Rodham Clinton's former Senate seat, fully enjoyed the moment, as the New York Observer reported in April 2011:

"For my friends and colleagues, this is a factual statement — current law already prevents federal money from paying for abortions," [Senator Gillibrand] said, referring to the Hyde Amendment, the perpetual rider that's been in place since 1976. "This has been the law of the land for over thirty years."

So embarrassed by his ignorance and the hysterical laughter that erupted at his expense, Senator Kyl had his remark stricken from the Senate record. From Politico's Pulse: "Senator Jon Kyl has quietly removed his infamous comment that 90% of Planned Parenthood's business is abortion from the Congressional Record.

Senators are allowed to revise and extend their comments in the record, and his statement now simply says: 'If you want an abortion you go to Planned Parenthood and that is what Planned Parenthood does.' Kyl's office could not be reached for comment.'"

What makes it worse is that it's not like the abortion rights opponents want to join in to make abortions rare either, with medical science improving the chance to make "rare" a real rarity. Through birth control and abortifacients like the morning-after pill, RU-486, and its cousin from France, ellaOne, which works up to five days after unprotected sex, women can control emergency situations themselves. Add abstinence, but not as the only preventative, because it doesn't work. Ask Sarah Palin's daughter, Bristol. So, why hasn't rare turned into *really* rare? Because the right, in whatever political party it lives, will not champion contraception and reproductive health care access as public policy imperatives. In the twenty-first century we're still battling the moral and religious judgment equivalent of the 1950s, while keeping young people hostage to those unrealistic notions, when what's really important is preventing unplanned pregnancies.

Instead of refighting the politics of sex battles we've already settled, why aren't we finding common ground by talking about preventing unplanned pregnancies? It isn't because the Democrats won't engage. It's the Republicans' fault. Because we have the medical and pharmaceutical tools to go beyond "safe, legal and rare," it's just that the right won't admit women's individual freedoms are non-negotiable. They're still fighting to make us surrender, which is never going to happen.

So, why did Democrats pull their punches on women's individual freedoms, including reproductive health care? Is it moral cowardice in the face of religious pressure, or guilt?

Kathleen Parker stubbornly wrote in late 2005 that Hillary could win the nomination and the presidency if she'd only run on ending abortion and women's freedom. Parker forgets that Democratic women, as well as feminist men, would never have stood for her nomination if she had. She also fails to understand what Hillary means when she says human rights are women's rights, and that a fundamental tenet is planning your life as you see fit, which includes family-planning, too.

Let's look at this through a philosophical lens for a minute, even though we all know that abortion rights revolve around a game of emotions. I'm just a flawed, "frozen chosen" sinner, so listen to Dr. Wayne W. Dyer in his book *Inspiration*, quoting the holy Hindu book, the Bhagavad Gita, which was Gandhi's guide:

> The Self dwells in the house of the body,
> Which passes through childhood, youth, and old age.
>
> So passes the Self at the time of death,
>
> Into another body.
>
> The wise know this truth,
>
> And are not deceived by it.

Dyer further quoting from Krishna:

> Not pierced by arrows nor burnt by fire,
>
> Affected by neither water nor wind,
>
> The Self is not a physical creature.
>
> Deathless is the Self in every creature.
>
> Know this truth, and leave all sorrow behind.

Is what a woman is carrying, before the fetus can live on its own, a life, and is a soul at issue? If the soul passes at the time of death into another body, what is this fight all about? Better yet, why are we waging it? If the self cannot be killed because the soul lives on, where is the death, the "killing"?

If whatever is inside the woman cannot live without her, whose life is it anyway?

Or is the entire philosophical argument a cover for controlling women, and pushing one view of family values and America? Because if you are someone who cares about preventing abortions and lowering their numbers, wouldn't you do everything in your power to make contraception, including pharmaceutical methods of stopping pregnancy, available to all women?

We have a moral obligation to make women safe as they exercise their individual rights of freedom. Women have a responsibility to themselves as well, but also ethically. Ultimately, though, the woman must come first, because it is her life on which the growing cells depend, long before they become a life. Nothing can survive if the woman does not.

When Hillary Clinton posited that human rights are women's rights, it shook people's consciousness, especially the women in China whose individual freedoms are not respected. She and President Clinton were vilified for their respect for women's individual freedoms after twelve years of Reagan-Bush, both of whom fought against those freedoms. But Hillary was fighting on the ultimate grounds of life when she said in Beijing, "It is a violation of human rights when women are denied the right to plan their own families."

Griswold v. Connecticut was the beginning for us. Heard by the Warren Court and decided in 1965, the case was based on the premise that the Bill of Rights provided numerous zones of privacy. The Ninth Amendment in the Bill of Rights establishes that the people have rights not specifically named in the U.S. Constitution. Examples of this are found in the First, Third, Fourth and Fifth Amendments.

The Griswold case revolved around a Connecticut law that prohibited "any drug, medicinal article or instrument for the purpose of preventing conception" and provided that "any person who assists, abets, counsels, causes or hires or commands another to commit any offense may be prosecuted and punished as if he were the principal offender." Planned Parenthood League of Connecticut offered birth control advice to married couples, which resulted in Estelle Griswold, executive director, and Dr. Charles Lee Buxton, medical director of the league and a professor from Yale Medical School, being arrested, convicted and fined $100. Outraged at the repercussions of the Connecticut law, Griswold and Buxton appealed their convictions. The Warren Court found the Connecticut law unconstitutional as an invasion of marital privacy, thus establishing the right to privacy that became the foundation for the decision that would be rendered in *Roe v. Wade*.

> Conclusion: Though the Constitution does not explicitly protect a general right to privacy, the various guarantees within the Bill of Rights create penumbras, or zones, that establish a right to privacy. Together, the First, Third, Fourth, and Ninth Amendments, create a new constitutional right, the right to privacy in marital

relations. The Connecticut statute conflicts with the exercise of this right and is therefore null and void.

> — *Griswold* rules on privacy, *Roe v. Wade* specific to it, saying that abortion is legal until the *"point at which the fetus becomes 'viable'"*

I can't believe we're still fighting about abortion in the twenty-first century, when we should all be joining together to prevent as many unwanted pregnancies as possible, with everyone accepting that a woman's individual rights and freedoms should be no less than any man's.

So no, a zygote or nonviable fetus is not a person. That is, unless it can live outside the woman on its own, sustaining life, including through medical means.

God, do I hate this part of the conversation.

But since Sarah Palin went on a "mama grizzly" warpath, with Tea Party extremists taking up so much oxygen, now seen through the candidacies of Ron Paul, Michele Bachmann, Rick Perry and Herman Cain, among others, questionably unconstitutional laws directed at women and impacting men, too, are being enacted. I'm starting to get that 1950's feeling, because Democrats don't seem to have any intention of fighting for women.

In a speech to the Susan B. Anthony List, Palin said Obama was "the most pro-abortion president ever to occupy the White House." This statement is not only hyperbole, it's a lie. This was the same day Palin launched the "mama grizzly" line, coupling it with her own story to share, which for abortion rights opponents would be heresy if it didn't come from Saint Sarah. From Lisa Miller's *Newsweek* article:

> Palin has already overshared: Nothing makes a person, let alone a politician, appear more vulnerable, more ordinary, and more unambiguously female than a scene in a bathroom where she pees on a stick. But then she defies a generation of pro-life activists who preached that the life of the fetus is sacred, no matter what an individual woman wants. For a split second, Palin — already at the limits of her time and energy — stops to consider the chaos another baby will create in her life. These are really less than ideal circumstances, she thinks. And then the inconceivable. I'm out of town. No one knows I'm pregnant. No one would

ever have to know. Any woman who has faced a pregnancy test with hope or with dread can picture the governor sitting there, alone with her dilemma, certain that her future will change. We know, of course, how the story ends. Trig, diagnosed in utero with Down syndrome, was born just months before his mother's vice presidential run.

Phyllis Schlafly could never have pulled this stuff off. It's one reason Palin rose to conservative heroine status. Not only are her policies right-wing perfection, but women want to be like her; she's seen as glamorous, attractive and fun. Unlike any other woman in Republican history, Sarah was a triple-threat Republican conservative, which has made wing-nut conservatism cool, even if it isn't particularly informed.

The whole "mama grizzly" dynamic reeks of the same type of stigmatizing women used to go through if their choices didn't include children, a husband and "traditional values," only Sarah's way is a tougher, hipper code, complete with fierce, western, wildlife imagery. Of course, the notion that frontier women didn't experience unwanted pregnancy is ludicrous, and they didn't have birth control. The stark truth is that on rare occasions even birth control can fail you.

Back in the late 1970s, I was on the road with a hot dinner theater show, before I landed on Broadway. My long-term boyfriend and I were very careful about sex, never forgetting to use contraception. In fact, we both protected ourselves. It happened anyway. There's a lesson for you.

Panicked, there wasn't a moment I didn't know what I had to do. The trouble was there were no doctors in the Virginia area we could find to help. I also had to orchestrate it so no one knew, as the stigma was unbelievable at the time, which meant seeing a doctor on our day off of a grueling performance schedule, making sure I was back at work and ready to perform by Tuesday night.

The kicker was it meant driving across several states to get the abortion.

It was an outpatient procedure, the long trip a horrific experience, the procedure loud and unnerving, though the doctor couldn't have been more professional, kinder or more comforting. Once back at home, I went to bed to rest up so I'd be ready to perform the next day — high cancan kicks, jumping splits, acting, full performance and all.

Everyone asked where we were going on our day off, then why I wasn't feeling well on Tuesday, with that lasting most of the week, though I did have to miss rehearsal. As I was the choreographer and lead dancer of the show, it turned into a real soap opera. Stomach flu was my excuse. I was queasy all week, but the show went on. No one thought anything different than what we told them.

Because I felt I had to skulk around and quickly get back to work, which included performing when I should have been resting, what eventually ensued was a nightmare. One day as I walked through a mall I started hemorrhaging and almost passed out. Rushed phone calls to the doctor, meds — it was awful. But in the end, I kept the real reason quiet. I was very lucky my health was preserved, because of the extremes I had to go through to keep it a secret.

There was absolutely no way I could have had a child.

To this day I think of poor women who don't have the support or means to take care of themselves. How much more difficult it would have been if my boyfriend hadn't helped me pull it off. The desperation women must feel when they have no system on which they can rely, so they're forced to endure a pregnancy and a child they cannot handle, or desperately reduced to putting their own life in danger to save themselves. I put myself in their place and I shudder at what might have been for me, the lengths I might have gone to in order to rescue myself.

No one has yet explained to me why poor women's individual freedoms are less important than mine or those of women with means. There's nothing Christian about sacrificing these women to a bootstrap philosophy that can ruin their lives and be culturally costly.

Life happens when you're planning your future. I was lucky. That abortion saved my life, because I couldn't have handled a child in any way. I would have been in real trouble, so I don't regret it for a second and never have. It's a difficult experience on all levels, but I did what I had to do to save my own life. This is no exaggeration. Not because I was physically threatened by childbirth or in danger for my life through my health, but for other reasons just as grave and intensely personal. You have to be emotionally prepared for a child and have the reserve to deal with the responsibility. I always knew the life I was saving was my own.

> Here's the simple truth.... You did not originate from a material particle as you've been led to believe. Your conception at the moment of your parents' blissful commingling was not your beginning. You had no beginning. That particle emanated from the universal energy field of intention, as do all particles. You're a piece of that universal mind of Creation, and you must see God inside of you and view yourself as a divine creation in order to access the power of intention in your life.

> — Dr. Wayne Dyer, *Inspiration*, 2006

Dr. Dyer's words are not given as an excuse or to establish a reason, but instead to offer that the language we've used in battling over whether a woman has a basic human right to control her own body is being manipulated in ways that serve no one. Stipulating "pro-life" versus "pro-choice" makes a mockery of the actual challenge any woman faces at a time of physical and emotional crisis, when pregnancy isn't an option. The pro-life *marketing* label is a selective endeavor, as it leaves the woman out of the equation, just as pro-choice is meant to reduce a woman's dire decision to a choice, instead of acknowledging it as fundamental human right for her to control her own body. A woman also has a responsibility to make every effort to prevent her own unwanted pregnancy, and if she can't, it's horribly tragic, but United States law makes abortion legal, something Republicans and even some Democrats ignore.

In late March 2010, NPR released updated guidelines on the language of women's rights. It was a long time coming:

> On the air, we should use "abortion rights supporter(s)/advocate(s)" and "abortion rights opponent(s)" or derivations thereof (for example: "advocates of abortion rights"). It is acceptable to use the phrase "anti-abortion," but do not use the term "pro-abortion rights...."

> — David Sweeney, managing editor, NPR

Mr. Sweeney's stated objective was to be as "clear, consistent and neutral as possible" in the words spoken and written on NPR. Sweeney obviously understands the charged nature of the language of pro-life and pro-choice, as evidenced by his explicitly stating that "pro-abortion rights" should not be used.

Certainly we can all agree that no one is pro-abortion, but the right and Tea Partiers won't do this, because they want to use it as a punch line to push their ideology.

Democrats let Hyde stay in play. In fact, after the legal cases that enshrined women's rights, the Hyde Amendment simply opened up the argument again, keeping it perpetually in motion. We'll never get beyond this unless we reverse the Hyde Amendment, finally getting to the fundamental human rights question that regardless of means, a woman's human rights, her civil rights, depend on access to full reproductive services, which includes reproductive counseling and birth control, as well as abortion.

Conservatives rail that the real beef for Democrats against Sarah Palin and other conservative women is that they're abortion-rights opponents. The conservative website Life News put it this way, under the subhead, "Valuing Human Life Especially Bad":

> Of course, the first most-cherished tenet of the feminist movement has always been abortion-on-demand — the "right" of women to put their "interests" (and moods and convenience) before giving birth to an unwanted child. This "inconvenience" has cost over fifty million babies their rights to Life, Liberty and the Pursuit of Happiness since the Supreme Court enacted *Roe v. Wade* in 1973.
>
> — Life News, September 28, 2008

The woman herself is never respected as a human life to be considered in any equation formulated by these particular conservatives and their extremist partners.

Laura Ingraham, guest-hosting the *O'Reilly Factor* on November 2, 2009, had a segment with Sally Quinn and Kellyanne Conway, with the topic for discussion, "Are Feminists Jealous of Sarah Palin?" Part of it went like this:

QUINN: ...I mean, she clearly believes in equality for women.

INGRAHAM: And babies in the womb.

CONWAY: But most of the criticism of her came from females, and we should make that point from the beginning. And the fact is, this woman's right to choose was to have five children and help raise a grandchild out of wedlock. She's pro-life. And the feminist movement is rooted in the fact that no matter who you are and what your background is, if you dare think you're going to become president or vice president of the United States as a woman, the calling card cost at the beginning, the cost of admission is that you be pro-choice.

I respect Sarah Palin and other women's views, but they do not respect mine or those of us who believe that what we do with our bodies is none of their fucking business and certainly isn't the government's. But I couldn't care less whether you're a feminist or not. If some hack tried to force me to get a sonogram at the worst moment in my life, I'd find a way to sue their ass.

Conservative women didn't seem to need feminism on Ladies' Night 2010, even after Sarah went to the Susan B. Anthony List breakfast to proclaim "a new conservative feminism." Unfortunately, no one is buying it, because what you cannot soft-pedal with conservative women who proclaim they are feminists is that they are actually *anti*-feminist. The right seems to believe that feminism hasn't been good for women; that sex outside marriage is immoral and that, when married, it's part of a woman's biological fate and wifely duty; and that choosing to be a single career woman *and* mother is heresy.

For Republican women, why isn't *anti*-feminism the field on which they want to play? It's wide open and it fits. Michele Bachmann was the first to figure it out.

In an interview with Fox News Channel talking-head and Daily Beast contributor Kirsten Powers in late June 2011, Bachmann rejected the idea of feminism, saying she was simply an "empowered American." It was a first for Republicans and the right, who'd tried desperately over decades to seem relevant to women as feminism elevated the fight for freedoms and individual rights for modern women. In quietly crying uncle, Michele Bachmann finally opened a new path for conservatives at a time when more women were worried about economics. The right was never going to defeat feminism, because whether they want to accept it or not, conservative women and their daughters are also beneficiaries of what feminism accomplished through battles in the courts.

Among the new generation of women, reproductive freedom is now taking a back seat to economic realities. This includes the anti-feminist "baby Palins" featured in the September 2011 issue of *Elle* who enjoy more freedoms because of feminism's successes now enshrined in law. Women today are focused on economics, whether they're single, moms or career-oriented. We're breadwinners and heads of households (even having husbands who stay home with the children). Women are staying single longer before bearing children, or happily choosing child-free lives. We're creating independent lives that force economics onto the forefront, or embracing the role of wife and mother who also has to be the CFO of her family and make ends meet.

The nonchalance by women of younger generations about feminist philosophy ignores the fact that women around the world are still kept down, driving home that the "post-feminism" the right tried to push does not exist. American women have also seen this play out through our involvement in Afghanistan, but also through the awakening in the Middle East, which has revived my hope that people will come to understand our non-military, soft-power support can make the difference to women who are just now finding freedom.

Secretary Clinton in March 2010:

> The status of the world's women is not only a matter of morality and justice. It is also a political, economic and social imperative. The evidence is irrefutable: When women are free to develop their talents and contribute fully to their societies, everyone benefits. When women are free to vote and run for public office, governments are more effective and responsive to their people. When women are free to earn a living and start small businesses, they become drivers of economic growth. When women are afforded the opportunity of education and access to health care, their families and communities prosper. When women have equal rights, nations are more stable, peaceful and secure. Advancing women's equality is at the heart of the foreign policy of the United States.

In Kenya, according to the Guttmacher Institute, "Forty percent of births are unplanned, and one in four married women have an unmet need for contraceptives." In fact, a Kenyan woman has a "one in thirty-nine chance of dying from pregnancy-related causes."

Those numbers have shifted, according to the medical journal *The Lancet*, cited in the *New York Times* in April, 2010:

> For the first time in decades, researchers are reporting a significant drop worldwide in the number of women dying each year from pregnancy and childbirth, to about 342,900 in 2008 from 526,300 in 1980....
>
> The researchers analyzed maternal mortality in 181 countries from 1980 to 2008....
>
> For instance, from 1990 to 2008, the maternal death rate dropped 8.8% a year in the Maldives, but rose 5.5% in Zimbabwe. Sub-Saharan Africa has the highest maternal death rates. Brazil improved more than Mexico, Egypt more than Turkey. Six countries accounted for more than half of all the maternal deaths in 2008: India, Nigeria, Pakistan, Afghanistan, Ethiopia and the Democratic Republic of Congo.

The issues converge with the global practice of child marriages, which continue regardless of the UN Convention on the Elimination of All Forms of Discrimination Against Women. They include violence against women. But even with international laws against child marriages, we all know they exist and happen too frequently. The resulting physical damage to girls of 14 or younger if pregnancy occurs, which can easily happen without birth control, is devastating beyond our western imagination — not just physically but emotionally. The damage can be life-threatening as well.

In Yemen, the *New York Times* reported in 2008, young girls in rural areas wed at the age of 9 or 10. The story told in "Tiny Voices Defy Child Marriage in Yemen" spoke of two such girls that startled the country awake, beginning a movement to ban child marriages. The result of which is not only pregnancy too young, but births to babies that are not normal. Powerful tribal customs held deeply undercover for generations are being given the light of the global press and the Internet, revealing that young girls are preyed upon and beaten if they don't comply.

The *Independent* of London reported that when Afghanistan's president Hamid Karzai was running for re-election, he made a deal with fundamentalist Islamists in his country that came back to bite him in the guise of an international uproar. The Shia Family Law was basically forced marital rape. In 2009 under Karzai, the law would have forced women to comply with their husbands' sexual demands; restricted women's rights to leave the house; and made child marriage legal.

> Details of the law emerged after Mr. Karzai was endorsed by Afghanistan's Supreme Court to stay in power until elections scheduled in August. Some MPs claimed President Karzai was under pressure from Iran, which maintains a close relationship with Afghanistan's Shias. The most controversial parts of the law deal explicitly with sexual relations. Article 132 requires women to obey their husbands' sexual demands and stipulates that a man can expect to have sex with his wife at least "once every four nights" when travelling, unless they are ill. The law also gives men preferential inheritance rights, easier access to divorce, and priority in court. A report by the United Nations Development for Women, Unifem, warned: "Article 132 legalises the rape of a wife by her husband."
>
> — The *Independent*, March 31, 2009

To protest the law, more than three hundred women gathered, forcing police to protect them from men surrounding the group and shouting "Death to the enemies of Islam!"

The *Independent* broke the story online, proving that the biggest impediment to men and the regimes around the world who want to continue their violence against women, is the free, unfettered global information network offered by the web. We saw evidence of this during the Iranian Green uprising, then in Tunisia, Egypt and throughout the Middle East during the Arab Spring, with YouTube, Facebook and Twitter playing important roles as well.

Remember the *Time* magazine cover in July 2010 showing a woman identified as Aisha, whose "brother-in-law held her down while her husband pulled out a knife. First he sliced off her ears. Then he started on her nose." It's hard to believe such barbarism is happening at the dawn of the twenty-first century.

On *Forbes* online, Melik Kaylan reported about a young girl in Bangladesh who was punished with 101 lashes for the crime of being a rape victim who became pregnant as a result. In remote areas of the world where ancient tribal customs and codes have patriarchal tyranny embedded in them, as Kaylan notes, it's impossible for the West to have a dramatic impact by enforcing our codes. But what cannot be ignored is the worldwide sympathy and outrage that is now engendered when these cases are reported and discussed, including the widespread coverage they get on blogs, locally and internationally. Some people were not even aware these sorts of crimes against women even still went on until the web made the information accessible and easy to share.

Could the Green uprising in Iran have made such an impact without websites and Twitter? Secretary Clinton's intervention to get Twitter's maintenance schedule changed was certainly a first. There is speculation that Twitter didn't help people mobilize inside Iran, however, there is quite a bit of evidence that the people who did have access to the web got information out to the global audience, as well as to the Iranian diaspora. This world communication network was responsible for the outrage when Neda Agha-Soltan was murdered on the street in Tehran, which galvanized the world against the Iranian regime.

Over 2009, I spent innumerable hours attending think tank events and policy forums in Washington, D.C. I live in the Beltway and became a regular at the New America Foundation, where Steve Clemons, a senior fellow there, also Washington editor at large for *The Atlantic* and editor in chief of *Atlantic* Live, hosted experts and discussions on Afghanistan, Central Asia, Iran and many other pressing issues. Steve and I have had many lively exchanges over the years, especially where the intersection of Afghanistan, the women there and our need to withdraw converge. I supported President Obama's initial policy, then our continued presence in Afghanistan, though mainly because of the women. But that changed in June 2010, when Lt. Gen. Stanley McChrystal unloaded in his interview with Michael Hastings in "The Runaway General" for *Rolling Stone*. Clemons is one of the most important independent voices on foreign policy today.

Daniel Levy and Amjad Atallah are co-directors of NAF's Middle East Task Force, with Daniel's morning salons with leading voices on current issues invaluable. NAF is where I also had the pleasure of meeting and speaking with late Ambassador Richard C. Holbrooke on Afghanistan. Learning and listening to leading experts on foreign policy, including the dilemma the U.S. faces where women are concerned in these areas of the globe, nothing I've learned has convinced me we did not make a huge difference aiding women in Afghanistan at first. However, the U.S. has now done all we can do militarily. Women and children in war torn countries suffer incredibly. Afghan women must fight their battles among their own, though now the whole world really is watching, pushing their backward country and misogynistic culture and customs to catch up. Changing Afghanistan will take a lot more time than the U.S. can afford, and it can never be coerced by outsiders to happen.

When we publicize the treatment of women inside closed societies, and we show cultures that a woman with a trade has a way to make money for her family, perhaps by sewing, it can help families prosper and save a village, save a woman. Spilling blood in these far-off places is always controversial and usually unwise. But challenging ancient tribal beliefs and customs that freedom belongs to men but not women is one of the most important foreign policy goals for the twenty-first century. It must be done using soft power beyond military interventionism.

> In Syria, as elsewhere, many conservative Muslims — including women — see any creeping sympathy for rape victims as the beginnings of westernization by stealth, the tip of the iceberg of feminism. In plenty of Muslim countries — Morocco, Yemen, Bangladesh — honor killings are often not punishable by law if they're deemed "justified," and not infrequently the rapist benefits from customary codes of mercy in place of the victim. This is especially true where a weak central state gives way to tribal law in remote regions or even in overcrowded and unpolicable urban areas. In some places the problem barely exists — in Iran, for example, and in Turkey outside of the Kurdish areas. But everywhere this central principle applies: Tribalism equals Islamic conservativism equals bad news for women.
>
> — *Forbes*, "No More Honor Killings," January 2010

In 2009, Syria's Bashar al-Assad amended his country's honor killing laws, scrapping Article 548 of the penal code that decriminalized honor killings in that country, replacing the one-year maximum sentence for that offense with a minimum of two years in jail. Of course, this is small comfort, because according to reports by the BBC, the new law protects men who "unintentionally" kill their wives or do so when they suspect them of being unfaithful. Syria's amended law also covers men who murder the lover of a woman, with enforcement doubtful. Syria presents a very dicey situation, and the carnage President Assad caused as the Arab Spring swept across the Mideast has left the country bloody and broken.

There is no way to chronicle all the challenges facing women fighting for their freedoms, which extend far beyond America's borders. Think of Israeli and Palestinian women caught in a never-ending cycle of violence within patriarchal as well as religious structures that keep them from living full lives, including something as basic as working. There are so many more, but I hope giving just a puny few examples will send a message to the "post-feminist" crowd that if one country's women are kept down we still have work to do, and that the United States benefits when we make the investment in partnership with the world community.

Just ask any woman in Central Asia or Pakistan how political her personal life is. Or how the politics of sex impacts her life. Rana Husseini has spent years exposing the "so-called crimes of honor" in Jordan, though they occur in Pakistan, Afghanistan, areas of Turkey, Egypt, Syria and beyond, including cases in the United States, something once unheard of by Americans. Jordan is one of the most aggressive in the region on exposing the inhumane practice, because of Husseini's work, which is groundbreaking.

However, the shifting sand on cultural tides changes on a misogynistic whim in countries across the world. What was law in 2010 could change even by the time you read this book. But it won't stay hidden. It's what makes the web, Twitter, YouTube, Facebook and other advanced social networking platforms so important.

Look at what happened in Egypt in March 2011 after Mubarak fell and women in that country were flying high before International Women's Day 2011, when Secretary Clinton released this message to the world: "They have now insisted that their voices be heard. And in the coming months and years, the women in Egypt and Tunisia and other nations have just as much right as the men to remake their governments — to make them responsive, accountable, transparent."

But on this celebratory day, women were met with fury and misogyny when they tried to march in Tahrir Square (Freedom Square). No one will ever forget CBS reporter Lara Logan's horrific assault during the uprising. The *Washington Post* reported Clinton's statement juxtaposed against tweets from Egypt.

Egyptocracy tweeted: "So, anti demo logic was as follows: Women aren't allowed on the streets, but if they are then touch and grab them."

Mo-Ha-Med tweeted: "Got to Tahrir 30 minutes ago — to catch a group of women being massively harassed by the mob. Will Egypt ever change?"

The Arab Spring was cataclysmic enough for the women of the region to inspire *Vogue* magazine to run a "Women of War: Liberating Libya" feature in the all-important September 2011 fall fashion issue.

In some countries, patrolling Sharia or Islamic police, watch for women who are not following Islamic law. In the Aceh province of Indonesia, as of January 2010, tight pants or jeans were banned. In Sudan in September 2009, thirteen women were arrested, fined and flogged for wearing pants, which was judged against Sharia law.

But get this: In Saudi Arabia in May 2010, when a woman walking with a man was confronted by the Virtue Police, she turned on the cop and beat him up! A month later, however, a group of men and women mingling were sentenced to lashings and prison. *Lashings.* It's not the twenty-first century everywhere on earth.

In Iran in July 2010, Mohammadi-Ashtiani, a 43-year-old mother of two, was sentenced to death by stoning for adultery, which her family denied. Canadian Prime Minister Stephen Harper's wife Laureen came out against the action.

In Arizona in October 2009, Noor Faleh Almaleki's father, Faleh Hassan Almaleki, ran her over with his Jeep Cherokee, killing her, because he felt she was too "Westernized." Mr. Almaleki tried to flee but was caught, tried and found guilty in February 2011 of second degree murder, in what prosecutors in Arizona called an "honor killing."

In 2009, Liberia President Ellen Johnson Sirleaf, the first woman elected head of state in Africa and a Nobel laureate as of October 2011, called out a Liberian family living in Phoenix, Arizona for disowning their eight-year-old daughter. She'd supposedly brought "shame" on the family, which decided they didn't want her anymore. They blamed the young girl when it was discovered she was a victim of gang-rape by four Liberian boys, also refugees. The AP and CNN covered the story, with President Sirleaf saying on CNN that the child had been "victimized," and appealing to the parents to "protect their child," saying the young men "infringed upon her." She then went on to talk about the problem of rape, which now is a criminal offense in Liberia: "Things have changed in Liberia; no longer do we tolerate this.... This is not a question of shame on the family. It is the question of an assault on a young child. That cannot be tolerated."

Contending that sexual education and birth control availability are part of a young girl's path to staying free may seem like a stretch for some. That her freedom can change the path of her own country does too. But nothing thwarts potential like an unexpected pregnancy, with customs and cultural impediments to progress hurting a nation's stability. It's the same in every country all around the world.

In 2010, France took an unprecedented step in outlawing the burqa. It was a historic moment for a country that has always championed sectarian society, fighting against any religion, from Catholics and Jews to Muslims, which want to change France's foundation. Chalk this one up as a win, denying fundamentalists the power to demand women stay invisible. We've got to find a way to support moderate Islam and create a space for twenty-first century Muslims to gain power. Banning the full veil is the place France bravely chose to start.

Secretary Clinton was the first to visit the war state of Congo, a country whose vast natural resources, including diamonds, gold, copper and tin, among other minerals, have created a perpetually combustible and very toxic environment. Clinton was there specifically to focus on the violence and atrocities committed against women who are regularly subjected to rape, another weapon of war in Africa, but particularly brutal in the Congo. "This problem is too big for one country to solve alone," she said.

The *New York Times* reported that foreign minister Assunção dos Anjos said of Clinton's visit to Angola, that it was "the most sublime, most magnanimous moment" that "changes everything."

Of course, Hillary Clinton knows better; it takes more than just one visit by a political rock star, but her trek to the Congo and other war-ravaged areas of Africa was a monumental step. Clinton long ago answered and closed the debate on the question, is freedom just for men? President Obama showed his support and made a statement by appointing Melanne Verveer to be the first ever Ambassador-at-Large for Global Women's Issues in U.S. history to work with Secretary Clinton.

Even in the Bush administration, through *Fortune* magazine and the U.S. State Department's Most Powerful Women mentor program, which continued under Obama, women from around the world get the chance to be mentored inside the U.S. I got to watch some of the mentees in this program, who were nominated by the U.S. embassies in their home countries, enjoy a night at the State Department few would have once dreamed possible. All of this before they were on their way to spend a month with a U.S. company that would show them the business ropes.

Freedom is not just for men, and Hillary Clinton has been one of the loudest and most resounding voices in American history to say so, continuing what she began in 1995 at the State Department. Her work in the Obama administration has made an impact through exposing the silence and shadows where global misogyny lives and breeds, as the U.S. continues to lead in the efforts to expose violence against women.

Of course, we can't change cultures, but aided by the interconnectedness of the world today, fundamentalist countries with misogyny and sexism built into their cultures, customs and history over centuries now have klieg lights trained on them. It was Hillary Rodham Clinton who turned up the wattage just before the dawn of the twenty-first century, saying that regardless of culture and hundred-year-old habits, freedom is not just for men.

Chapter 5: **Blaming Bill**

Democrats are nothing if not politically self-loathing. Republicans don't have that problem; they're permanently self-righteous. The moral of this chapter is that Democratic self-loathing simply sets up Republicans and their culture of permanent self-righteousness, which makes losers out of Democrats.

William Jefferson Clinton proved both hypotheses. Democrats "always wanted to look purer than Caesar's wife," Clinton told author Ken Gormley. This predilection helped cost Al Gore the presidency. It also helped defeat Hillary.

> I think this President has shown a remarkable disrespect for his office, for the moral dimensions of leadership, for his friends, for his wife, for his precious daughter. It is breathtaking to me the level to which that disrespect has risen.
>
> — John Edwards, circa 1999

It's impossible to think of Hillary without Bill as background. But the lengths to which some people will go to make every political utterance or occurrence Bill's fault borders on a national psychosis. Still, it was part of the dynamic Hillary combated even to be named secretary of state, with Bill Clinton doing everything that was asked in order to make that happen, even as the press reported otherwise.

Apropos of perpetuating the Democratic self-loathing dynamic, see *Vanity Fair*'s anonymously sourced, July 2008 "Comeback Id" column, which was subtitled "Bubba Trouble," by Todd Purdum, Dee Dee Myers' husband. Purdum's "disappointed by his shortcomings" and "sins against decorum and the dignity of his office" prove the point and the perpetual fetish of blaming Bill.

Jay Carson, spokesperson for former President Clinton at the time, unloaded on Purdum's vacuous scattershot, offering this statement: "The ills of the Democratic Party can be seen perfectly in the willingness of fellow Democrats to say bad things about President Clinton. If you ask any Republican about Reagan they will say he still makes the sun rise in the morning, but if you ask Democrats about their only two-term president in eighty years, a man who took the party from the wilderness of loserdom to the White House and created the strongest economy in American history, they'd rather be quoted saying what a reporter wants to hear than protect a strong brand for the party. Republicans look at this behavior and laugh at us."

There was just no road map for what Hillary Rodham Clinton, with her former-president husband by her side, was about to do, though the rearview mirror provided plenty of foreshadowing of the minefields. One six-time Peabody winner for CNN, John Camp, interviewed for the video made of Joe Conason and Gene Lyons' *Hunting of the President*, said there was a "huge gangbang in the national media taking place" during the '90s. It was a period when reporting the truth about the Clintons got you labeled a "Clinton apologist." But Watergate fever had swept through the national press corps over Whitewater, everyone thinking they were going to be the next Woodward or Bernstein. The coverage of Clinton evolved into a never-ending journalistic farce.

Of course, the history of the Clintons might have been different if either Bill or Hillary was as cunningly smart as their daughter Chelsea. When asked at a campaign event about the Lewinski imbroglio, she showed her parents how it was done, responding, "Wow, you're the first person actually that's ever asked me that question in the, I don't know, maybe seventy college campuses that I've now been to, and I do not think that's any of your business."

It's none of your business; if only Bill Clinton had begun there.

The political force that is Bill Clinton is inescapable in American politics, as President Obama found out during the 2010 election cycle, with Bill able to campaign in places, more welcome than any other Democrat. But in 2008, he was used as a cudgel against Hillary.

You gained experience from your husband's presidency? Prove it. If Hillary hadn't had Bill during the primaries it might have worked out better. Seriously? She couldn't control him. No kidding. He was off the reservation, compounded by more befouled dish and blind quoting coming out of the primaries than there was time to debunk the avalanche. Blaming Bill was the natural fallback position. The fact that he was off his game didn't help. Heart bypass surgery will do that to anyone, even William Jefferson Clinton.

Puritanical America can stand a lot of things — lying about war, torture, eavesdropping on Americans, David Vitter's diaper and hooker fetish, John Ensign's ethically challenged hypocrisy that resulted in his resignation, Larry Craig's wide stance, Republicans obstructing unemployment insurance, and threatening to stiff first responders, both parties feeding the rich — but Bill Clinton getting caught having a consensual affair was a bridge too far. Today's buttinsky piety-obsession would have deprived us of John F. Kennedy.

Barack Obama even utilized the Clinton era as a springboard to help make his case why he should be the nominee, deriding "the Washington battles of the 1990s." Little did Obama's fans know that this line would foreshadow a lack of fight from Obama that would become the hallmark and pitfall of his first term. However, his campaign team was cagey enough to know Hillary would be vulnerable to this attack and callous enough to wage it. Democratic self-loathing made blaming Bill possible, so Obama seized upon the meme. But then as the economic crisis deepened during Obama's first term, the Clinton '90s were again being recalled fondly, starting with the largest tax increase in modern times, which helped set up the '90s boom.

On Memorial Day weekend 2010, Josh Gerstein's Politico article reached back for an oldie-but-goodie storyline: "Bill Clinton's picture is again a fixture on cable news. Republicans are sternly demanding a special prosecutor. And legal commentators are bickering over the finer points of federal criminal statutes on bribery and graft. It feels like 1997 — but it's 2010. And Barack Obama can't be happy."

It came with the headline, "Clinton 'Whiff of Scandal' Returns," because the White House admitted enlisting former President Bill Clinton in lobbying Joe Sestak to stay in the House and not run for Senate against Arlen Specter. Never mind that it was Mr. Obama's White House, through his then-chief-of-staff Rahm Emanuel, who asked Mr. Clinton to get involved in the first place. Pimping the Clinton scandal meme, Politico knew it would draw eyes, regardless of the bottom line.

"This is just a ridiculous diversion back to the future," said Larry Sabato, professor of politics at the University of Virginia.

"They're trying to regenerate negative feelings about Bill Clinton that have long since disappeared in the electorate.

As for "the Washington battles of the 1990s," the budget vote in August 1993 would end up being historic for the Clinton family. See, it was Chelsea's mother-in-law, then-Rep. Marjorie Margolies-Mezvinsky, upon President Clinton's personal request, who cast the deciding vote to pass Clinton's budget, her last-minute switch making the difference. That vote would end up costing Margolies-Mezvinsky her House seat, with jeers of "Goodbye Marjorie" ringing through the chamber immediately afterward. Rep. Barney Frank, also proud of that budget win, wrote about it on Huffington Post, offering a '90s history lesson for candidate Obama. The most important thing Rep. Frank wrote became what Hillary's campaign was all about: fighting the good fight on behalf of battles not yet completely won.

> Few fights that we had in the period when Senator Obama is denigrating our battles [were] more important than the successful effort to pass President Clinton's tax plan in 1993. That battle was so hotly fought that it contributed, sadly, to the Republican takeover the next year, because a number of the Democrats who had voted for a progressive tax plan which made the tax code less unfair and provided important revenues for important programs lost their seats because of it. I make no apologies for having fought that fight, and in fact I hope that whoever is the President of the United States in 2009 will take up the battle against excessive tax cuts for the wealthiest people in the country, both as a matter of fairness and as a matter of being able to afford fundamental programs essential to the quality of our lives. I also remember fighting hard during that period for the rights of working men and women to join unions, and while we lost that once the Republicans took power in '94, we did score one victory when we were still in the majority in passing, in a "bitter partisan battle," the Family and Medical Leave Act — the need for us to wage that battle is once again as strong if not stronger in 2008 than it was in 1995....
>
> If Senator Obama was denouncing the outrageous tactics of Gingrich and DeLay, I would be very much in support of his comments. Instead, he evenhandedly denounces the "bitter partisanship" of that period and

seems to me to be distancing himself equally from the Gingrich/DeLay attack and the efforts of many of us to combat it.

— Rep. Barney Frank, Huffington Post, January 9, 2008

Once in the White House, President Obama not only didn't "take up the battle against excessive tax cuts for the wealthiest people in the country," he defended, then extended the Bush tax cuts, which candidate Obama first said he wouldn't do, then said he'd fight against them in the future, just in time for reelection season. Not even the example of Ronald Reagan raising taxes eleven times during his presidency could stir Republicans or Democrats to act responsibly.

President Bill Clinton got blamed for anything that took us in the opposite direction of Ronald Reagan. The right hated him for it, while Bill's legacy cast a wide shadow over Hillary, including with many progressives who were tired of all things that represented corporate Democrats. That they didn't have a clue Obama was one, too, has become their embarrassment.

Meanwhile, the right won't get caught dead doing self-analysis on its own hypocrisy. Take Rep. Henry Hyde, the driver of Clinton impeachment. During Iran-Contra, Hyde wasn't so picky about lying by Republicans. In the sex versus Iran-Contra model, Democratic president versus Republican, Hyde's choice was simple, as quoted in the *Washington Post*, December 8, 1998:

"It just seems to me too simplistic to condemn all lying. In the murkier grayness of the real world, choices must be made."

The irony of Henry Hyde's crusade against Bill Clinton is that he'd messed around with a married woman, ruining her marriage, a hidden affair buried deep until his impeachment crusade began. David Talbot, editor of Salon at the time, published the account of the cuckolded husband in a September 1998 article called, "This Hypocrite Broke Up My Family."

Hyde had also been a cheerleader for Ollie North during Iran-Contra, as well as John Poindexter, something Sidney Blumenthal recounts in his book, *The Clinton Wars*. "'It is an emotional and gut-wrenching experience to go through these hearings and to see good people who have made errors in judgment have to sit here and go through the tortures of the damned,'" Blumenthal quotes Rep. Hyde saying about North.

The whole impeachment drama, which was the denouement for "the Washington battles of the 1990s," was the setup for the ugly campaign battles, with Hillary getting tagged with the scandal, too. The whole thing was an offensive strike at Bill Clinton's presidency. It began in 1992 and it matters, because if we're going to talk about one of candidate Obama's favorite lines invoked to smack Hillary, it's important to remember who shot the first volley. It wasn't the Clintons.

In 1992, Chief Justice Rehnquist, who was appointed to the Supreme Court by Nixon and named chief justice under Reagan, replaced a current judge on the three-court panel that appoints special prosecutors with the most right-wing judge in the federal judiciary, U.S. Appeals Court Judge David Sentelle. A man who was nominated to a North Carolina district court by Senator Jesse Helms, a notorious Clinton-hater who led the Republican right-wing political machine. It was Judge Sentelle who also overturned the Iran-Contra convictions of Oliver North and John Poindexter, something that no doubt tickled the man spearheading impeachment, Rep. Henry Hyde.

Rehnquist also pushed to have Robert Fiske, a respected American Bar Association president and the original independent counsel, removed and replaced with Ken Starr, an activist conservative lawyer with ties to helping Paula Jones, and that's not even getting into the funding being funneled through Richard Mellon Scaife to spearhead the effort. Judge Sentelle pushed Attorney General Janet Reno to replace Fiske, citing that her involvement in his appointment was bad for appearances.

Clinton had been targeted by conservatives from the start. Joe Conason and Gene Lyons have written extensively on this, as have others. E.J. Dionne provides color, from the September 30, 1997 edition of the *Washington Post*:

> But appearances didn't seem to bother Judge Sentelle when he lunched with Sens. Jesse Helms and Lauch Faircloth, both North Carolina Republicans, shortly before he replaced Fiske. The same Senator Faircloth had accused Fiske of a "cover-up." Five past presidents of the American Bar Association issued a statement saying the

meeting was "unfortunate, to say the least" and gave rise "to the appearance of impropriety."

This is all part of "the Washington battles of the 1990s," much of which was orchestrated not by Bill Clinton and certainly not by Hillary, but by the conservative right, helped along by the traditional media smelling Pulitzers. They were pulling every string to unravel the Clinton presidency, hoping to take that haughty, shrill, "feminazi" Hillary down, too.

Sally Quinn, in her innumerable columns shredding Hillary, continually ignored the Rehnquist-Sentelle-Jesse Helms-Ken Starr-Paula Jones linkage. Maybe she's ignorant or just not interested in political history, but it's likely she prefers the *Peyton Place*-era gossip of her generation, spinning lies into truth. Quoting again from one of Quinn's impeachment-era columns, her willful cluelessness is clear.

> Independent counsel Ken Starr is not seen by many Washington insiders as an out-of-control prudish crusader. Starr is a Washington insider, too. He has lived and worked here for years. He had a reputation as a fair and honest judge. He has many friends in both parties. Their wives are friendly with one another and their children go to the same schools. He is seen as someone who is operating under a legal statute, with a mandate from the attorney general and a three-judge panel, although there are some lawyers here who have questioned some of Starr's most aggressive tactics.
>
> — *Washington Post*, November 2, 1998

Talk about rewriting history. "Some lawyers" included the most knowledgeable person on the issue you could find:

> The initial wrongdoing was not criminal and did not, in contrast to that of Richard Nixon, entail the abuse of power.
>
> — Elliott Richardson, attorney general under President Nixon (resigned in what came to be known as the Saturday Night Massacre)

In a Federal News Service Report published December 1, 1998, in the *Washington Post*, attorney Alan Dershowitz agreed. "'You could not fit into this room or into this building all of the people who testified more perjuriously than President Clinton and were not ever prosecuted,'" Dershowitz was quoted saying.

After what President George W. Bush and Dick Cheney orchestrated in their two terms in office, it gives "restoring honor and dignity to the White House" new meaning. But Democratic self-loathing means blaming Bill into eternity, though the American people long ago gave up that one, most never having taken it up in the first place.

However, continuing the storyline that it's all Bill Clinton's fault was a way the boys club could tag Hillary with what happened in the '90s without holding the media accountable.

The degree to which the media, the establishment Democratic elite and many others hung Bill's every transgression on Hillary is important to note. It weighted her candidacy down in ways she had no control over, which is made clear by the fact that the establishment's preferred candidate turned out to be Barack Obama. The Democratic Senate elite fell into Rep. Henry Hyde's self-righteous trap. Their self-loathing made them do it.

In an interview with Paul Gigot of the *Wall Street Journal*, Hyde admits, "we got sex," but impeaching Clinton wasn't what he really wanted. With evangelicals, it's always about the culture war.

> [Hyde] acknowledges that "this was a culture war," and maybe the 1960s generation "revels in this guy's success. I don't know."
>
> — *Wall Street Journal*, February 12, 1999

Ah yes, the 1960s presidency of William Jefferson Clinton, symbolizing the birth control era of *Griswold* privacy, which begat *Roe v. Wade*, which begat the Hyde Amendment, which begat President Bill Clinton, who despoiled the place after the sainted Reagan years. Oh, and let us not forget First Lady Hillary Rodham Clinton, who had the audacity to declare that human rights are women's rights. Because, fer Christ's sake, people, we can't have women running around with their individual freedoms flapping in the goddamn breeze. This is America.

So when President Clinton served up an opportunity, the House piety squad jumped on the sexually voracious Bubba from the sticks, letting him know who was boss. Never mind that the Clintons were entirely cleared of the story that got "the Washington battles of the 1990s" rolling, Whitewater. Ever heard of the Pillsbury Report?

> The Pillsbury Report found no evidence that Whitewater's losses had been subsidized by taxpayers in the savings and loan bailout. But even if they were, it concluded, the Clintons were not at fault: "There is no basis to assert that the Clintons knew anything of substance about the McDougals' advances to Whitewater, the source of the funds used to make those advances, or the sources of the funds used to make payments on the bank debt...."
>
> — Pillsbury Report text, from *Hunting of the President*, by Gene Lyons and Joe Conason, 2000

The hunt worked, but it also came back to bite the self-righteous Republicans at the ballot box, something people too often forget.

> "Republicans need to remember that they screwed up '98 when they were about to win an election and win twenty House seats in 1998, and they decided to spend the summer talking about Monica Lewinski, which is a fascinating conversation for talk radio and doesn't move votes. And Republicans lost five seats, because they were talking about Monica Lewinski."
>
> — Grover Norquist, C-SPAN, August 2010

What has always been ironic is that Bill Clinton embodied the Republican "pick yourself up by your boot straps," philosophy, with his life the embodiment of the American dream; same with Barack Obama. Something George W. Bush couldn't boast, with his family considered an American dynasty not unlike the Kennedys, though without the glamour, magic and polish. William Jefferson Clinton was just too damn glib and gifted, with brains and communication skills to match, along with a pedigree that went all the way to Oxford, where Reagan fell well short.

As for Hillary, she was a goddamn feminist of the first order. That's all the Phyllis Schlafly cliterati club needed to know.

More than ten years after he left office, everyone is still blaming Bill.

Mary Matalin, Republican strategist who's married to James Carville, said the Bush-Cheney administration inherited "the most tragic attack on our own soil in our nation's history" from President Clinton. Matalin's claim that Clinton somehow bequeathed 9/11 to Bush-Cheney is astoundingly uninformed. In fact, it's a lie. The Bush administration was warned. From the *9/11 Commission Report*, Chapter Six:

> In December, Bush met with Clinton for a two-hour, one-on-one discussion of national security and foreign policy challenges. Clinton recalled saying to Bush, "I think you will find that by far your biggest threat is Bin Ladin and the al Qaeda." Clinton told us that he also said, "One of the great regrets of my presidency is that I didn't get [Bin Ladin] for you, because I tried to."

When Gen. Hugh Shelton's book, *Without Hesitation: The Odyssey of an American Warrior,* came out, there was a media kerfuffle about one section where the president's aide loses the "biscuit," a.k.a. the nuclear codes. Right-wingers, as well as national media outlets including ABC News, translated this into President Clinton losing the codes, because it fit their fantasy rhetoric about any Democrat being incompetent on national defense. Ed Morrissey, over at the aptly named Hot Air blog, blared the headline: Second Book Claims Clinton Lost Nuclear Codes While President.

Gen. Hugh Shelton responded to the media misinformation by writing at the Command Post blog, explaining how badly the media had mangled the story. Cutting to the chase, it boiled down to this: "The President never did have [the codes], but he assumed, I'm sure, that the aide had them like he was supposed to."

David E. Hoffman, over at Foreign Policy, adds more with one part of his October 22, 2010, blog post that's worth mentioning since there are so many lazy-ass squealers out there who are running with any headline that blames Bill:

> "The president does not possess the actual codes to authorize the launch of nuclear weapons. What the president does carry (or an aide) is a small laminated card which is used to authenticate the president's identity in the event of an emergency. The cards contain date-time groups and alphanumeric codes in columns and rows, according to Bruce Blair, president of the World Security Institute who has written several books on nuclear command and control. In an emergency, a president would use this laminated card to verify that he is the commander in chief making decisions."

It should also be noted that none of the news organizations opining and ripping truncated stories out of Shelton's book seemed to have actually read the thing. I was sent a copy so it was easy for me to check. Beyond Shelton's "the number of redundancies is staggering" to "within minutes we reissued replacement codes," the detail of the story simply was too troublesome for traditional and new media who often prefer their sound bites simple and their stories negative where Clinton and national security are concerned.

The news media completely ignored that Gen. Hugh Shelton also obliterated the infamous wag-the-dog fantasy narrative when Clinton ordered strikes on December 16, 1998, in Iraq, because Saddam Hussein wouldn't cooperate with weapons inspectors. Senator Trent Lott, the Republican majority leader, accused Clinton of launching the strike to save his presidency, saying the timing was "suspect" and "cursory." Now-disgraced Rep. Tom Delay asked Secretary of Defense William Cohen in a closed House session instigated by departing House Speaker Newt Gingrich, whom Clinton had beaten in Newt's government shutdown disaster, whether he believed "that national security would be endangered if the House were to proceed with an impeachment trial the following day," to quote from Shelton's book. Gen. Shelton makes fools of Lott, Delay and Gingrich, whose idiocy was blasted across the media in a national press pile-on that represented the feeding frenzy at the time. The truth was quite the contrary.

> Even today, if one were to Google "Clinton Wag the Dog" — almost twelve years after the impeachment hearings — the search would yield more than fifty thousand alleging that the President orchestrated his own personal Wag the Dog.
>
> It may sound ironic when considering what prompted the impeachment in the first place, but the way I see it, President Clinton demonstrated exemplary leadership skills in his decision to strike on the sixteenth. He acted firmly, quickly, and with complete integrity, basing his decision totally and completely on what was best for the country and safest for our pilots, even though he was well aware that by making such a decision he would be personally battered by accusations. I gained a tremendous amount of respect for the president that day.
>
> — *Without Hesitation*, Gen. Hugh Shelton, 2010

"The Washington battles of the 1990s" included at its epicenter an ethically challenged independent counsel. Whatever Bill Clinton did wrong, and he should have his head examined for his libidinous recklessness, his adversaries used means and methods to get at him that were more fundamentally un-American than Clinton's original promiscuity, in which Ms. Lewinsky was a willing and eager participant. The "bracing" of Monica Lewinsky, which amounted to the entrapment of her by the Office of Independent Council, is proved in Ken Gormley's book, revealing Lewinsky's terror of the OIC's tactics.

> "I wouldn't have touched her with a ten-foot pole," said the lawyer hired to examine the episode, Jo Ann Harris, breaking her silence about her findings on the effort to lure in Lewinsky for questioning. "The minute she says, 'Can I call my lawyer?' you stop.... And when she says it for the sixth or seventh time, you really stop.... There are limits."
>
> — *The Death of American Virtue*, Ken Gormley, 2011

We learn through Gormley that one of Kenneth Starr's prosecutors got a judge to put Ms. Harris' assessment under seal. We can't have anything that would prove Ken Starr and the OIC were able to flay Bill Clinton on impeachment only by using unethical means, now can we? It ruins all the fun. Harris was appointed on January 16, 1998, to investigate the alleged improper questioning of Monica Lewinski at the Ritz-Carlton Hotel in Pentagon City, just outside of Washington, D.C. This was the same day Attorney General Janet Reno approved the expansion of Starr's investigation, which Judge Sentelle's three-judge panel approved, and one day before President Clinton was to give his deposition in the Paula Jones lawsuit.

The *Washington Post* was one of the media outlets that benefited from the "serious and repetitive" leaks from Starr's office, though hardly the only one. It cited sources like "prosecutors," "the prosecution," "sources with knowledge of the investigation," "law enforcement sources" and "Starr's deputies" in its reports.

Hillary's baggage from Bill, beyond his mistakes and the self-loathing Democratic obsession with "the Washington battles of the 1990s," included the longest economic expansion in American history: more than twenty-two million new jobs; the lowest poverty rate in twenty years; the largest budget deficit in American history converted into the largest surplus; the highest home-ownership in American history; the lowest unemployment in thirty years; the largest expansion of college opportunity since the GI Bill; connecting to the Internet of 95% of schools; lowest crime rate in twenty-six years; adding one hundred thousand more police for our streets; enacting the most sweeping gun safety legislation in a generation; passing the Family and Medical Leave Act for twenty million Americans; the smallest welfare rolls in thirty-two years; higher incomes at all levels; the lowest teen birth rate in sixty years; the lowest infant mortality rate in American history; deactivation of more than seventeen hundred nuclear warheads from the former Soviet Union; protection of millions of acres of American land; paying off $360 billion of the national debt; the lowest government spending in three decades; the lowest federal income tax burden in thirty-five years; growth of family stock ownership to an all-time high; appointing the most diverse cabinet in American history, which includes the appointment of the first female attorney general, first female secretary of state and first Asian American cabinet secretary. This is part of the historical record from the official White House website that existed during the Presidency of William Jefferson Clinton. Clinton also restored women's individual freedoms to where they belonged, including American aid around the world by reversing Ronald Reagan's "Global Gag Rule," which forbade NGOs that receive federal monies from offering abortion services or giving advice on abortion, infuriating Republicans and the right the most. President Clinton did all of this after twelve years of Reaganism, while being hounded in the press and hunted by the right.

That last point isn't a small one, either. People forget what Reaganism did to Democrats and what Bill Clinton and Al Gore standing together meant to many of us. Unlike Barack Obama, who was lifted up by the disdain for George W. Bush's and Dick Cheney's policies, Clinton came into Washington after the conservative king's reign, with Bush 41's loss crushing, because it was the end of an era. Obama came into Washington with the people and the press at his feet and the world cheering him on, with the political establishment also agog at the new president. This wasn't the case with Bill Clinton, who wasn't seen as half what Reagan was, even though he had a stronger educational background and executive experience as governor, leaving office with a much better record than Reagan. Clinton was equally the epitome of the American dream fulfilled, in spite of being hunted and impeached for lying about a consensual relationship, which doesn't come close to Iran-Contra under Reagan's watch.

This is one reason why when Barack Obama lauded Ronald Reagan over William Jefferson Clinton during the primaries it pissed so many people off and rightly so. Ironically, it was Clinton's third-way-ism that paved the way for Obama's conservative compromises and capitulations. Yet, succeeding under the shadow of Reagan's ghost, Bill Clinton is beloved for a reason. He taught Democrats what it felt like to be winners after Reagan's reign, while also showing us how to fight again, something Hillary had in her political veins as well, but Obama does not.

Of course, NAFTA was a horrible policy, and President Clinton's a corporate Democrat through and through, which is one of the reasons he'll never be beloved by many movement progressives. But he also knew where to draw a line in the sand with Republicans, something Barack Obama can never claim. Bill Clinton is best friends with Wall Street too, but at least he can talk and relate to Main Street. Clinton ended up admitting "I was wrong" about not regulating derivatives, which was a colossal error. As for the end of Glass-Steagall, the Gramm-Leach-Bliley Act that Clinton signed, allowing banks to enter the investment arena, it received a veto-proof majority, so there's plenty of blame to go around. It should start with Larry Summers, even if blaming Bill is what's most popular.

Many progressive activists also have very real philosophical differences with him, especially his DLC, "third way" concoction, which they rightly argue leaves Democrats with people like Evan Bayh sniping on cable for Democrats to move to the center. Never mind that George McGovern got elected in South Dakota, and the 2010 midterms had most progressive Dems winning their seats, while Blue Dog Dems took a beating.

You'd think Hillary would have at least gotten credit from the Democratic boys club for helping save her husband's presidency, not to mention the Democratic Party from total implosion. Her public approval numbers soared, including in old-fashioned Iowa where standing by her man was seen as valiant, but to the

Democratic establishment, nursing their perpetual self-loathing was more important.

Segue to the late David Broder, who was one of Sally Quinn's poison-pen, anti-Clinton pals at the *Washington Post*:

> The former president's intervention — volunteered during a campaign appearance on her behalf in South Carolina — raised the second, and largely unspoken, issue identified by my friend from the Clinton administration: the two-headed campaign and the prospect of a dual presidency. In his view, which I share, this is a prospect that will test the tolerance of the American people far more severely than the possibility of the first female president — or, for that matter, the first black president. No one can reasonably expect that partnership to end should Hillary Clinton be elected president. But the country must decide whether it is comfortable with such a sharing of the power and authority of the highest office in the land. It is a difficult question for any of the Democratic rivals to raise. But it lingers, even if unasked.

> — David Broder, *Washington Post*, November 15, 2007

Ooh, it lingers... out there... *unmasked*... SOMEWHERE.

But it's telling that Mr. Broder found Bill Clinton's presence in the White House as first spouse more of a challenge to the American people's tolerance than the possibility of the first woman or African American president. Broder, like Sally Quinn, Chris Matthews and many others, were co-creators of the anti-Clinton propaganda system from the start. Much of the elite media in Washington hold a personal grudge for the Lewinski affair, which was never Hillary's fault.

> "This is a contractual city," says Chris Matthews, who once was a top aide to the late Speaker of the House Thomas P. "Tip" O'Neill. "There are no factories here. What we make are deals. It's a city based on bonds made and kept." The president, he went on, "has broken and shattered contracts publicly and shamefully. He violates the trust at the highest level of politics.... There has to be a functional trust by reporters of the person they're covering. Clinton lies knowing that you know he's lying. It's brutal and it subjugates the person who's being lied to. I resent deeply being constantly lied to."

Senator Claire McCaskill, an early Obama supporter, even spun her own gossip gold out of '90s Clinton tales. During a *Meet the Press* interview, McCaskill confirmed former President Bill Clinton was coming in to fundraise for her campaign. Russert then asked, "Do you think President Clinton was a great president?" To which she replied, "I do. I had a lot of problems with some of his personal issues." And then to prove just how self-loathing *and* self-righteously moral she was, McCaskill finished by saying, "I said at the time, I think he's been a great leader, but I don't want him near my daughter."

Oh, how perfect! McCaskill willingly walked Russert's moral plank over Clinton's affair ten years prior, with her splash the stuff of drenching teenage cannon balls. It was a reprehensible statement from the Missouri senator that reveals the spiteful streak in Democratic politics that is poisonously pompous. This self-loathing virus runs through the Democratic Party, yet Republicans are rarely affected by their own. Jesus, David Vitter's still in the Senate.

Rumors abounded during the 2008 primaries about shenanigans going on during regular trips Bill Clinton was allegedly taking to Las Vegas. In Nevada at the time, I heard reporters were scouring Sin City to get the dirt, but no one could get anything worth printing or they would have done so. What happened in Vegas... remained rumors.

After Iowa, President Clinton's strategic, behind the scenes role changed. He became fully involved in the primary and often became the story, as well as the scapegoat on many occasions. He certainly underestimated the Obama fan base and the backlash some of his remarks would bring. He also knew Hillary faced an unfriendly media, so poking the press didn't always pay off. In the twenty-first century, multi-platform media era it's a deadly gamble.

Bill Clinton's comment, "Give me a break. This whole thing is the biggest fairy tale I've ever seen," touched off a firestorm in New Hampshire. You can argue it was tone-deaf or unhelpful, but it wasn't referring to Obama's candidacy. What President Clinton was talking about is that once Obama was in the Senate, his votes on Iraq were exactly the same as Hillary's, so the focus on his anti-Iraq speech was overblown. The media went wild.

The *Washington Post*'s Courtland Milloy took it out of context and said African Americans took it to mean that Obama's candidacy was a "black magic fable." Former *Newsweek* editor Jon Meacham also got it wrong, saying "Bill Clinton appeared to dismiss Obama's campaign as 'the biggest fairy tale I've ever seen.'" The late Robert Novak, known as the "Prince of Darkness," a moniker he enjoyed, also jumped on it, writing that President Clinton had "referred to (Senator Barack) Obama's candidacy as 'a fairy tale.'" Media Matters for America documented the whole predictable media pile-on.

Below is former President Bill Clinton's remark in full context from the event where it happened, a transcript of which was provided by the *Congressional Quarterly*:

> PRESIDENT CLINTON: ...Second, it is wrong that Senator Obama got to go through fifteen debates trumpeting his superior judgment and how he had been against the war in every year, enumerating the years and never got asked one time, not once, "Well, how could you say that when you said in 2004 you didn't know how you would have voted on the resolution? You said in 2004 there was no difference between you and George Bush on the war, and you took that speech you're now running on off your website in 2004, and there's no difference in your voting record and Hillary's ever since." Give me a break. [applause] This whole thing is the biggest fairy tale I've ever seen.

The trouble with Bill Clinton playing Hillary's champion, coming to the rescue of his wife, saying things she couldn't, is that the entire storyline was fraught with minefields. Besides, Hillary didn't need his help. It also smacked of sexism for Bill to assume the role of dragon-slayer, which came off as if he had to fight Hillary's battles for her, conjuring up Oval Office dramas to come, which was never far from the collective borg mind of the national and new media. President Clinton walked right into the buzz saw every time.

In Nevada, when Hillary won, though the delegates were split, talk swirled that former President Clinton's involvement sent Barack Obama and his campaign team into a tailspin. Everything I heard confirmed it. The Big Dog strutting through casinos talking to workers, walking around revving up Hispanics, union members and

Nevadans to vote for his gal Hillary. The local news was filled with Bill, which I saw first-hand.

Alleged union worker coercion caused quite a stir. So did the caucuses, with a lot of ill will afterward and websites set up with YouTube clips alleging voter intimidation. But everyone had the same playing field, and Hillary should have known the challenges of caucuses; Bill went through the same gauntlet. It's not a perfect system, and caucuses should be abolished for primaries. However, no beef about alleged intimidation, none of which was proved conclusively, can replace Mark Penn's caucus malpractice. That had to weigh on Bill Clinton, too, because there was simply no excusing it, and Penn was his guy.

Former President Bill Clinton was also obviously off his game. He was spending long hours and traveling constantly, but he'd also never before been subjected to the new-media, twenty-first-century world while playing a new role, spouse in chief. He was lousy at it. All emotion, very little tact, which was blasted everywhere in ways that made Bill look bad. According to Jonathan Alter's book, *The Promise*, at one point in the primary, Rahm Emanuel, now mayor of Chicago, dressed Bill Clinton down saying, "'stop acting like the fucking hack in chief.'"

Heading into the politically volatile landscape of South Carolina, former President Bill Clinton misread the mood and the moment, making a mistake he'd never have made at his political peak.

Nothing hit William Jefferson Clinton harder than when his own credibility with African Americans was challenged. The whole scene in South Carolina became an emotional elixir that eventually poisoned everything Bill Clinton said. When Obama trounced Hillary in South Carolina, it was clear it was a loss hard for them to take. One remark from former President Clinton invoking Jesse Jackson did him in: "Jackson ran a good campaign. And Obama ran a good campaign here."

It was taken to mean that Obama won South Carolina because he was black, his candidacy equal to Jesse Jackson's. *Kaboom!* The facts didn't matter, but they were that Jesse Jackson had also won the South Carolina caucuses back in 1988, but John Edwards had won it in 2004. So what? After New Hampshire and

Nevada, after the "fairy tale" line at such a critical campaign juncture, no one took Bill at face value anymore. Clinton was seen to be spinning the bad outcome by comparing the two campaigns. But as comparisons go, the difference between Obama and Jackson is in leagues, not caucus-winner candidates twenty years apart.

The comment President Clinton made comparing Jackson and Obama ricocheted like a rubber ball. The ravenous media knew they had a big one and went after it, as did the Obama blogs. It washed over former President Bill Clinton and neutered his advocacy, rendering him untouchable, at least for the moment. It was as if his lifelong advocacy for civil rights had gone up in smoke. The collective amnesia and venomous judgments from the press from all sides were further proof that the little objectivity that had existed had just gone *pfft*!

But there wasn't a doubt in my mind the race-baiting that occurred in the 2008 primaries wouldn't stick to former President Bill Clinton. I also have no doubt that Barack Obama never believed it of either Clinton. You don't tap a bigot to be your secretary of state, especially if you think her husband is a racist. It was simply a useful political cudgel for Obama, Axelrod and company at a time candidate Obama needed a knockout punch. It was scorched-earth warfare. His team was also sure the charge would be sucked up by traditional and new media.

During the 2010 midterms, former President Clinton was on a loyalty tour, giving his support to Democrats who'd supported Hillary's candidacy. As Josh Green wrote in the *Atlantic Monthly* in August 2010, while candidates were asking whether Obama would help them or hurt them, a stunning development given where Barack Obama's popularity was when he arrived in Washington, the "surrogate of choice for embattled Democrats" was overwhelmingly former President Bill Clinton.

If Mr. Clinton was actually a racist or if anyone really believed it, former President Bill Clinton would never have recovered. But he has and for good reason. His roots belie the race-baiting lies of a partisan fight, which goes back decades to Bill Clinton's foundation. From Ken Gormley:

> From the start, Clinton also had an uncanny ability to forge
> a bond with African American voters. Judge L.T. Simes II
> understood why this was so: Simes had grown up picking

cotton in Helena, Arkansas, at a time when the Mississippi Delta of Arkansas was predominantly segregated and inhospitable toward African Americans.... Simes immediately took note that Clinton, unlike most of the stodgy "old-boy" professors, treated black students with the utmost fairness and respect in the classroom. After becoming governor, Clinton bucked the system by appointing highly qualified blacks to key positions in state government. Simes himself became the first African American to serve as chairman of the Arkansas Soil and Water Commission. Although Clinton paid dearly, in political terms, for eschewing the prevailing culture by appointing blacks, that didn't slow him. During the governor's 1980 reelection campaign, Clinton brought Simes along to a country club in an elite section of eastern Arkansas where segregation was still firmly entrenched....Clinton was defeated by Frank White that fall.... "We'll be back," he said. "We're not going to let the people down."

— Ken Gormley, *The Death of American Virtue* 2010

Sean Wilentz encapsulated the race-baiting feeding frenzy that took place in the primaries whose sole purpose was to marginalize the Clinton legacy and dislodge African American supporters from their historic identification with the Clintons. It wasn't enough to expect that Obama and the Clintons might split the vote or fight on equal turf, with the twenty-first century bringing a colorless contest, at least on the Democratic side. Instead it was like a flashback to the 1860s and the fight of Cady Stanton and Susan B. Anthony versus Frederick Douglass over the Fourteenth and Fifteenth Amendments, with hurt left on all sides.

Historian Sean Wilentz, writing in the February 27, 2008 *New Republic*: "More than any other maneuver, this one has brought Clinton into disrepute with important portions of the Democratic Party. A review of what actually happened shows that the charges that the Clintons played the 'race card' were not simply false; they were deliberately manufactured by the Obama camp and trumpeted by a credulous and/or compliant press corps in order to strip away her once formidable majority among black voters and to outrage affluent, college-educated white liberals as well as college students."

Eugene Robinson was part of the "compliant press corps" and had plenty of company. In a column published January 15, 2008, in the *Post*, he wrote, "Is it possible that accusing Obama and his campaign of playing the race card might create doubt in the minds of the moderate, independent white voters who now seem so enamored of the young, black senator? Might that be the idea? Yes, that's a cynical view. But history is history."

In February 2008, former *New York Times* columnist Frank Rich opined that the Clinton "campaign's other most potent form of currency remains its thick deck of race cards."

What Robinson, Rich and everyone else making these scurrilous accusations and charges never considered was a question historian Sean Wilentz asked that no one ever answered: How does playing the race card help Hillary Clinton win the Democratic nomination? Pause... *crickets* ...more silence. There is no answer that explains why playing the race card in any way would benefit Hillary. The only outcome would be blowback. Besides, there's scorched earth, then there's a white woman playing the race card against the first African American wunderkind. People thought she was fucking stupid.

So, ask the next question. How does playing the race card help Barack Obama win the Democratic nomination? How would Jesse Jackson Jr.'s race-baiting after the New Hampshire primary help Barack Obama? How does it help Obama in South Carolina?

Wilentz again:

> Playing the race card against Obama could only cost her black votes, as well as offend liberal whites who normally turn out in disproportionally large numbers for Democratic caucuses and primaries. Indeed, indulging in racial politics would be a sure-fire way for the Clinton campaign to shatter its own coalition. On the other hand, especially in South Carolina where black voters made up nearly half of the Democratic turnout, and especially following the shocking disappointment in New Hampshire, playing the race card — or, more precisely, the race-baiting card — made eminent sense for the Obama campaign. Doing so would help Obama secure huge black majorities (in states such as Missouri and Virginia as well as in South Carolina and the deep South) and enlarge his activist white base in

the university communities and among affluent liberals. And that is precisely what happened.

— Sean Wilentz, *The New Republic*, February 27, 2008

Anyone who saw Bill Clinton campaign in the 1990s, which I did, but also weather the right-wing storms and political hunting he had to endure, saw a man who knew not only how to fight, but also the script you needed to get the job done. By the time Hillary Clinton ran for president that man had changed, some of it for the better, but not all.

Traditional and new media took aim at every statement. It's impossible to imagine conservatives doing the same to Ronald Reagan. President Bill Clinton actually has a better record and was the only Democrat able to win two presidential terms since FDR and go out with superlative economic and employment records of achievement, with the U.S. and its president beloved around the world.

During the primary campaign season of 2008, Bill seemed changed. He wasn't the unflappable former president. After Iowa, a defeat that everyone knew was a very ominous sign, even if they weren't saying it out loud, the charismatic, brilliant Bill became emotional and unpredictable, a political live-wire whose performances were uneven. He began grabbing headlines beyond what the candidate herself could control.

The primary persona of Bill Clinton often revealed his hair-trigger temper, with reports out of closed meetings damning. Justified or not, it just wasn't something he'd ever allowed to surface before, even during the most trying days of impeachment, but now could be caught on YouTube. That's not to say he wasn't brilliant too, and a clear asset many times. At one campaign event he responded to right-wing, anti-abortion protesters, calling them out on their goal to criminalize women and doctors, standing up to the thugs while supporters cheered him on. It was classic Clinton. The problem was he clearly was caught off-guard when he became the target of fellow Democrats.

Of course, Clinton's temper was legendary among those surrounding him going back to his presidency, but their stories came out from things witnessed in private. What was different is that Clinton exploded several times during the campaign season.

The former president then went on a tirade that ran from the media's unfair treatment of Hillary to questions about the fairness of the votes in state caucuses that voted for Obama. It ended with him asking delegates to imagine what the reaction would be if Obama was trailing by just 1% and people were telling him to drop out. "It was very, very intense," said one attendee. "Not at all like the Bill of earlier campaigns." When he finally wound down, Bill was asked what message he wanted the delegates to take away from the meeting. At that point, a much calmer Clinton outlined his message of party unity. "It was kind of strange later when he took the stage and told everyone to 'chill out,'" one delegate told us.

— *San Francisco Chronicle*, April 2, 2008

Bill's "temper tantrums" made headline news from coast to coast to Fox News, with Hillary always taking the hit more than Bill. It hurt doubly when the talking point was repeated by liberals like Katrina vanden Heuvel, which got picked up by the conservative NewsBusters website and many others, who quoted someone close to the Clinton campaign as having said, "People are looking at him like a Little League dad who's having these temper tantrums in every state." George Stephanopoulos, hosting *This Week*, said in the same segment in which Ms. vanden Heuvel appeared, "Some people are concerned about this, even inside the party. I have no indication at all though that President Clinton's going to stop."

President Clinton set up a perfect opportunity for cheap-shot artists like Patrick Healy of the *New York Times*, which was exploited in a Healy piece headlined, "Bill Clinton, Stumping and Simmering," which ran in January 2008. "Mr. Clinton's temper has been an issue for him as long as he has been in public life," Healey wrote. "But it has played an unusual role during the current campaign, his face turning red in public nearly every week, often making headlines as he defends his wife and injects himself, whether or not intentionally, into her race in sometimes distracting ways."

It's a mystery why Hillary never stepped in to stop him long before things careened in South Carolina. It can only be laid at her feet that she did not; if she could not that's another story entirely and we're left to ask why not?

168

William Jefferson Clinton was now the husband of a woman running for president, whom he loved deeply and had a personal investment in her succeeding. But the emotional and physical stress of campaigning for Hillary wasn't the only component that caused Mr. Clinton to career wildly from political cheerleader to Obama critic, ripping his presidential status to shreds in the process.

Now, I'm not going to get into a long dissertation about heart bypass surgery and its aftermath on a person's mind and physical limitations. There are as many opinions on this issue as there are patients, and you need the specifics of each case to justify a final verdict, which can only be given by a qualified specialist. No heart specialist is going to give you a definitive answer without knowing the specific health condition of former President Clinton, including the private details to which no one is privy and shouldn't be.

However, I have witnessed people close to me after quadruple-bypass and noticed the change in their personalities and stamina in many ways, especially in the early recovery months and years; luckily most of these are reversed eventually, but people can be changed significantly afterward. Everyone is different. But anyone under extreme stress, as former President Bill Clinton was during the height of the 2008 primary season, is going to show it physically and particularly emotionally.

No one ever mentioned the possibility that part of former President Clinton's reaction might have been due to his health. No network or political writer, not even a medical correspondent, dared bring it up or broach the subject. We were talking about the invincible Bill Clinton, super-politician, after all. It would be unseemly, even embarrassing to mention that the stress was making him emotionally volatile because he wasn't healthy enough to stand the strain. He couldn't be affected by the stress of the onslaught Hillary was receiving, or the fact that the man he'd trusted to run her campaign, Mark Penn, had blown it, and he couldn't change the course they were on.

Clinton's heart bypass was on September 6, 2004. A 2001 Duke University study published in the *New England Journal of Medicine* proved that up to 20% cognitive impairment is a factor, even up to five years after bypass. People change after heart bypass surgery, with the rigors of a presidential campaign something that few have to endure. In fact, there isn't another circumstance in U.S.

political history similar to what former President Bill Clinton experienced during the '08 election season. After quadruple-bypass surgery people have to change their lifestyles, including their diet, work habits, exercise, rest, you name it, it's on the table. A high-pressure situation like what Hillary was in isn't part of that package.

You don't need a medical journal or diagnosis to know that Bill Clinton of 2008 wasn't close to the politician he was in the '90s, with his health very likely a component. This isn't meant as an excuse; it's simply a statement about the human and physical limitations and stressors that impact people in high-stress situations, especially after life-altering health challenges, which former President Clinton certainly suffered.

From my vantage point, what we were witnessing through former President Bill Clinton was a political tragedy; a situation that his adversaries used to full advantage, which you cannot blame on them alone, because a man's got to know his limitations. Not only was he married to the candidate, but his spouse was under fire from all corners, both from her opponent and from the media, who had clearly picked sides. But his emotions were running wild, as was his rage at what he judged to be unfairness toward a woman he deeply loves and wanted to help, while having to be on stage 24/7. The media's sexism alone would be enough to set off any husband watching what Hillary had to endure. However, this was her battle, not his, so at times it was positively infuriating. The episodic nature of Bill Clinton's blowups, however, proved that if someone was talking to him, he wasn't listening to anyone.

By 2010, Bill was back on his game. When Mark Critz was in a tight race for the late Jack Murtha's old district, Pennsylvania-12, who did the Dems send? Bill Clinton, and Critz won. Unfortunately, Critz turned out to be an anti-women's-rights Democrat, one of fifteen so-called Democrats who voted for the offensive "Protect Life Act" in the House. As CREDO said in its campaign to stop the Democratic Congressional Campaign Committee from funding anti-women's-civil-rights candidates like Critz, Mike McIntyre and Jim Matheson, the offensive bill "would make it legal for hospitals to refuse to perform a life-saving abortion on a woman as an emergency procedure."

Using his signature pragmatism out of loyalty in Arkansas to help his friend Blanche Lincoln, Bill Clinton railed against "outside special interests," which included movement progressives marshaling a formidable challenger against Lincoln, Bill Halter, who forced her into a run-off. Bill Clinton attacked labor unions and movement progressives as "outside special interests," an unforgiveable move that will not be forgotten, but after 2008, it's unlikely he gives a shit. However, he was wrong to do it, loyalty or not, because unions make the middle-class possible, including by keeping non-union companies honest, even if their role and goals have to change in the twenty-first century. The battle in Wisconsin over collective bargaining in 2011 proved it.

By the end of the 2008 primary season, former President Bill Clinton had to win back his place in the Democratic hierarchy, as the new crowd had written him off. Bill and Barack, two alpha males, but also members of the most elite presidents' club, with Clinton's understanding of winning in tough times always worth tapping.

A July 1, 2010, Siena College Research Institute (SRI) Survey of U.S. Presidents called on 238 presidential scholars, historians and political scientists to weigh in. Former President Clinton comes in thirteenth (rising from eighteenth place in 2002), higher than Ronald Reagan. Barack Obama comes in at fifteenth, with Reagan at eighteen. George W. Bush is among the bottom five worst presidents in American history. FDR remains first with no equal.

By the time the Clinton Global Initiative rolled around in 2010, former President Bill Clinton was enjoying a renaissance, with Clinton nostalgia exploding, and for good reasons. According to Mr. Clinton in an interview with Joe Scarborough and Mika Brzezinski, "two-thirds of all the kids in the world who are alive who have AIDS, get medicine from our foundation" is just one reason.

Contrary to predictions, as of President Obama's third year in office, there remains a very vibrant Clinton wing inside the Democratic Party. In a bad economic era, with people feeling insecure and jobs scarce, Bill Clinton's presidency, which was hardly perfect, is once again remembered for what it should be instead of simply "the battles of the '90s. "

In January of 2010, when Rep. Marion Berry expressed concern over the upcoming midterms, Obama scoffed at any warnings or problems in his path. When Berry specifically referenced a possible '94 reoccurrence, Obama reportedly gave the concern "no credibility." Berry told the *Arkansas Democrat Gazette*, reported also by Jake Tapper of ABC News, "They just kept telling us how good it was going to be."

In the newspaper and television reports, Berry went further, quoting President Obama as saying, "'Well, the big difference here and in '94 was you've got me.' We're going to see how much difference that makes now."

It didn't mean squat.

Former President Bill Clinton has been on a roller coaster ride his entire political life, with his quadruple-bypass on September 6, 2004, changing his world more than he knew or anyone, including the media, admitted. During the 2008 primary season, his political star fell to earth. Almost. By September 2010, according to an NBC/*Wall Street Journal* poll, his approval/disapproval rating was at 55-23, making him the most popular politician in America.

Hillary's campaign team simply didn't have near enough discipline, which former President Bill Clinton proved by becoming the story too often, even if much of the incoming his way was overblown or bordered on political swift-boating. You can't expect the candidate to do everything; at some point the people around her have to assume some heavy lifting, step up and deliver. It circles us back around to the people she chose, as well as those Bill Clinton brought along. Should that be laid at Hillary's door for being a bad manager? After all, in the end it was *her* campaign to win or lose. But it does bring to mind what ran through my head when the campaign started and Hillary was churning out slogans. I just kept hearing, "I've learned a lot from my husband, but this is not his campaign."

Chapter 6: **It's All the Woman's Fault**

It wasn't Hillary's fault that on the same day as 17,481 pages of her schedule as first lady were released by the National Archives, ABC decided to proclaim in a blaring headline "Hillary at White House on 'Stained Blue Dress' Day." Stained Blue Dress Day? The assholes at ABC just couldn't help themselves. Oh, and it came complete with composite Reuters/AP photos showing Hillary, Lewinski and the blue dress, just in case you didn't get it. Brian Ross reported the National Archive release with words like "fateful" and "infamous blue dress" up front, with Ross's heavy breathing the only thing missing. ABC didn't get or didn't care that Hillary had nothing whatsoever to do with Bill's stupidity or Lewinsky's choices. The whole report was over-exercised and a clear attempt to titillate and bring web traffic to ABC. Humiliating Hillary was simply a bonus.

There has never been any evidence or anything close to proof that Hillary has ever been unfaithful, let alone that she murdered someone, so it's not her fault when bullshit artist and right-wing hack Sean Hannity spewed his hate about Hillary in "The Clinton Chapters" on his Fox News show. He posited questions like, "Did a close friend of Hillary Clinton commit suicide, or was it a massive cover-up?" close to fifteen years after the tragedy of Vince Foster's untimely death occurred. Hannity went further, pulling factoids out of thin air, asking if perhaps Foster had papers on Whitewater in his possession when he died, while also ghoulishly salivating over the details while trying to drum up suspicions: "In the minds of some, these questions may have provided a motive for foul play." Who exactly were "some," no one knew. In Hannity's weird world, it's not about facts or what you can prove, but simply about making shit up to make Hillary look bad. Hannity and his ilk could have cared less how crushed the Clintons were about Mr. Foster's suicide, which Ken Gormley reveals fully in his book. For Sean Hannity, a professed Catholic, exploiting a man's tragic death simply is a gift to be used to concoct foul-play scenarios and blame the Clintons, Hannity's idea of compassionate conservatism.

Talk radio king Rush Limbaugh and his fraternity of hacks like Hannity, as well as Sean's mini-me, Mark Levin, spew misogynistic drivel all day long as part of the freedom-is-only-for-men crowd, while personally demeaning or lying about any liberal woman who stands up to them. Spewing invective like "feminazis" or using "Hillary Rotten Clinton, her thighness," a sexist slur Levin directed at Secretary of State Clinton, is what masquerades as "entertainment" on right-wing talk radio. Don Imus, the "nappy-headed ho" gasbag, has referred to Hillary as "Satan."

There has also never been any evidence that Hillary was gay, so it's hardly her fault that even the leading gay magazine chooses the gutter over substance, giving the *New York Daily News* their banner headline, "Hillary Clinton: I Am Not a Lesbian." In September 2007, Sean Kennedy of the *Advocate* decided it was a burning question to ask the first viable female candidate running for the presidency, "How do you respond to the occasional rumor that you're a lesbian?" How 'bout, fuck you? This whole line of questioning is completely worthless, but it's considered not only appropriate but important to ask a married woman who was running to be the first female commander in chief. The *Advocate* was evidently titillated by the rumors and ran with them, perhaps hoping to mine a larger gay readership through bullshit.

"People say a lot of things about me, so I really don't pay any attention to it," Hillary responded. "It's not true, but it is something that I have no control over. People will say what they want to say."

The *Daily News* delighted in making this a larger story by asking the *Advocate* to verify a non-story: "I one-hundred-percent believe she's a straight, heterosexual woman," said Kennedy. I'm *so* relieved, because dykes are damn dangerous. Look at Ellen DeGeneres, Rosie O'Donnell, Rachel Maddow — I mean, what more needs to be said?

According to Chris Matthews, it was all the women's fault when Hillary was endorsed by the *Des Moines Register*. Matthews on *Hardball* in December 2007: "...She may have gotten the *Des Moines Register*'s endorsement the other day thanks to her husband's lobbying, with its female editors and publisher, but voters have spotted the dagger. They don't like what it looks like."

The *New York Times* had set it up: "The other day,...former President Bill Clinton held forth on a sofa in the publisher's suite at the *Des Moines Register*.... Ms. Hollingsworth, Carolyn Washburn and Carol Hunter have been wooed these last days by multiple members of the Clinton campaign."

Ben Smith of Politico sucked it up through a straw: "The endorsement reads as if it were written with the help of [chief

Clinton strategist] Mark Penn over those cocktails the Clintons shared with the edit board at Azalea...."

Right, because Hillary Clinton had no prowess on policy and issues that actually impressed women like Carol Hunter, who said in part, *"The choice, then, comes down to preparedness: Who is best prepared to confront the enormous challenges the nation faces."* It was impossible to believe Hillary had won them over herself. Never mind what good the sucking up did them, because Hillary got her ass handed to her in Iowa. In today's post-newspaper, new-media world, endorsements don't mean squat.

It wasn't Hillary's fault that David Bossie had made a career out of Clinton-hating. Bossie was linked to tape-doctoring when he was on Rep. Dan Burton's staff, alleging that Web Hubbell "was hiding information to protect the first lady," as Ken Gormley put it, but instead, Bossie ended up resigning. Bossie never gave up his Clinton-hunting, getting really creative once Hillary was running for president, concocting a documentary, *Hillary: The Movie,* which was to be shown on pay-per-view and cable right before the Democratic primaries but went straight to DVD instead, because the feds blocked it. The case spawned a lawsuit that eventually made it to the Supreme Court and ended up changing campaign finance forever. *Citizens United v. Federal Election Commission* became the foundation for an explosion of mass corporate involvement and buying of elections and candidates, which will be in full evidence in 2012.

The targeting of Clinton by Bossie and the right-wing boys will never be seen again, considering the right's anti-Clinton campaign spanned sixteen years. Besides, in the new-media age, right-wing talk radio is finally seen for what it is: the last sexist outpost of an outdated medium run by men, where women are merely tolerated as totems; a dying, misogynistic format with a mid-twentieth-century mindset. They've got their choir, but the majority of Americans just don't take their sexist, hate-screed rants seriously anymore; certainly new generations will not. When Rush Limbaugh retires, it's over. The point driven home when Dr. Laura Schlessinger was forced off talk radio after an n-word blizzard that left her apologizing, then opining on Larry King that it was "now the era of the Internet." Glenn Beck emphasized this fact when he left Fox for the web.

It wasn't Hillary's fault that a leading progressive new-media site channeled Tucker Carlson when it came to all things Clinton. When Mark Penn was demoted from chief strategist of Clinton's campaign, Josh Marshall of TPM ran a headline blaring, "Full Firing? Or Just Gelded?" Melissa McEwan, who once worked in the John Edwards campaign, eviscerated Marshall on her Shakesville blog:

> Are you fucking kidding me, Josh Marshall? Because I quite honestly can't believe that a person who identifies as a progressive and has two brain cells still knocking together doesn't understand why it's *problematic*, to put it charitably, to frame Hillary Clinton pushing her male chief strategist from power as "gelding" him.

> — Shakesville, April 7, 2008

McEwan's blog ran a stunning series called "Hillary Sexism Watch" that numbered more than 111 items, all of the posts laying out how it's all the woman's fault because, you know, feminists are all such ballbusters. That went double for Hillary.

Who didn't laugh when an all-male panel on *Morning Joe*, comprised of Joe Scarborough, Willie Geist and David Shuster, who has joined Olbermann's *Countdown* on Current TV, listened in as Mike Barnicle said Senator Hillary Clinton looked "like everyone's first wife standing outside a probate court"? It's Hillary's fault because of her toughness, that strong steely countenance and no-bullshit manner that lets you know if you cross her you're going to hear about it. It's all just so, I don't know, *emasculating*, so first-wives'-club. Mr. Barnicle traded in this stuff regularly where Hillary was concerned, but it was disheartening to see on *Morning Joe*, the one place on MSNBC where Clinton wasn't ravaged. But, you know, get Shuster and Barnicle going on Hillary, and boys will be boys. It's not Hillary's fault that Mike Barnicle couldn't give up his Clinton derangement to consider the wasted taxpayer money on Clinton investigations over the years, preferring to lend his sympathies instead to Tom Delay, letting go a gaseous whine in the summer of 2010 when he complained that the six-year investigation of Delay was "inexcusable." Barnicle evidently slept through the '90s.

The Associated Press disseminated a widely published, sexist diatribe in December 2007 from Fred Thompson about Hillary, as he opined on the virtues of a man being president, maybe even his daughter, but most definitely not Hillary.

> "Who are we going to set on the road — what man are we going to set on the road — to lead us and to stand against this assault?" he asked, emphasizing the word "man." He couched his comments by saying, "I say the word man advisedly. Now, I've got a daughter that's going to be president some day, I know it, and I am all for a woman president, just not this year, not next year."

> Without saying Clinton's name, he added: "There is no woman on the horizon that ought to be president next year, let's all agree on that."

Thompson obviously thought invoking his daughter inoculated him from the sexism charge, which shows you just how clueless the right is.

Long after Hillary's fall lead of thirty points vanished, not even then was Clinton ever awarded underdog status. How could Hillary be an underdog? She's Hillary! Politico's Roger Simon made a mess of the whole victim-versus-underdog dance in a post entitled "Clinton Plays Victim and Victimizer," without sensing he'd written irony into his very first line: "The stage has been set for a Hillary Clinton comeback on Tuesday." Any normal candidate trying to make a "comeback" is not in the driver's seat; he or she is behind, trying to catch up. It's also hard for someone trying to make a "comeback" to "victimize" the person who's leading; at least it is if you're talking about two men.

If we weren't talking about Hillary here, there is no way you would ever consider a woman able to victimize a man while running for president. In over two hundred years, Hillary Clinton was the first viable female candidate in presidential history. That's not all the women's fault.

> "White women are a problem; that's, you know — we all live with that."

> — Bill Kristol, Fox News, February 3, 2008

What's a man to do? Can't kill her; obviously can't live with her, and sure as hell can't elect her as president.

It's good to have women reporters because they won't ask the stupid questions, right? From an interview with Couric and Clinton, circa February 2008:

COURIC: Someone told me your nickname in school was Miss Frigidaire. Is that true?

Aha! We all knew Hillary was a cold-hearted bitch. I'm so relieved some serious journalist finally nailed her on that one, and we all know this persona is all Hillary's fault.

After Hillary's moment of emotional vulnerability in New Hampshire, the right went berserk. Glenn Beck, during his show when he was with CNN Headline News, said, "Apparently, Hillary Clinton isn't just running for president, but she's also making a run for the best actress nomination." The only thing Beck's worthy of judging is the standard for amateur carnival barkers.

Bill Kristol chimed in on Fox News' *Special Report*: "And I don't believe it was genuine. I think no Clinton cries without calculating first. This — and I think this was — if it was genuine, it was entirely solipsistic and narcissistic. It's all about her."

Michelle Malkin for the *New York Post*: "So long, feminist hero. Hello, weeping willow. Anyone who believes Hillary spontaneously teared up and got emotional on the campaign trail has been in a coma the last three decades."

Newsweek went for history: Hillary Clinton's Emotional Moment: A Muskie Moment, or a Helpful Glimpse of "the Real Hillary"?

Wall Street Journal: "Emotional Moment for Clinton in N.H."

ABC News did three different headlines to capitalize on the moment: "Clinton Gets Emotional on Campaign Trail"; "Rivals React to Teary Clinton"; and, "Can Clinton's Emotions Get the Best of Her?" But the article was even worse. Phrases like "noticeably agitated" and "a little bit louder" clearly meant to convey Hillary as an emotional woman out of control. To drill their point home, the ABC report focused on interviews from a few carefully selected college professors. Julian Zelizer, professor of history and public affairs, said now that she's shown emotion, Hillary can't get "too vicious." Diana Owen, a Georgetown professor, said "she lost her cool."

John Edwards, that paragon of political virtue and national security wunderkind, had this to say about the teary Clinton: "I think what we need in a commander in chief is strength and resolve, and presidential campaigns are tough business, but being president of the United States is also tough business."

Yeah, yeah, broads cry, film at eleven.

Matt Taibbi, in "Hillary Clinton: The New Nixon," went with the inauthentic card, while saying Clinton was actually "a Republican at heart," though there wasn't and still isn't a Republican anywhere who champions women's rights and freedoms more than Hillary.

> The crying incident was Hillary's own personal Checkers speech, a painful bit of self-mutilation tossed off on the last step before the political gallows — a pure sea-cucumber tactic, scaring us off with a display of vulnerable green guts. We missed the chance to finish her off, and now she's back in charge, setting the tone for a campaign that gets dumber and meaner and dirtier by the day. Thanks to you, New Hampshire, the Clintons still have us to kick around.
>
> — Matt Taibbi, *Rolling Stone*, January 30, 2008

Taibbi is right about Mark Penn being the Democratic Karl Rove, though Penn was actually twice as toxic and half as effective.

Meanwhile, Barack Obama revealed a moment of class. "I didn't see what happened," he was widely quoted saying, and adding, "I know this process is a grind. So that's not something I care to comment on."

To Obama's point, not one outlet did a piece about how many events Clinton had done, her travel time, the energy expended in a campaign or the grueling demands these candidates endure to become their party's nominee. However, Ezra Klein, now blogging for the *Washington Post*, but writing on the American Prospect blog during the '08 election, could relate: "And Christ Almighty," he wrote, "I've been on the campaign trail for a week and want to cry. Anyone who doesn't get worn out and a bit emotional after the grueling process these candidates are undergoing is inhuman."

What about someone in the national media doing an analysis of what it meant for Clinton to go from "inevitable," with a thirty-point juggernaut lead, to being an underdog after Iowa, coming in third, which rendered most people shell-shocked at the time? The media focused solely on the emotional element, because after all, who knew Hillary could cry?

Some tried to make the case that her feelings were calculated. Obama's national co-chair, Jesse Jackson Jr., even questioned whether Hillary had cried for Katrina victims.

Chris Matthews painted horns on Hillary, also calling her a "she-devil" for his NBC show, asking one question: "Smart politics for GOP to demonize Hillary?" Oh, and of course the "insiders" who answered the question said yes, eleven-to-one. Crying was a political winner! Next question: "Will Hillary use it again?" Just kidding, that question wasn't asked, but who would have been surprised if it had been?

Camille Paglia's misogynistic drivel on Salon during the Clinton campaign was an embarrassment for the site. "Hillary's Slick Willies" was particularly venomous.

> I agree that the male staff who Hillary attracts are slick, geeky weasels or rancid, asexual cream puffs.... If I were to hazard a guess, I'd say Hillary is reconstituting the toxic hierarchy of her childhood household, with her on top instead of her drill-sergeant father. All those seething beta males (as you so aptly describe them) are versions of her sad-sack brothers, who got the short end of the Rodham DNA stick.
>
> — Camille Paglia, Salon, April 9, 2008

I happen to have engaged with many of Clinton's top males on her team, including Howard Wolfson, now counselor and deputy mayor for New York, but also my friend Peter Daou, among others, all of whom are the exact opposite of what Paglia describes. Leaving me to guess that she likely never met and didn't know any of them, which is hardly the point for Ms. Paglia. I had no interaction with Mark Penn, but it's hard to argue he isn't a "slick, geeky weasel."

Joan Walsh, then Salon's editor in chief, now editor at large, wrote the following on her blog regarding the sexism at the time: "If you disagree, and you'd like to argue on behalf of calling female politicians "fucking whores," please marshal your best arguments in my comments section. But also, if you feel that way, please feel free to stop reading Salon. I passionately want to grow our audience, and I'm proud to have tripled it in the three years I've been editor in chief. But truly, some readers we can live without. There must be someplace where people who want to call female leaders "fucking whores" will feel welcomed and at home, but this isn't it."

Well, at least Ms. Paglia didn't call Clinton a "fucking whore," for which I guess Salon readers are to be grateful. That was talk radio host Randi Rhodes' specialty.

It wasn't Hillary's fault that *Vanity Fair*'s Michael Wolff has a problem with women, especially strong women of a certain age. He not only declares there wasn't any sexism, but misses the irony of his own misogynistic myopia that came squirting out of his sexist column, "It's the Adultery, Stupid," in June 2008:

> The Hillary story is — and how could it not be? — largely a sexual one. This is not so much a sexist view as a sexualist view.... So what exactly is the thing with Hillary and sex, with the consensus being that she simply must not have it (at least not with her husband; there are, on the other hand, the various conspiracy scenarios of whom else she might have had it with). It's partly around this consensus view of her not having sex that people support her or resist her. She's the special-interest candidate of older women — the post-sexual set. She's resisted by others (including older women who don't see themselves as part of the post-sexual set) who see her as either frigid or sexually shunned —they turn from her inhibitions and her pain.

Honestly, I got nothin' on this one. It squeals for itself.

On May 28, 2008, CNN's Wolf Blitzer stood like a potted plant as his panel discussed Hillary and sexism, while Alex Castellanos said she deserved to be called a "bitch." Wolf didn't say squat. Now, he's the moderator/anchor, but are we really suggesting that journalistic standards require standing by and condoning this shit? Jeffrey Toobin defended Hillary, with Castellanos saying, "Some women are named that and it's accurate." Also sitting shamefully mute were Gloria Borger and, predictably, Donna Brazile, both women not uttering one word of defense on what had happened to Hillary in the media. It's all her fault, because, as Castellanos also said, "she's Hillary Clinton."

Maureen Dowd helped define the insider camps in Washington, all of whom hated Hillary for her ambition, which in a man is considered strength.

> The town is divided into two camps: those who think that, after sixteen years of Hillary pushing herself forward, the public will get worn out and reject her, and those who think that, after sixteen years of Hillary pushing herself forward, the public will get worn down and give in to her.

> ...As Leon Wieseltier, the literary editor of *The New Republic*, once told me: "She's never going to get out of our faces.... She's like some hellish housewife who has seen something that she really, really wants and won't stop nagging you about it until finally you say, fine, take it, be the damn president, just leave me alone."

> That's why Hillary is laughing a lot now, big belly laughs, in response to tough questions or comments, to soften her image as she confidently knocks her male opponents out of the way. From nag to wag.

> — Maureen Dowd, *New York Times*, September 30, 2007

A younger woman would not have been experienced enough, while someone of Hillary's caliber either had too many wrinkles, because of the "toll of the campaign," or was called a bitch for being determined, which was like "some hellish housewife." It's always the woman's fault, which when it came to Hillary included that her *cackle* was simply a cover-up for trying to presume to be human.

Women eventually got it, but it was too late. In January 2008, the *New York Times* ran an article entitled "Women's Support for Clinton Rises in Wake of *Perceived* Sexism" (emphasis added). One woman talked about the likability question for Hillary in the debate, which she said "wouldn't be coming up if she weren't a woman."

> In interviews, some Democratic women over 40, who said they had experienced stinging sexism at school and in the workplace, seemed too long for the election of a female president — they said Mrs. Clinton would fill the role just fine — as a grand moment of validation. But younger women, who have grown up in a world of greater parity, seemed less likely to allow gender to influence their vote.

This feeds perfectly into the "let's not refight the battles of the '90s" argument, as well as the Independent Women's Forum chant that "feminism should be erased from the American lexicon," which their president Michelle Bernard wrote in a June 2010 *U.S. News* column. Sprucing up Phyllis Schlafly's 1950s talking points, re-written for the twenty-first century, Bernard used the term "second-wave feminism" and then took off on a tangent.

"These feminists also refused to acknowledge that there are differences between men and women. Recognizing this fact is an affirmation of a biological reality, not patriarchy."

The "women are women and men are men" platform died in the 1970s, but thanks for playing. The Independent Women's Forum was founded by a group of females, along with a who's who list of Republicans, who backed Clarence Thomas for the Supreme Court. One of these was Barbara Olson, who died on 9/11, when the plane she was in crashed into the Pentagon, and who was a savage Hillary-hater, writing a book entitled, *Hell to Pay: The Unfolding Story of Hillary Rodham Clinton*.

Bernard's anti-feminism morphs perfectly with Maureen Dowd's shoulder-pad feminism. Only women of a certain age get Hillary, because she's just so classic-movies, Greatest Generation stuff.

> But Hillary — carried on the padded shoulders of the older women in Texas, Ohio and Rhode Island who loved her "I Will Survive" rallying cry that "I am a little older and I have earned every wrinkle on my face" — has been saved to fight another day.
>
> — Maureen Dowd, *New York Times*, March 5, 2008

In the same piece, Dowd proclaimed, "Hillary doesn't make it look like fun to be a woman." It's not a lot of fun to be hunted for sport. Ms. Dowd represented the people who felt uncomfortable calling out sexism, preferring the I-have-been-victimized campaign.

God bless Tina Fey. *Twice.* Her "bitch is the new black" cry from *Saturday Night Live* resounds still, making the ravings of Dowd, Bernard, the "baby Palins" and the anti-feminist block of the white-pearl set seem not just quaint, but antiquated *and* clueless. Fey declaring with pride during the height of the primaries that Hillary's the bitch who "will get stuff done," which is what the Republicans and feeble anti-feminist whiners were afraid of in the first place — Clinton's competency.

It's not surprising it took awhile for the elite and even many women to catch on to what was happening to Hillary right before their eyes, with people blaming feminism, thus women, for what Bernard perceives as "victimhood." Anti-feminist conservatives want to make it uncool to call sexism out, because feminism has always been the right's worst enemy. The crusade to abolish the term feminism and the state of free mind *and* body, which didn't work when they proclaimed the age of "post-feminism," was being tried once again by stating feminism is just so yesterday.

The *Los Angeles Times* proved this problem by devaluing the importance of women's and children's issues when Clinton's White House records were released.

> As for overseas travel, the papers show that Clinton did spend some time conferring with foreign leaders on strategic issues. But the records suggest she spent a lot more time fulfilling the traditional role of the first lady: meeting the leaders' wives and focusing on women's and children's issues.
>
> — Los Angeles Times, March 20, 2008

When Republicans talk about women's and children's issues, they're put on a pedestal of "family values." When Hillary did it through her first lady outreach role of helping women, coupling it with her women's-rights-are-human-rights campaign, it is downplayed and seen as less important than "strategic issues," even though soft power is the very definition of strategic.

What some younger women don't understand is that in our society it took a woman of Hillary's age and status to get those eighteen million cracks, because if any woman forty-something would have tried for the presidency they'd be considered too young and not ready to be commander in chief. Yet Hillary's ambition was seen as too much.

In January 2010, Ms. Jay Newton-Small asked a question on *Time* magazine's Swampland blog that told a story few even noticed was a problem for all women. Certainly members of the anti-feminist brigade who think feminist battles no longer need to be fought missed it. "But when her top advisor who also happens to be a famous champion of women politicians endorses Obama," Ms. Newton-Small wrote, "does it send the signal: Is there room in Washington for both a Speaker Pelosi and a President Hillary?"

There's only room for one powerhouse female politician? It's an either-or proposition? It was a question no one ever asked of Barack Obama or Harry Reid or any other male president coming into office where a male was in charge of the House or Senate. But all of a sudden two women at the top, especially Democrats like Pelosi and Hillary, were just too much. *Time* magazine might as well have sounded the alarm that the Estrogen War was coming and would lead to political paralysis, panic and national pandemonium.

Sadly, even Nicholas Kristof, the man who champions women in his "Half the Sky" campaign, got into the act against Hillary, writing in a March 27, 2008, *New York Times* column it would be all Hillary's fault if she turned into the Nader of 2008, while implying she's the only one at fault for the "brawl":

"If Mrs. Clinton can run a high-minded, civil campaign and rein in her proxies," Kristof wrote, "then she has every right to continue through the next few primaries, and the Democrats might even benefit from the bolstered attention and turnout. But if the brawl continues, then she and her husband may be remembered by many people who long admired them as having the same effect on Mr. Obama this November that Ralph Nader had on Al Gore in 2000."

ABC News' Jennifer Parker was another one who got caught up, wondering just how far Hillary would go to beat Obama: "The question is — what will Clinton have to do in order to achieve it?" I don't remember anyone asking what George W. Bush would have to do to achieve victory after McCain trounced him in New Hampshire, though we sure as hell found out in South Carolina, through Bush's illegitimate "black child" campaign.

According to Parker, if Democrats lose, it will be all the woman's fault, because the ruthless bitch would rather burn the house down than let Obama win. You hardly need CPAC "Stay out of my village, bitch" t-shirts when anonymous Democratic officials and the national media will do their job for them.

In Andrew Sullivan's January 25, 2008, "The Corruption of Feminism" post on *The Atlantic*'s website, it's all the "Clintonian" feminists' fault, using "Clintonian" to mean they —*we* — are dishonest, because in Sullivan's political fantasy world, the Clintons supposedly "smeared" women, or worse, back during impeachment.

However, as Ken Gormley proved through exhaustive research, there was no such thing orchestrated out of the White House. Besides, whether we're talking about Kathleen Willey, Paula Jones, Monica Lewinski or Jennifer Flowers, you can certainly say Mr. Clinton was a philandering jackass, but it doesn't prove sexual harassment from a man who didn't have to harass anyone to indulge in extramarital escapades. And last time I checked my feminist handbook, thong-flashing a married man is a bridge farther than a come-hither look. As for Ms. Willey's affectionate notes to President Clinton after the alleged "harassment," women don't write thank-you notes after being threatened.

Sullivan's "feminism" excludes anyone thinking Hillary Rodham Clinton is worthy of esteem. His irrational Hillary hysteria is revealed in emotional, diuretic screeds entitled "Evita!," where Sullivan lets a reader email devolve into sexual innuendo; and "Hillary's Big Balls," a regurgitation no real feminist would print under that title. Then there's his "Steinem Women, Paglia Women" competition, inspired by another reader email, which turns hilarious when you consider Salon's Camille Paglia is a huge fan of Sarah Palin, which Gloria Steinem is decidedly not. It proves yet again that Sullivan's ravings have no coherent through-line at all.

Paglia thinks Palin is an "Amazon Warrior." Steinem thinks she's the "wrong woman." Sullivan's heroine, Paglia, is laughing at him when she lifts Palin up as the "biggest step forward in reshaping the persona of female authority since Madonna." So, considering Sullivan is following Gloria Steinem's lead in standing up against Sarah, the real problem with Sullivan is he needs to learn a lot more about feminism.

It's one thing to debate whether Hillary was the right candidate for president, which was what the fight was all about. It's another thing to eschew facts for character assassination, because of who she is. But it did explain the viciousness of right-winger Roger Stone's 527 group, Citizens United Not Timid, whose name was obviously chosen so they could use the acronym CUNT.

Being blamed for simply being a woman, for being who you are, the sexism during the Hillary era of politics was painfully obvious. But that doesn't mean Hillary didn't make mistakes. Sometimes there really is no one to blame but yourself.

"I remember landing under sniper fire. There was supposed to be some kind of a greeting ceremony at the airport, but instead we just ran with our heads down to get into the vehicles to get to our base." — Hillary Clinton, in a speech at George Washington University, March 17, 2008.

What the hell was she thinking? There wasn't one mention of sniper fire in Bosnia in her autobiography, *Living History*, which compounded the embarrassing story suddenly popping up out of campaign air.

"I think the only 'red-phone' moment was: 'Do we eat here or at the next place,'" was how Sinbad commented in his routine. When a comedian rebuts your story you know you're in deep shit.

Glenn Kessler on "Fact Checker" for the *Washington Post* gave Clinton the lowest possible distinction, the highest rating for whoppers, four Pinocchios.

> Numerous reporters, including the *Washington Post*'s John Pomfret, covered her trip. A review of nearly one hundred news accounts of her visit shows that not a single newspaper or television station reported any security threat to the first lady. "As a former AP wire service hack, I can safely say that it would have been in my lead had anything like that happened," Pomfret said.
>
> According to Pomfret, the Tuzla airport was "one of the safest places in Bosnia" in March 1996, and "firmly under the control" of the 1st Armored Division.

The other problem was that a little girl named Emina had read Clinton a poem upon her arrival in Bosnia, saying "There is peace now, because Mr. Clinton signed it. All this peace. I love it."

Damage control was swift.

Lissa Muscatine, First Lady Hilary Clinton's chief speechwriter in 1996, who had accompanied Clinton on the Bosnia trip, contacted the *Post* to rebut their appraisal of the situation. This was added as an update to Kessler's "Fact Checker" post:

I was on the plane with then-First Lady Hillary Clinton for the trip from Germany into Bosnia in 1996. We were put on a C17 — a plane capable of steep ascents and descents — precisely because we were flying into what was considered a combat zone. We were issued flak jackets for the final leg because of possible sniper fire near Tuzla. As an additional precaution, the first lady and Chelsea were moved to the armored cockpit for the descent into Tuzla. We were told that a welcoming ceremony on the tarmac might be canceled because of sniper fire in the hills surrounding the air strip. From Tuzla, Hillary flew to two outposts in Bosnia with gunships escorting her helicopter.

This line was picked up by die-hard Clintonites, who eviscerated me in emails for "betraying" Hillary when I wrote my blog post, "Clinton Blows it on Bosnia." The myopic absurdity in offering an excuse when what Hillary said cannot be excused away was stunning, but that's the nature of partisan loyalty, what I call fan politics. Emails flew, hate mail slammed my inbox and comment sections, her fans believing the only thing to do was back Hillary up.

Clinton's damage control continued into Saturday. Another update from Kessler:

Gen. Nash says that I misquoted him in saying he was unaware of any "security threat" to the first lady. While he was unaware of any "sniper threat," he now tells me there were a couple of "security concerns" that day, which he found out about after returning to his headquarters after greeting Clinton at the airport. There was a "non-specific report" of a possible truck bomb in the area. The military also had information that "some of the communications associated with the first lady's visit were being monitored."

"In both cases, we took appropriate security action," said Nash, adding that Clinton's visit was not disrupted.

Meanwhile the headlines were devastating, as were the Obama campaign's talking points to their media allies. Andrew Sullivan mentioned me in a post at the time, writing that if I'm calling Clinton out on Bosnia, you know it's bad. He was right, it was, and it was all Clinton's fault.

Liz Cheney got her access to power by being the daughter of former Vice President Dick Cheney, parroting her dad's neoconservative talking points, which she does through her Keep America Safe PAC. It's where Cheney launches her attacks against President Obama and Democrats, but also Republicans, including demanding then-RNC chair Michael Steele resign when he went way off the GOP reservation by saying our involvement in Afghanistan was "not something the United States had actively prosecuted or wanted to engage in."

An interesting story that didn't get much traction, but reveals Ms. Cheney's penchant to let her ideology be her guide, revolves around Cheney being duped, putting her own credibility on the line by siding with Norma Khouri. Khouri was caught lying and perpetrating fraud through concocting an "honor killing" fiction about one of her friends, which was spotlighted in the 2007 Australian documentary, *Forbidden Lie$*, which aired on Showtime in 2009. *Vanity Fair* covered it in April 2009.

> Eerily, Forbidden Lie$ draws a dotted line from Khouri to the Bush administration via Dick Cheney's eldest daughter, Elizabeth, the U.S. deputy assistant secretary of state for Near Eastern Affairs from 2002 through 2004. Elizabeth, it turns out, wrote a letter of support for Khouri when she was applying for residency in Australia.

If nothing else, coming from Cheney's former position in the State Department as deputy assistant secretary of state for Near Eastern affairs, then named a principal in that department, she should have known how tightly watched honor killings are in Jordan. Considering Jordan was part of Cheney's portfolio at State, which included the Middle East, it doesn't say much for her analytical skills or attention to detail and facts. But it does reveal her national security stance is less based on facts and evidence than it is on preconceived ideology, the same type of thinking that brought us George W. Bush and the Iraq war. She's a chip off her dad's block.

Much more serious, Ms. Cheney's lack of analytical skills got her into real trouble when she tried to swift-boat Department of Justice lawyers for representing detainees, calling them "terrorist sympathizers" and questioning the attorneys' core values. Cheney's McCarthyism was considered so over the top it was called out by *conservatives*, including top lawyers for the Bush administration.

Ben Smith of Politico posted their letter, which was signed by Philip Zelikow and Kenneth W. Starr, among many others.

> ...The American tradition of zealous representation of unpopular clients is at least as old as John Adams's representation of the British soldiers charged in the Boston massacre.
>
> ...To suggest that the Justice Department should not employ talented lawyers who have advocated on behalf of detainees maligns the patriotism of people who have taken honorable positions on contested questions and demands a uniformity of background and view in government service from which no administration would benefit.

Raw Story reported that Paul Mirengoff, a fellow at the conservative Claremont Institute, stated Liz Cheney's ad "could be worse than some of the assertions made by [Joe] McCarthy."

But when you think of self-inflicted embarrassments, what was Sarah Palin thinking when she quit the governorship? It was the quintessential anti-Hillary move. And scribbling notes on her hand? Her fans loved it, but why should they, just because Sarah did it? It's all shrugged off as some elitist criticism, Sarah saying it's just a "poor man's teleprompter," though it's unthinkable to imagine the conservative heroine Margaret Thatcher devolving into such kindergarten antics.

Sarah's paranoia about the press has morphed into a Tea Party credo, seen through the Sharron Angle-ism, spoken back in the Nevada candidate's 2010 midterm Senate campaign, that journalists should "ask the questions we want to answer so that they report the news the way we want it to be reported." Palin's disastrous 2010 Delaware Senate pick, Christine O'Donnell, parroted this position with Piers Morgan before walking off the set. So, when you think of Camille Paglia's special pedestal for Palin, she falls far short of coming anywhere close to Paglia's claim that Sarah's the "biggest step forward in reshaping the persona of female authority since Madonna." Sarah's attempt to mimic Reagan through her *Alaska* reality series certainly added to Palin's wealth, which no one begrudges her, but it won't make anyone think she's any readier to be president than she was in 2008.

In March 2007, the late Elizabeth Edwards knew much more than she was sharing. The story is Shakespearean in its betrayal of public trust, because the Edwardses defrauded their supporters in a willful, stunning manner. It also revealed their perfect family hypocrisy.

The tragic grandeur of the John and Elizabeth soap opera turned self-servingly embarrassing when Elizabeth chose to go on Oprah Winfrey's show on the condition that no one speak the name of Rielle Hunter, the woman who had an affair with John Edwards and gave birth to his child. The first public disclosure of Elizabeth Edwards' private pain came in the book *Game Change* and was excerpted in *New York* magazine under the title "Saint Elizabeth and the Ego Monster." The co-authors took a lot grief for their revelations, which had never been disclosed before. The backlash toward Mark Halperin and John Heilemann proved we haven't learned very much from this political fraud the media went out of their way to ignore and only the *National Enquirer* would report. If you're beloved by the press, you'll likely get a pass no matter how scurrilous your behavior, which is often not even investigated.

There is also rightly a great deal of empathy toward the late Mrs. Edwards because of the tragedies she suffered, as well as the heroic life she lived while waging a war against terminal cancer. I understand in one sense, because I sat through more than a decade of my mother's harrowing battles with lymphoma. After one of her last operations, she came out of it with her entire head in a cast, only one eye peeping out, the surgeon having to break bones to rip the cancer from her body for the umpteenth time. We used to celebrate every three-month hurdle when her checkups proved she was cancer-free. After this operation, we worked together, me helping her learn to speak clearly again. But never once in these torturous years did my mother lose her dignity or her faith, or ever think of taking advantage of someone else.

No matter what Elizabeth Edwards suffered through, there was no excuse for colluding with her husband to perpetrate the "perfect family" fraud, which is no different from the right's "family values" hucksters who force their cultural piety on the rest of us while often harboring secrets that prove their morals aren't worth the spit it took to pronounce them. Mrs. Edwards' story breaks your heart. However, Elizabeth Edwards had choices, lots of them, unlike many women. But not even she could make them, not even to save herself from ruining her own life, and reputation, which she didn't have enough time to reclaim.

From a June 2010 *Today Show* interview with Matt Lauer:

LAUER: So, at this moment have you found some portion of peace in your life?

EDWARDS: I have, I mean, I really feel I have. I still really feel I need to break free of the media-imposed image. I'm not just a cuckolded wife. You know, I think about it because so many stories have been in the news recently. But I think about Sandra Bullock — who I don't know at all — what an incredible year she's had. She won the Academy Award for an incredible performance, and more than that, she took that story and integrated that into her own life in this healthy, happy way. And yet, the stories you hear are not about all those great successes, but about the failure of her marriage. And I thought that's not who she is, and in a sense I know she, I don't know her, but I assume she wants to reclaim who she is in the same way I want to reclaim who I am. I hope the next time I am on television it's to talk about some policy I really care about.

After the late Geraldine Ferraro's disastrous vice presidential bid, the first time in U.S. history a woman was on a national party ticket, you'd think women in politics would have realized the reality they face when it comes to their men.

> What has the women's movement learned from her candidacy for vice president? Never get married.
>
> — Gloria Steinem, May 1987

Reinvention is crucial for women, especially as we pass from teenage years into our twenties, thirties, forties and fifties, until in our sixties when we are to have arrived.

In all Hillary's travails, one of the things that dogged her with many women, especially those of younger generations, was her inability to walk away from her philandering husband. Never mind that it was no one's business. In American politics, "family values" interrupts, then obliterates privacy zones.

Hillary may have made the media explode with her "I'm not some Tammy Wynette standing by my man" remark, but in that statement is the foundation of Clinton's philosophy of her relationship with her husband. The translation comes in many forms, but one of them surely is that the Clinton marriage is real and foundational, with consequences being paid on both sides for their choices, which are freely made. Clinton's actions implied, "I know what I'm getting into and choose to handle what comes, whether the public approves or not, because it's *my* life."

But women did judge her choice of steadfastness and couldn't get beyond it or understand it or relate. If you've read the Starr Report, you likely know why. After that humiliation delivered on Hillary she would have been justified in whatever she decided. I would have drop-kicked his ass and so would have most other women, judging from what I've read and the correspondence and comments I've gotten over the years. But a marriage is a complicated beast, created uniquely, sometimes demanding beyond convention, with the Clintons the only ones who can understand the unconventional turns and eruptions of their partnership, which has benefited this country greatly and about which no one else should care.

But what the hell was Silda Wall Spitzer thinking when she stood by her "Luv Gov" husband? A collective *this is enough* cry rose up one last time from women. But this woman of wealth and accomplishment, the founder of Children for Children, may be the last woman to take a page out of First Lady Hillary Rodham Clinton's book. Mr. Spitzer was yet another powerful man who handed his enemies the dagger with which to kill him, when he went after AIG's Maurice "Hank" Greenberg, then Wall Street weenie Dick Grasso, which brought out the billionaire bullies' club and fat-cat Kenneth Langone, as well as right-wing hit man Roger Stone.

Silda Wall Spitzer urged her man to stay in office, but his bull-in-a-brothel style didn't allow for political friends or foes sticking by him. The public didn't know the Wall Street back- story hit job that brought Spitzer down, even if his own personal foibles launched it. But why did Democrats cut him loose, while Republicans suck it up and let their sexual scalawags, Newt, Rudy, et al., stay? Self-loathing on the Democratic side loses to Republican self-righteousness every time.

Seeing Mr. Spitzer relegated to CNN talking-head, which he is no longer, was an insult and waste considering he sniffed out what was going on first, and just after he was pulled off the job of policing Wall Street, the entire U.S. financial system came crashing down.

Jenny Sanford let her love-struck husband, Appalachian Trail gigolo Gov. Mark Sanford, stand alone. She then divorced him, a first for the conservative "family values" crowd, for which she rightly received no criticism, another first. But before the finale, Mr. Sanford humiliated his wife through embarrassing statements declaring his love for his Argentinean mistress, Maria Belen Chapur, through incredible press conferences that defied the drama of previous political philanderers in recent history. Bill Maher weighed in to say it was "sweet" that Gov. Sanford was "really in love," an odd statement of sentimental support from the perennial-bachelor peanut gallery. It was certainly a first.

One Sanford love letter went like this:

You are glorious and I hope you really understand that. You do not need a therapist to help you figure your place in the world. You are special and unique and fabulous in a whole host of ways that are worth a much longer conversation.

Another like this:

As I told you before, you brought happiness and love to my life and [I] will take you forever in my heart. I wasn't aware till we met last week, the strong feelings I had for you, and believe me, I haven't felt this since I was in my teen ages, when afterwards I got married. I do love you, I can feel it in my heart, and although I don't know if we'll ever be able to meet again this has been the best that has happened to me in a long time, You made me realized [sic] how you feel when you realy [sic] love somebody and how much you want to be beside the beloved. Last Friday I would had [sic] stayed embrassing [sic] and kissing you forever.

We'd never read or heard anything like it.

Conservative rising star and now governor of South Carolina, Nikki Haley, an Indian American, had to talk about her conversion to Christianity from her Sikh faith beginnings, proving she was properly Christian enough for Republicans to represent them and hold office in South Carolina. But it was during the primary campaign when Haley was attacked with charges of infidelity, having to fend off two charges. She stood up, denied them, said she'd resign if they were proven, but didn't blink. The strong push-back without any hint of sexist "shrill" charges revealed something had indeed shifted as the Hillary Effect resounded out. The "raghead" slur was denounced even by Republicans, who don't approve of such things when it targets one of their own.

Then there's Christine O'Donnell, the serial Senate candidate without a clue, who keeps on trying for the job anyway, failing every time. Her piety parade was assaulted when Gawker ran an anonymous smear of some alleged sexless encounter that was supposed to prove, hell, I don't know what, and neither did Gawker. Ms. O'Donnell defended herself on Facebook, with the event politically historic for the chaos-politics of the 2010 midterms, because it united all sides to condemn the ethically challenged screed.

Nothing could ever unite left and right on Hillary's behalf, no matter how vile the assault. It took Hillary taking a fatal political hit before what she'd endured would benefit others.

Conservatives have helped fuel the category of "it's all the woman's fault," because of the vitriol they wield against liberal women. They are represented by the bankruptcy of the Phyllis Schlafly theory of womanhood and marriage, which is getting reinvigorated by the Tea Party movement. In 2010, Schlafly brought new outlandish charges against women, when she talked about single women voting for Democrats because "when you kick your husband out, you've got to have big brother government to be your provider."

But in the woman's-fault game, feminism is often pointed to when it comes to relationships, again by the entire right, because in the modern era it has changed love, marriage and "family values" forever. It's the economic equality, stupid.

Today, if a woman's unhappy she can change it, and if she doesn't, she has only herself to blame. Bad relationships are the same way. We pick whom we think we deserve. We stay with a man because we don't have the courage to fight for ourselves or for what we rightfully deserve. It used to be that religion held the bonds of marriage tightly, but it doesn't any longer. The other issue is that our longevity outlasts our love sometimes, especially if the relationship starts early. When news of Al and Tipper Gore's separation hit the airwaves, it inspired a national discussion that led to catharsis. Women and men live fuller, more independent lives these days, and people sometimes grow apart. That's what the Gores have said happened, which is just part of modern living at that level of equal achievement and opportunities.

The talk the day the Gore announcement hit was that the Clinton marriage lasted longer. How ironic. However, when you look deeper you see the definition of marriage is obviously different for each couple. What made the Gores grow apart, by accounts from their friends quoted in the media, were their busy lives. For the Clintons, their busy lives are a part of a marriage that is made up on different grounds.

There are as many types of marriages as there are couples. There is no saying what is right or wrong in the modern era. However, when you live a public political life you'd better be prepared to explain it or suffer through analyses like mine (or worse) that try to make sense of what we're seeing versus what we're hearing and what it could mean in a political, historical and cultural sense.

But when pondering why Hillary stayed with Bill or why Elizabeth Edwards chose to be a shield for her shit-heel husband, you might as well ponder why Jackie stayed with John F. Kennedy. That would also take us into Jackie's father, Black Jack Bouvier, and his notorious behavior, something that obviously stuck in the former first lady's mind, and is another page in the voluminous series of Good Girls Loving Very Bad Boys.

You don't make choices to please others and the choices we do make often come through our hearts or loins, not our heads. We can handle what we choose as long as we accept we have no one to blame but ourselves when things go south. That goes for Elizabeth Edwards, Monica Lewinsky, Rielle Hunter, Jenny Sanford, Silda Spitzer and on and on, as well as Hillary Rodham Clinton, none of whom escaped humiliation for being addicted to their love.

There's a big difference between making our own mistakes and the outside world blaming us for something over which we have no control, both realities something Hillary faced, with the media and her adversaries' gender-based charges something she had to live down and rebut, even though they were usually groundless and almost always sexist.

Erica Jong took the issue on in "Hillary vs. The Patriarchy," in the February 4, 2008, *Washington Post*.

> I'm hardly the only woman who sees my life mirrored in hers. She's always worked twice as hard to get half as far as the men around her. She endured a demanding Republican father she could seldom please and a brilliant, straying husband who played around with bimbos. She was clearly his intellectual soul mate, but the women he chased were dumb and dumber.
>
> Nothing she did was ever enough to stop her detractors. Supporting a politician husband by being a successful lawyer, raising a terrific daughter, saving her marriage when the love of her life publicly humiliated her — these are things that would be considered enormously admirable in most politicians and public figures. But because she's a white woman, she's been pilloried for them.
>
> She's had to endure nutcrackers made in her image, insults about the shape of her ankles and nasty cracks from mediocrities in the media like Rush Limbaugh, Chris Matthews and Kristol.

What made it worse is that if you did stand up and call out the patriarchal sexism coming at Clinton, the incoming *methinks you doth protest too much* avalanche would drown out any serious discussion, because of who that debate would have targeted, which almost always included those denying the misogyny in the first place.

The endurance needed to take on the media gauntlet Hillary experienced in her run for president illustrated many things. Having a woman run her campaign like a man, because she thinks that's the only way to prove she's as strong as any man, is not like having a woman represent a new kind of leadership that goes beyond what men have offered before and be willing to talk and run like a woman to prove it. Sarah Palin comes out of the neocon cloth, as does Liz Cheney, and they sound like the men. Hillary's vote on Iraq, her stance on Iran, Libya, and Mubarak before he fell, as well as her politics on Israel — all run along the same militaristic, macho national security reflex dialogue that most women in the Washington political game mimic. Samantha Power and U.N. Ambassador Susan Rice reportedly wanting to move militarily on Libya is a prime example. Women are not going to offer a different outcome on national security if we follow the same talking points, the same philosophy and tactics as men. During the 2010 midterms, "man up" became the conservative women's Tea Party mantra, and it doesn't really matter whether they're trying to win over men by proving their toughness through macho lingo or not. In order to change the game, we've got to confront the male stereotypes with a new dialogue all our own.

It's a catch-22, but only women can break out and we aren't there yet. Whether it's Hillary or other highly visible women in politics like Sarah Palin or Michele Bachmann, channeling men's language on security issues seems to be the route, even if it's wrong. Senator Kirsten Gillibrand showed signs of strength and independence in 2011 with her campaign to end the war in Afghanistan more swiftly through a timetable, but she stopped short of suggesting immediate withdrawal.

When DNC chair Debbie Wasserman Schultz defended entitlements and challenged Rep. Allen West to do the same, his response via email, which Politico's Ben Smith posted, was to go nuclear and call her "vile... despicable... not a lady." There's another Republican vote for the subservient model. But why aren't Wasserman Schultz and other Democrats defending entitlements against President Obama's priority to "reform" them, while wars wage on?

Do women have to talk like men in order to present to voters what they're accustomed to seeing and hearing so we can pass the commander in chief test? Will we, by parroting male talking points, get voters accustomed to women talking as men, using it as a bridge to introduce new ideas that only a woman could offer, finally setting us apart and free to consider national security alternatives? The answer is critical and it's way too soon to tell.

Ms. Rosin, in "The End of Men," discovered the same thing, if on a different plain.

> In fact, the more women dominate, the more they behave, fittingly, like the dominant sex. Rates of violence committed by middle-aged women have skyrocketed since

the 1980s, and no one knows why. High-profile female killers have been showing up regularly in the news: Amy Bishop, the homicidal Alabama professor; Jihad Jane and her sidekick, Jihad Jamie; the latest generation of Black Widows, responsible for suicide bombings in Russia. In Roman Polanski's *The Ghost Writer*, the traditional political wife is rewritten as a cold-blooded killer at the heart of an evil conspiracy. In her recent video, "Telephone," Lady Gaga, with her infallible radar for the cultural edge, rewrites *Thelma and Louise* as a story not about elusive female empowerment but about sheer, ruthless power. Instead of killing themselves, she and her girlfriend (played by Beyoncé) kill a bad boyfriend and random others in a homicidal spree and then escape in their yellow pickup truck, Gaga bragging, "We did it, Honey B."

The last political gender war over Hillary's presidential campaign, which wasn't Hillary's fault even as her attackers said it was, happened simply because she was Hillary Rodham Clinton. After Clinton's defeat, most could finally recognize when someone is blaming the woman through the prism of gender, instead of critiquing her on her substance and merits. People are also braver to call it out and land the criticism where it's warranted — not at the woman, but at the person leveling the sexist rant at her. It's also clear when it's actually her fault or when someone is simply saying it's all the woman's fault, however it's phrased, because they want to continue the status quo. We can tell through the language, swagger and coded references, but also because of who's talking. The differences are clear no matter who's flinging the assault, which in the '08 election season came from all directions.

Chapter 7: **Eating Your Own**

You certainly won't get the view I saw of Obama versus Hillary from David Plouffe's book, *The Audacity to Win: The Inside Story and Lessons of Barack Obama's Historic Victory*. It is indeed a truly remarkable story. But the subtitle of Plouffe's book should have been: *Marketing Barack Obama's "New Kind of Politics" and the Craft of Political Mythmaking*. Because I assure you, the story Plouffe tells, while true for him, is only half complete. His ability to cherry-pick the most laudable campaign plums, leaving the scorched earth of the Obama team and their surrogates out, really is a lesson in how the winners write the history. The Obama campaign was anything but a "new kind of politics," but most of the media sucked it up like an intoxicating elixir, though there were a very few exceptions who saw it.

John Heilemann, co-author of *Game Change*, writing in *New York* magazine, March 28, 2008:

"For all its rhetoric about practicing a new, more virtuous brand of politics, the Obama campaign has been going after Clinton hammer and tongs. Rarely a day passes without his people dubbing her a liar and a fraud. (Although when it comes to Snipergate, it's hard to blame them.) They have accused Bill Clinton of McCarthyism and invoked the infamous blue dress on which he left his, er, DNA — the latter coming on a blog post arguing that he actually makes McCarthy look benign. Indeed, it sometimes seems as if the Obamans are actively trying to cede the moral high ground."

The history of winning campaigns is about myth-making, with Obama's historic candidacy headed for enshrinement. David Plouffe's book intends to obliterate what had come before. It was a brilliant strategy, especially when embodied through a talented politician like Barack Obama, the first African American to become president. But when Plouffe talks about the "toxicity of the campaign," leaving the Obama campaign's substantial contribution out, it rewrites the history of the bruising battle into a fictional tale. Team Obama offered as toxic a component to the primary campaign trail as anyone ever has.

Former President Bill Clinton pointed this out at a January 7, 2008, campaign event, as transcribed by *Congressional Quarterly*: "But, you know, the idea that one of these campaigns is positive and [the] other is negative, when I know the reverse is true and I have seen it and I have been blistered by it for months, is a little tough to take. Just because of the sanitizing coverage that's in the media doesn't mean the facts aren't out there."

That Obama was actually the establishment candidate, the media's choice as well, with Hillary the outsider, is represented well in a piece John Judis wrote for the *New Republic*, in May 2008, which unmasks all the mystery about Obama and the press:

> Clinton's second great political mistake lay in how she dealt with Obama's challenge. Sometime in December, having realized that Obama was going to be a genuine rival for the nomination, she and her campaign decided to go negative on him....
>
> John McCain and Mitt Romney were doing similar things to each other — and Obama did some of it to Clinton, too. But there was a difference between her doing this to Obama and McCain's doing it to Romney... Obama, too, was, and is, history — the first viable African American presidential candidate. Yes, Hillary Clinton was the first viable female candidate, but it is still different.... And if some voters didn't appreciate the potential breakthrough that Obama's candidacy represented, many in the Democratic primaries and caucuses did — and so did the members of the media and Obama's fellow politicians.

Barack Obama's candidacy was obviously historic, but so was Hillary Rodham Clinton's. They were both firsts — equal, except to the media covering the race. As with Plouffe's rewriting of primary history, the media wrote their own script. It's how the Obama campaign's negative campaigning got a pass. After all, how else could he beat the bitch?

It began in June 2007, when Patrick Healy of the *New York Times* reported on a not-for-attribution-basis memo-dump by team Obama. One portion of the memo dealt with fund-raising from Indian Americans, with Obama's team providing a "scathing analysis," as Healy put it. The clincher was that the Obama campaign identified Hillary as "Hillary Clinton (D-Punjab)," eviscerating Clinton for courting the Indian American community, with the language in the Obama team memo bordering on racist. Bill Burton wouldn't explain it, with candidate Obama forced to admit the document circulated by his campaign was "stupid and caustic," a "screw-up." This is how the "change" candidate and his team *began*.

Hillary's first-lady role made it easy to attack her on free trade, as she'd never stood up against NAFTA, a controversial policy, especially among progressives. David Axelrod was quoted in *USA Today* in March 2008 saying Hillary's stance amounted to the "political equivalent of consumer fraud. And she owes an apology to the people of Ohio and an explanation to the people of this country."

But as Sally Bedell Smith and Carl Bernstein both reported, Hillary was against NAFTA, "primarily because it could take jobs away from American workers," a quote from Bedell Smith's book, *For Love of Politics*. But as first lady, she was rendered mute in the face of her husband's presidential agenda, though many evidently expected Hillary to take on Bill publicly on the issue, which was a ridiculous assertion. As Sally Bedell Smith explained, Mickey Cantor, who was U.S. Trade Representative at the time and charged with making sure NAFTA worked, was sent in to cajole Hillary into siding with her husband on the issue. Carl Bernstein, not exactly a fan — he wrote a biography on Hillary Clinton, *A Woman in Charge*, that includes details about Hillary's father that are chilling — also recalled that she'd been against NAFTA, which he voiced on CNN back on January 30, 2008:

"Hillary Clinton's economics, the ones she preached to her husband in the White House are much closer to John Edwards than you would think. She argued with Bill Clinton when she was first lady.... She said 'Bill, you are doing Republican economics when you are doing NAFTA.' She was against NAFTA."

Once in office, President Obama became a free-trade addict, once again taking a page from former President Bill Clinton's playbook.

After the eleven thousand pages of Clinton's daily schedules as first lady were released from the National Archives, Robert Gibbs, Obama's press secretary at the time, accused Hillary Clinton of "hiding the truth." Candidate Obama said Clinton was being "disingenuous."

It was very smart for Obama to run against Washington while draping the insider role over Hillary, but the way in which his campaign did it day in and day out was not the politics of hope, far from it. In his stump speeches, candidate Barack Obama said Democrats could win "not by nominating a candidate who will unite the other party against us," which clearly aimed the "divisive" label squarely at Hillary, and did so while tagging her as siding with Republicans on vital issues from trade to national security. The AP, on January 30, 2008, described it like this: "Obama depicted Clinton as a calculating, poll-tested, divisive figure who will only inspire greater partisan divisions as she sides with Republicans on issues like trade, the role of lobbyists in politics and national security."

If that sounds like a vaguely familiar description, it should. It's what a whole lot of movement progressives and die-hard Democrats are saying about President Obama today.

Ironically, in February 2008, Sam Stein of the Huffington Post reported that Obama was the one who had spent more on polling, $2.55 million to Clinton's $1.92 million. Stein followed that up more than two years later, reporting in July 2010 that the Obama administration spent more on polling in its first eighteen months than George W. Bush did in his first twenty-four months:

"While Gibbs routinely chides members of the press for obsessing about the day-to-day temperamental swings of the American public, behind the scenes the White House has poured plenty of money into conducting its own public opinion polls. Through June 9, 2010, the administration, via the Democratic National Committee, has spent at least $4.45 million on the services of seven different pollsters, according to records compiled by the Center for Responsive Politics. That total represents only eighteen months into the administration. During the first twenty-four months of the Bush administration, the Republican National Committee spent $3.1 million on polling according to a 2003 study done by Brookings."

In a campaign memo, the Obama campaign said Hillary "will say and do anything to win." Now, negative campaigning is as American as a cheeseburger with fries. But it gets tricky when the first wunderkind African American comes out of nowhere to claim a "new kind of politics," challenging the first viable female contender, while whining about the "battles of the '90s." Never mind that from time immemorial men have been saying and doing anything to win, with Obama certainly no exception.

Just ask Alice Palmer. Barack Obama came to power by challenging signatures on Ms. Palmer's nominating petitions, leaving her short. It was a huge controversy at the time, and people I spoke with in early 2007 — none would go on the record even after numerous conversations — said Obama played hardball "the Chicago way." What does that mean? *He did anything to win.* That's fine. However, when Hillary did it, the Obama campaign judged it as unseemly, even if they were doing the very same thing. National traditional media, new media and cable yackers let him get away with it every time.

In another campaign memo, March 8, 2008, the Obama campaign accused Clinton of tactics that were "an attempt to deceive the American people just so that they can win this election... this is exactly why people don't trust their leaders anymore."

David Plouffe, in early March 2008, attacked Clinton's honesty, in a back-and-forth over the Clinton-papers release, saying "You have to wonder whether she'll be open and honest with the American people as president," calling Hillary Clinton "one of the most secretive politicians in America today."

Oh, the irony, as revealed by Politico, March 30, 2011:

> President Obama finally and quietly accepted his "transparency" award from the open government community this week — in a closed, undisclosed meeting at the White House on Monday. The secret presentation happened almost two weeks after the White House inexplicably postponed the ceremony, which was expected to be open to the press pool.

Samantha Power revealed the thinking of the Obama team and many supporters when she called Hillary a "monster" on camera in an interview in the U.K., which quickly resulted in outrage that forced her resignation. She eventually apologized to Secretary Clinton, and became an important administration advisor who, along with Hillary and U.N. Ambassador Susan Rice, was one of the women who reportedly took a leading role in making the humanitarian case for bombing Libya.

Obama and his team targeted Bill Clinton, too, even when the press wouldn't pick it up. Marc Ambinder, now with the *National Journal*, reported that one Obama aide asked when the media was going to pick up the scent of Bill Clinton's sex life. One can only imagine if this had been a Clinton aide questioning and floating a story about Obama. Howard Kurtz reported on it through the lens of the different press the two candidates received:

> There was also a lack of media pickup when the *Atlantic*'s Marc Ambinder reported that an Obama aide had sat down next to him and "wanted to know when reporters would begin to look into Bill Clinton's post-presidential sex life."
>
> — Howard Kurtz, Washington Post, December 19, 2007

Howard Fineman, in the same article, said other campaign operatives complained about the media coverage, and also said about Obama, "He's getting a free ride." That's because he was.

When the late Robert Novak reported that Hillary's team had "scandalous information" about Obama, Obama's team released a statement quoting Novak, even though there was no proof Novak really had any such information, let alone that it would come from Clinton. The statement also implied a threat to Hillary Clinton's reputation. It read in part, "But in the interest of our party, and her own reputation, Senator Clinton should either make public any and all information referred to in the item, or concede the truth: that there is none."

It was by no means the only time Barack Obama or his campaign team used Republican talking points to attack Clinton. In a July 27, 2007, *New York Times* story headlined, "Obama Says Clinton Is 'Bush-Cheney Lite,'" Obama is said to have told reporters, "I don't want Bush-Cheney lite. I want a fundamental change."

Marketing "fundamental change" was the Obama campaign's crowning achievement. What was delivered in many cases was politics as usual, which by the summer of 2011 was looking very "Bush-Cheney lite." From Salon's Glenn Greenwald, written in May 2009:

> Obama has been at least as aggressive as Bush was in asserting radical secrecy doctrines in order to prevent courts from ruling on illegal torture and spying programs and to block victims from having a day in court. He has continued and even "ramped up" so-called "targeted killings" in Pakistan and Afghanistan which, as Goldsmith puts it, "have predictably caused more collateral damage to innocent civilians." He has maintained not only Bush's rendition policy but also the standard used to determine to

which countries a suspect can be rendered, and has kept Bush's domestic surveillance policies in place and unchanged. Most of all, he has emphatically endorsed the Bush/Cheney paradigm that we are engaged in a "war" against terrorists — with all of the accompanying presidential "war powers" — rather than the law enforcement challenge that John Kerry, among others, advocated.

During the primaries, Obama attacked Clinton's integrity at every stop, with no hint of shame, for defying his own politics-of-change PR: "If you choose change, you will have a nominee who doesn't just tell people what they want to hear."

The avalanche of bullshit from the Obama campaign should have come with hip boots, because candidate Obama had no problem going negative against Hillary:

"I have no doubt that once the nomination contest is over, I will get the people who voted for her. Now the question is can she get the people who voted for me?"

I wouldn't call what Michelle Obama said on *Good Morning America* the day before Super Tuesday, February 2008, exactly "a different kind of politics" either.

GMA: Could you see yourself working to support Hillary Clinton should she win the nomination?

MICHELLE OBAMA: I'd have to think about that. I'd have to think about that, her policies, her approach, her tone.

Michelle Obama has been a groundbreaking first lady with regard to her work on childhood obesity and nutrition, including taking up Alice Waters' challenge to start a White House garden. But if former President Bill Clinton had said something like this about candidate Barack Obama, heads would have exploded across national politics. Andrew Sullivan would have called for Clinton's scalp, with Christopher Hitchens willingly stalking the former president in order to perform the honors himself!

This is a good place to talk about my own scorched earth, "eating your own" partisan analysis during the campaign once I sided with Hillary, which didn't happen until July 2007. I was tough and partisan, but I never pretended otherwise. At least I was transparent, while many closeted Obama supporters instead feigned independence and balance, then went on cable spewing invective at Clinton. I make no apologies for doing background work on candidate Obama, revealing what I heard and read, as well as what his record revealed. From his flyover of the first Carson City debate to showing up at the Nevada health care forum unprepared, beginning in early 2007, I delivered political analysis and honest critique that wasn't getting done elsewhere by many. There is no doubt I was tough, even rough, on candidate Barack Obama, which is why I earned so many enemies that spawned innumerable attacks against me personally, including amateur diary blog posts, mostly from male Obama supporters, but today my analysis holds up to scrutiny as being correct. When I wrote a column laying out how the Republicans would use William Ayers, it was as if I'd killed a litter of kittens; it hardly mattered that it came true. I never believed President Obama would fight for Democratic Party principles, because he'd always rather deal and compromise, which he admitted in his interview with George Stephanopoulos in May 2007. His loyalists now need smelling salts when they remember candidate Obama versus President Obama, a presidency that's evolved exactly as I warned it would.

In the summer of 2010, when I came to First Lady Michelle Obama's defense, after a Republican hit piece in the *New York Daily News* about the vacation she took to Spain, this is just one of the emails I got from the right:

"Taylor, I never heard of you before. But you [*sic*] just one of the thousands of stupid elitist media whores out there, pimping for that fat Nazi bitch Michelle. Spare us already! — sl"

When I didn't miss a beat after Hillary conceded, immediately supporting Obama, it engendered hate from Hillary supporters that was red hot and vicious, some of which remains to this day. This email came in December 2009, after I blasted the Democratic health care bill in a debate on MSNBC, because the idea of mandates without a public option makes absolutely no sense to me.

"Taylor how does it feel to be called a white bitch by Obama supporters after your appearance on MSNBC? All the obots are lashing sexist, disgusting names at you," the writer said, using the "Obot" term of derision for unthinking Obama fans. "And that's the kind of people you wanted to be associate [*sic*] with. You're getting karma ten fold my friend. Admit you were wrong, join forces with Hillary supporters who are true progressives to save any last ounce of dignity you have left. — pumashouldhavevotedhc"

Obama even went down the road of attacking what some Democrats would say was the most important decade in modern times, the 1960s, implying that since Clinton was part of that generation — said like he was uttering an expletive — Hillary couldn't possibly reach the new generation of Obama voters. Never mind that a Democrat can't get elected without pro-Clinton Democrats. President Obama has packed his administration with Clintonites as well. It brought up another falsehood Obama's team was pushing, that Hillary was the only divisive one.

> I think there's no doubt that we represent the kind of change that Senator Clinton can't deliver on and part of it is generational. Senator Clinton and others, they've been fighting some of the same fights since the '60s and it makes it very difficult for them to bring the country together to get things done.
>
> — Barack Obama, as quoted on Fox News Channel via Breitbart TV, November 2007

Obama suggested that "it is fair to say that I believe I can bring the country together more effectively than she can," quoting a *Washington Post* article from August 2007, and that there was a break needed from the Clintons, because of "the ideological battles that we fought during the '90s that were really extensions of battles we fought since the '60s."

It was straight from Karl Rove and right-wing radio's playbook.

After the Obama campaign complained, CNN benched both James Carville and Paul Begala. Sam Feist, CNN's political director at the time, said "Carville and Begala are two of the best analysts around, and we look forward to seeing them on CNN plenty of times in the future, once the nominating process has ended." Meanwhile, one of the most divisive Democrats on CNN was left to spew venom in Hillary's direction. Donna Brazile presented herself as neutral but was anything but. Brazile started on Hillary first by saying her comeback would be about "sowing political seeds of doubt," then lowered the boom in a story via Yahoo! News:

"'In order to clinch the nomination, he must anticipate the worst attacks ever.... If these attacks are contrasts based on policy differences, there is no need to stop the race or halt the debate,' Brazile said. 'But, if this is more division, more diversion from the issues and more of the same politics of personal destruction, chairman Dean and other should be on standby.'"

Ms. Brazile evidently missed the Obama team's Rovesque plan for Clinton:

"A senior Obama adviser, speaking on condition of anonymity, said Obama's team will respond to Tuesday's results by going negative on Clinton — raising questions about her tax records and the source of donations to the Clinton presidential library, among skeletons in the Clintons' past." — Yahoo! News

It's the same type of story Politico mined in August 2011, when they interviewed Obama aides and advisers about their plans for Mitt Romney, whom they believe will be the nominee: "Obama Plan: Destroy Romney."

Brazile's commentary on CNN caused a lot of problems for her with Hillary supporters, with hate-filled emails bombarding her inbox. One email exchange between Ms. Brazile and a Hillary supporter, the text of which was posted widely on the blogs in April 2008, got a real rise out of Brazile:

Donna Brazile: "Blacks have been deeply wounded by the duplicity of the Clintons. Now, you may not like it or agree. But as a black person who helped save the Clinton presidency, please just respect what I am saying. Again, you disagree. But, I honestly believe the wounds will not heal. It's personal and the Clintons have shown their darker demons. Now, I will end it here.... I don't owe anybody a dime. And if I counted who has helped me since 2000, its [sic] Republican men and not Democrats. Go figure and good night."

In one appearance on CNN, in March 2008, Brazile brought up Rev. Wright saying he "did not turn on Clinton's husband during an hour of need for him," as the Los Angeles Times reported it, which was a constant part of her monologue aimed at Clinton.

Brazile also was a member of the DNC Rules Committee who "argued for a swift and harsh punishment for Florida," as reported in the Washington Post, but also for Michigan, whose votes Hillary fought openly and fiercely to be counted. Brazile also threatened to quit the Democratic Party if the superdelegates did not vote in line with the people. Every time she appeared on CNN, her tone against Clinton became harsher, yet CNN did nothing.

However, it was a quote from Hollywood mogul David Geffen that would rock the Hillary camp. According to *Her Way*, by Jeff Gerth and Don Van Natta Jr., Geffen had raised as much as $18 million in the 1990s for Bill Clinton and the Democrats. This time he'd raised over $1.3 million for Obama from a small soiree of forty Hollywood friends, territory that the Clintons had always owned. Dropping the quote to Maureen Dowd, Geffen called Hillary "polarizing," but then went on to vilify Hillary for being, of all things, ambitious.

"'Not since the Vietnam War has there been this level of disappointment in the behavior of America throughout the world, and I don't think that another incredibly polarizing figure, no matter how smart she is and no matter how ambitious she is — and God knows, is there anybody more ambitious than Hillary Clinton? — can bring the country together,'" Dowd wrote, quoting Geffen in a February 2007 *New York Times* column.

Going after a female for being "ambitious" is the height of sexism. But the Geffen quote was made for Ms. Dowd's 1950s world-view that girls are supposed to be seen and not heard from a microphone, for fear of becoming shrill. It was also brilliant advocacy, aiding Obama through a top Clinton-hater, Maureen Dowd, sending the message with samurai sword precision.

That wasn't the worst of it from Geffen in Dowd's column. "'Everybody in politics lies, but [the Clintons] do it with such ease, it's troubling,'" she quotes him as saying.

The Clinton camp went on the offensive, demanding Barack Obama return Geffen's money, which was a ludicrous demand, making them sound defensive and panicked. Clinton's Communications Director Howard Wolfson released a statement that spoke for itself. The whole thing ended up backfiring.

"While Senator Obama was denouncing slash and burn politics yesterday, his campaign's finance chair was viciously and personally attacking Senator Clinton and her husband. If Senator Obama is indeed sincere about his repeated claims to change the tone of our politics, he should immediately denounce these remarks,

remove Mr. Geffen from his campaign and return his money....
[There is] no place in our party or our politics for the kind of
personal insults made by Senator Obama's principal fundraiser."

What was going to be the worst shitstorm of the 2008
primaries, however, was foreshadowed by Rep. Jesse Jackson Jr.
after New Hampshire, where Barack Obama was clearly set back on
his heels after a historic win in Iowa. While Obama operatives were
dispensed to spin Hillary's New Hampshire win as "the Bradley
Effect," which stipulated that New Hampshire voters told pollsters
they were voting for Obama but actually didn't follow through at the
voting booth, hoping to dispel the reality that Hillary had connected
with voters. Before South Carolina, Jackson Jr. went all in for
Obama.

"There were tears that melted the Granite State," he said on
MSNBC, as reported all over the web. "And those are tears that Mrs.
Clinton cried on that day, clearly moved voters. She somehow
connected with those voters. But those tears also have to be
analyzed. They have to be looked at very, very carefully in light of
Katrina, in light of other things that Mrs. Clinton did not cry for,
particularly as we head to South Carolina where 45% of African
Americans who participate in the Democratic contest, and they see
real hope in Barack Obama."

It was exactly what John Judis had written, writing off what
people saw in Clinton's candidacy, expecting deference for Obama.
But at least he didn't come out and say "the ice queen melted."
Jackson Jr. dodged a question from Norah O'Donnell, formerly of
MSNBC and now White House correspondent with CBS, on whether
he thought Clinton's tears were "affected... staged." Rep. Jesse
Jackson Jr. played the race card by invoking the percentage of
African Americans, and plainly sent a shot across Clinton's bow,
implying that her emotions should be analyzed to see if whether she
cried for African Americans, too. Jackson's words seemed almost a
threat. Wait until South Carolina, bitch; we'll see who's boss.

The overt, sexist stereotype dripped from Mr. Jackson's
comments, but the uproar was nothing akin to what would have
happened if one of Hillary's surrogates had challenged Obama this
way. If Jackson had been in Clinton's campaign, his firing would
have been demanded, but there was no retraction or apology from
team Obama. The media was not outraged and in fact played along

by publicizing the challenge that the elitist white woman didn't feel everyone's pain equally. Obama's message muscleman was serving notice, and it went beyond Clinton.

Rep. Jesse Jackson Jr. went on to threaten primary challengers against African American lawmakers who were supporters of Hillary. The Associated Press quoted him this way: "Many of these guys have offered their support to Mrs. Clinton, but Obama has won their districts. So you wake up without the carpet under your feet. You might find some young primary challenger placing you in a difficult position."

The civil rights legend, Rep. John Lewis, had a flood of robocalls made against him, while Rep. Emanuel Cleaver of Missouri was also threatened for supporting Clinton. NPR reported the whole sorry spectacle in a February 15, 2008, piece titled, "Loyalty vs. Voters: A Superdelegate's Dilemma."

"I had a person in my district send out a newsletter, for which I know he didn't pay, distributed primarily in the African American community, in which he suggested that I had been paid by Senator Clinton to support her. I don't know if there's anyone [who is African American] who hasn't taken some grief for supporting Senator Clinton.... You don't abandon your friends," Cleaver was quoted saying.

I grew up in Missouri, mostly in St. Louis, and busing occurred at my high school, so no one has to explain to me the politics of race. As an aside, the man who got me interested in politics as a kid, my older brother Larry R. Marshall, was an assistant attorney general for the state of Missouri when John Ashcroft was attorney general. (Larry was also a Missouri state senator from 1972-1976, a pro-ERA Republican who became prochoice as well). To make a very long story short, when racism accusations started flying during Ashcroft's confirmation for U.S. attorney general, my brother was called by the *St. Louis Post-Dispatch*, eventually appearing on CNN. He also interacted with Senator Orrin Hatch's office, providing a statement for the confirmation hearing, which he stands by today, saying, "in his own mind this was totally untrue." He was in a position to know, because he was involved in both St. Louis and Kansas City desegregation cases and says "John Ashcroft never uttered one word during the entire time I was involved in both cases that was racist at all," and

214

also "never interfered" with his ability to do his job. Hey, but an ideological asshole is still an asshole, which describes Ashcroft to a tee for me.

It was the Obama campaign's South Carolina memo that would detonate like a campaign stink bomb. It was distributed under the name of the "South Carolina Press Secretary, Obama for America," Amaya Smith, complete with phone numbers so the press could contact her. I was one of the first people to get it, and the message was clear. Jumping off of Jackson's remarks after New Hampshire, then adding every quote possible, the Obama campaign was now implying in writing that the Clinton campaign was purposefully invoking race whenever they could. There simply wasn't a more incendiary charge to make.

The South Carolina memo began with Andrew Cuomo's quote that, "You can't shuck and jive at a press conference." The question Obama was asking was simple, which Ben Smith of Politico reported, getting quite a quote from Obama spokeswoman Candice Tolliver:

"There's a groundswell of reaction to these comments — and not just these latest comments, but really a pattern, or a series of comments that we've heard for several months," she said. "Folks are beginning to wonder: Is this really an isolated situation, or is there something bigger behind all of this?"

Translation: Is Hillary running a racist campaign against Obama?

Kathleen Parker had written a column about "Shuckin' 'n Jivin' with Hillary," in January 2006, because of a speech she gave at a celebration of Martin Luther King Jr. Obama regularly used the terms "bamboozled" and "hoodwinked" when campaigning in the South. Only Hillary's team got called for what wove throughout the entire campaign.

The Obama campaign had clearly decided that it would be scorched earth in South Carolina, and they were not just going to win the state, but damage Hillary politically. After all, people can't possibly say the campaign of the first viable black candidate to run for president is playing the race card. It didn't matter if the candidate himself was playing both sides of the racial aisle, utilizing "you've been hoodwinked, bamboozled," straight from Malcolm X, while having his campaign team corner the Clintons on an issue they'd worked their lives to tackle. The Clinton history of race relations would go up in a puff of smoke from a fax machine that delivered the bombshell to every media outlet and political operative they could find.

One heading in the Obama memo read: "Martin Luther King/Lyndon Johnson comparison: Clinton, Criticizing Obama For Promising 'False Hope,' Said That While MLK Jr. Spoke On Behalf Of Civil Rights, President Lyndon Johnson Was The One Who Got Legislation Passed." Another part of the memo invoked JFK's assassination: "Clinton Introducer Said JFK Gave Hope, But Was Assassinated." Yet another alleged that former President Bill Clinton had "implied Hillary Clinton Is Stronger Than Nelson Mandela," which appeared under the heading "NELSON MANDELA," in all capital letters.

When media outlets pressed for comment about the South Carolina memo, which Sam Stein broke wide on Huffington Post, the Obama campaign didn't respond. The South Carolina stink bomb would waft over the primary season until the gag-effect wore off. It was another Karl Rove moment for David Axelrod and company.

None of this is mentioned in David Plouffe's book, otherwise known as *The Audacity of Marketing Myth*.

When Obama won the South Carolina primaries, former President Bill Clinton teed one up for Plouffe and Axelrod.

"Jesse Jackson won South Carolina in '84 and '88. Jackson ran a good campaign. And Obama ran a good campaign here. He's run a good campaign everywhere. He's a good candidate with a good organization."

The whole quote above was rarely used, but instead was truncated to make the most out of the negative aspects of it, while leaving off the due Clinton gave to Obama, which was earned, no doubt. But to see Barack Obama was not to think Jesse Jackson, not even close. It's also not a graceful way to lose. The Obama blogs went nuts.

Blogging for ABC News under the headline, "Obama is Just Like Jesse Jackson" Mark Mooney characterized it like this: "Boy, I can't understand why anyone would think the Clintons are running a race-baiting campaign to paint Obama as 'the black candidate.'"

Many following the primaries at this point, including myself, heard the quote from Bill Clinton and thought, What the hell is he talking about? Obama wins South Carolina, and President Clinton brings up Jesse Jackson? It seemed like the mother of all non sequiturs. Because what does Jesse Jackson have to do with Barack Obama? They certainly are not remotely similar politicians. It defied logic when Bill Clinton said it, with Obama supporters and the media damning Clinton for what they deduced as belittling Obama's political prowess. Hillary Clinton felt forced to apologize: "You know, I am sorry if anyone was offended," she said, according to the Associated Press. "It was certainly not meant in any way to be offensive."

After it was all over, Bill Clinton felt compelled to state "I am not a racist" in an interview with Kate Snow, working at the time for ABC News. But how could anyone think Bill Clinton was a racist? There was absolutely nothing in his long political career or as president that even remotely hinted at such a thing. Where was the media in reporting this fact? Even Mark Mooney used "race-baiting – black candidate" suggestions, with it happily parroted throughout traditional and new media and across cable, except on *Morning Joe*.

Bill Clinton's history was established long before the 2008 primaries. The former president's flashes of anger and untimely rebuttals revealed a man infuriated at the rewriting of his own history. It's why he openly states that Rep. Jim Clyburn "used to be" a "longtime friend." Mr. Clyburn one of the people stepping in to help Obama's South Carolina strategy, which was to dismantle the attachment former President Clinton had with African Americans. Clyburn said President Clinton had "severely damaged" his reputation with blacks, to which Bill Clinton replied to Kate Snow, "Yeah, that may be. By the time he got through working on it, that was probably true."

In a January 29, 2008, *Washington Post* opinion piece called "Cards from a Worn-Out Deck," Eugene Robinson helped out by trying to concoct a reason the Clintons would use the race card:

"And the reasons to send that message would be to devalue an Obama victory in South Carolina; to inoculate the Clinton campaign against potential losses next Tuesday in Georgia, Alabama and Tennessee — Southern states with large African American populations; and, most important, to pigeonhole Obama as 'a black candidate' as opposed to a candidate who, among other characteristics, is black. That would help Hillary Clinton in other states, because the more prominent race becomes in this campaign, the more likely it is that she will win the nomination. They don't call us a 'minority' for nothing."

But as historian Sean Wilentz proved in his writings, none of Mr. Robinson's or anyone else's words on the subject proved how Hillary would gain from such a scurrilous attack of race-baiting against Obama. There is no way she'd come out on top.

Robinson's logic that Hillary's team was worried about Georgia, Alabama and Tennessee, so they'd stupidly played the race card to inoculate their candidate, is outright laughable to anyone knowing politics of the South, which Robinson certainly does. He was saying Hillary used the Southern strategy to bring out the bubbas, even if the bubbas already hated Hillary.

In fact, it was John Edwards and Mudcat Saunders who did what was being suggested. Only they went for a two-fer, also invoking Clinton, implying bubba won't vote black *or* female and only Edwards can beat the "Jesse Helms political machine." According to Edwards, only he knows "what you have to do to win in battleground states, and to win in tough, tough congressional districts," he told NBC's *Meet the Press*, "and what you have to do to put out your message that works in those kind of places." Ah yes, *those kinds of places.* Nobody said a word; well, I did, but no one cared. Besides, talk radio had long ago made Hillary toxic in Southern states.

It was no coincidence that on Super Tuesday 2008, Eugene Robinson wrote another *Post* opinion piece, "The Baggage Hillary Bears," which included this memorable passage: "When you Google the phrase 'unconstitutional third term,' you get references to a rogue's gallery of strongman leaders — Vladimir Putin, Alberto Fujimori, Olusegun Obasanjo, Islam Karimov, Hugo Chávez — who in recent years at least have flirted with the idea of holding on to power beyond statutory limits. Now the name Bill Clinton pops up, too."

There's Vladimir Putin, Hugo Chávez, then there's Bill Clinton? Christ. It might be outlandishly unfair to Hillary, but who gives a shit, right? It was stunning stuff to read from Eugene

Robinson, who actually won the Pulitzer Prize for this type of 2008 campaign-writing.

Another quote highlighted in Obama's infamous South Carolina memo was when Hillary Clinton made the statement about Martin Luther King and President Lyndon Johnson: "Dr. King's dream began to be realized when President Lyndon Johnson passed the Civil Rights Act of 1964. It took a president to get it done."

Historian Doris Kearns Goodwin said Hillary's statement "was absolutely right," even as privately it caused Senator Ted Kennedy to blow a gasket.

Rep. Clyburn, the highest-ranking African American in Congress and a legend in Southern Democratic politics, took umbrage publicly over the clumsy comment by Clinton, using the moment to tease that it might push him to endorse Obama. "We have to be very, very careful about how we speak about that era in American politics," Clyburn warned.

Even the *New York Times* editorial page got into the act, suggesting that Hillary's statement actually implied that "a black man needed the help of a white man to effect change." It was a rhetorical leap of Olympian heights.

It did not go unnoticed by Jonathan Martin of Politico: "There's no question that there's politics here at work too.... It helps [Obama's] campaign to... push these issues into the fore in a place like South Carolina."

Sean Wilentz summarized the tactic in the *New Republic*, February 27, 2008:

> The Clinton campaign, in fact, has not racialized the campaign, and never had any reason to do so. Rather the Obama campaign and its supporters, well-prepared to play the "race-baiter card" before the primaries began, launched it with a vengeance when Obama ran into dire straits after his losses in New Hampshire and Nevada — and thereby created a campaign myth that has turned into an incontrovertible truth among political pundits, reporters, and various Obama supporters. This development is the latest sad commentary on the malign power of the press, hyping its own favorites and tearing down those it dislikes, to create pseudo-scandals of the sort that hounded Al Gore during the 2000 campaign.

Jesse Jackson simply called the charges that Obama's South Carolina strategy was nothing less than swift-boating of Bill Clinton "more gotcha politics."

Politics ain't beanbag, the saying goes. That's right. Just don't try to sell everyone you represent a "different kind of politics" when you're as down and dirty as anyone — betting, *knowing*, that in the atmosphere of 2008, no one will have the nerve to accuse a brilliant African American politician of playing the race card in a historic primary season against a woman whose name is Hillary Rodham Clinton.

It was inconceivable that a person who'd spent her formative years working for minority rights would be accused of racism. That wasn't to say her surrogates didn't say stupid things, which included Bill Shaheen's off-the-campaign-reservation inferences about Obama's marijuana and cocaine use when he was young, of which most of us in certain generations couldn't care less. But that race-baiting or anything close was actually an orchestrated campaign directed by Hillary or encouraged by the people in her campaign was just plain nuts, because it would have been deadly to her. With people like me hearing most of what was being funneled to the press, if someone had tried this shit I not only wouldn't have touched it with a ten-foot pole; I would have reported it by blasting it across the web on every site that would have taken the submission.

It was likewise when New School president Bob Kerrey endorsed Hillary Clinton, which was really astounding, given Kerrey's antipathy toward her husband, once calling him an "unusually good liar." But the endorsement was clumsily delivered and horribly framed, so much so that political writer Marc Ambinder rightly judged Kerrey guilty of paraleipsis.

"I like the fact that his name is Barack Hussein Obama, and that his father was a Muslim and that his paternal grandmother is a Muslim," Kerrey is quoted as saying. "There's a billion people on the planet that are Muslims, and I think that experience is a big deal."

I didn't touch this quote. Jake Tapper asked why Kerrey endorsed Clinton in this manner. The better question was who in the Clinton campaign would be so stupid as to advise a statement like that, and why didn't someone throw him to the press?

Kerrey's support of Clinton inspired Chris Matthews to push his *Hardball* guests on the matter. Chris Cillizza wouldn't bite, so over it went to Chrystia Freeland, global editor at large of Reuters since 2010.

MATTHEWS: These lines look like they're being fed — well, let me find some outrage here. Can I get some from Chrystia? I'm not getting any from [Chris Cillizza]. Chrystia, do you — aren't you appalled at the willingness of these people to become castratos in the eunuch chorus here or whatever they are? What do you call them? I don't know what they are. What do you think of these people?

Castratos in the eunuch chorus. Again with Matthews' castrating bitch theme. The saga was never-ending. Freeland smartly wouldn't touch it, but rightly wondered the effectiveness of lines like Kerrey's.

Like her husband's, Hillary Rodham Clinton's history on race had never been questioned before, because her work on civil rights went way back, which was recounted in *Living History*, Hillary's autobiography.

The late Rep. Stephanie Tubbs Jones, a Clinton surrogate and an African American, defended the Clintons: "To say that there is a pattern of racist comments coming out of the Hillary campaign is ridiculous," she told Politico's Ben Smith. "All of the world knows the commitment of President Clinton and Senator Clinton to civil rights issues — and not only the commitment in terms of words but in terms of deeds."

Craig Crawford on *Morning Joe* in late January 2008 went even further.

> You know, I have sat down here in Florida for the last month. And I have watched the coverage, and I really think the evidence-free bias against the Clintons in the media borders on mental illness.... I mean, we've gotten into a situation where if you try to be fair to the Clintons, if you try to be objective, if you try to say, "Well, where's the evidence of racism in the Clinton campaign?" you're accused of being a naïve shill for the Clintons. I mean, I think if somebody came out today and said that Bill Clinton — if the town-drunk in Columbia [South Carolina] came out and said, "Bill Clinton last night was poisoning

the drinking water in Obama precincts," the media would say, "Ah, there goes Clinton again. You can't trust him." I really think it's a problem.

In March 2010, after being an analyst for MSNBC, Crawford finally cut his ties, then unloaded on Chris Matthews in an email exchange with Steve Krakauer of the Mediaite blog, which was founded by Dan Abrams:

"I haven't felt like a good fit for MSNBC since the presidential campaign, and the hard turn toward point-of-view programming. No particular event brought this on, just my desire to try other outlets and have more fun. As far as Chris is concerned, on *Morning Joe* after the West Virginia primary, he accused me of always defending Clinton and what he claimed to be her racially motivated campaigning. That's the problem. Trying to be fair became seen as bias in the new thinking over there. But I do wish my many pals at MSNBC nothing but good things."

What Crawford called "evidence-free bias against the Clintons in the media [that] borders on mental illness," applied to many people during the 2008 primaries, even those you'd least expect. Harold Meyerson, now an op-ed writer for the *Washington Post* and someone I knew only in passing from my time at the *LA Weekly*, wrote a post that was pulled, re-edited, caveats offered, with another post put in its place on the *American Prospect* blog, Tapped, entitled "Hillary Plays the Race Card." The original post began like this:

> I was visiting a friend in Los Angeles this morning when what can only be described as a Clinton Dirty Trick intruded upon us. My friend, I should say, is a notable political figure in L.A. who lives in a very upscale neighborhood — one in which few African Americans reside — and is a Clinton supporter (he greeted me holding a Hillary lawn sign). We were sitting in his kitchen when the phone rang. He answered it and looked startled. On the line, he said the moment he hung up, was a high-decibel gentleman with a very exaggerated, old style — *Amos 'n Andy*, in fact — black pattern of speech, singing the praises of Barack Obama.... And if this call was what it seemed to be, it looks like the Clinton campaign, or that of one of the groups campaigning on her

behalf, is playing the race card discreetly — and despicably.

A phone call during a heated primary contest is automatically assumed to be from the Clinton camp? *No* evidence. *No* proof. Just a racist phone call against Obama, which a seasoned reporter from a very respected, leading progressive site not only automatically assumed is Hillary playing the race card, but the man writes his rank speculation in detail without investigating whether it actually was from the Clinton campaign or not. However, Mr. Meyerson didn't stop there. He wrote a second post titled "The Race Card, Part 2," but only after the first post, "Hillary Plays the Race Card," had been completely scrubbed from the *American Prospect* website. Mr. Meyerson went on to admit he could not "empirically verify" the call came from anyone backing Clinton, but his own knowledge of L.A. elections pushed him to "believe" it came from that corner. He was wildly wrong.

Now, we all make mistakes. I've made doozies. But blaming Hillary Clinton without proof was a knee-jerk media reaction in '08, especially among loyalists doing the Obama campaign's bidding, which included progressive, pro-Obama blogs, with posts written by males who were all too willing to take a shot at Hillary whenever they could, evidence not required.

The Clinton campaign immediately denied any involvement whatsoever in the call, didn't bother to mention Meyerson by name, dismissing where it was posted because this stuff was happening regularly, putting the following on one of Hillary's campaign websites: "False Smear Against Clinton Campaign — There are accusations on a blog attributing an offensive phone call to the Clinton campaign. This is an outrageous and baseless allegation and is completely false."

The Obama campaign even used the opportunity of a blaring Drudge headline over a picture showing Obama in a ritual Somali costume to walk out talking points for the right-wing. David Plouffe, now a White House senior advisor, was eager to label this "the most shameful, offensive fear-mongering we've seen from either party in this election" and "part of a disturbing pattern." It took most people about two mouse clicks to find photos of leaders in all sorts of traditional costuming from other countries, including one of Hillary Clinton and Chelsea with the late Benazir Bhutto of Pakistan. But

David Plouffe wanted to make sure to take advantage of the long narrative the Obama team had built over months, helped along by baseless chatter that the Clinton campaign had distributed the photo, which was finally traced to a right-wing site.

Surrogate blowback during the 2008 primaries was nothing new for the Clinton campaign, but the JFK-assassination association from someone introducing Hillary was another pain-in-the-ass interruption that Clinton's team had to disavow immediately.

> Today, in Dover, Francine Torge, a former John Edwards supporter, said this while introducing Mrs. Clinton: "Some people compare one of the other candidates to John F. Kennedy. But he was assassinated. And Lyndon Baines Johnson was the one who actually" passed the civil rights legislation.... Phil Singer, a Clinton spokesman said: "We were not aware that this person was going to make those comments and disapprove of them completely. They were totally inappropriate."
>
> — *New York Times*, January 7, 2008

Close to the end of the primaries, Rachel Maddow got sucked into the negative narrative on Clinton, saying Hillary was readying "all-out, scorched-earth war" toward Barack Obama regarding the Michigan and Florida challenges. Maddow added to the Hillary-intends-to-steal-the-nomination hysteria, after an MSNBC appearance, in a post at now-defunct Air America titled, "Democratic Party Political Suicide Watch." An excerpt:

> Do you see where this is going? If there is an open, unresolved procedural issue involving the Florida and Michigan delegations, Senator Clinton will be able to cite that as her justification for staying in the race until the convention even though she is not ahead in the nomination contest at the end of the primary calendar. If she can ensure that the Florida and Michigan issue stays unresolved until the convention (and by appealing it every step of the way, I don't see how that can be avoided), then Clinton stays in the race until the convention. Staying in until the convention buys her three more months of campaign time, three more months to make her case to the party and the country, three more months for some potential political unfortunateness to befall Senator Obama.

Oh, for fuck's sake. In this fight up to my eyeballs at the time, I couldn't believe anyone was making such an outlandish suggestion. Is there anything in Hillary's life to date that reveals a reckless nature? It was not only implausible, but laughable. Hillary's fans pilloried me for this analysis, but anyone who had studied Hillary's commitment to Democratic ideals and policy prescriptions knew what Maddow was pushing was pure political fiction.

Few analysts understood what rooted many of Hillary supporters to her, people who weren't in the least ready for her to quit the fight, which was one of the reasons she waited until Obama had the numbers required to secure the nomination. Even at the convention there was still drama from some over whether she would release her delegates, which was never in doubt and people who knew Hillary's politics understood this. Some of Hillary's supporters wouldn't let go and wanted her to take their fan-politics passion to the convention floor. This would never happen. When it became clear during the primaries that the math just wasn't there, and I began writing about it, I was flamed and denounced. Getting out was Hillary's call and if she hadn't done what she did the way she did it, the Democratic Party would very likely have had a real problem on its hands, instead of the concocted scenario the media stoked.

Matt Taibbi wrote "Hillary's Bitter Victory: How the Democratic Campaign Turned into an Absurd and Acrimonious Culture War" in May 2010. It captured why Hillary wouldn't back down.

> See, we can laugh all we want, but they won't ... back ... down! THEY WON'T! BACK! DOWWWWWWWN!
>
> Somewhere in there is where you can find the emotional imperative underneath this campaign, and the reason why all the electoral math in the world doesn't mean shit to these people. Hillary calls them the "invisible Americans." There are a hell of a lot of them, and their anger is real.

There certainly were a lot of them and the fury was indeed *very* real. In fact, some hadn't let go of their grievances against me by the time the 2010 midterms approached, with one female posting on my Facebook page that I'd been "vilifying the Clintons" after I'd "originally stood with" them. It was pure fact-free fiction brought to you by fan-politics obsession.

For women competing in the male marketplace, especially in national politics, one of legendary organizer Saul Alinsky's rules rings loudest: Make the enemy live up to their own book of rules. Hillary's Wellesley College senior honors thesis was on Alinsky. Though the competition need not be "the enemy," sometimes it ends up that way, especially when the media isn't holding your competition to the same standard, which in the primaries of 2008 was certainly the case.

Clinton endured a decade of training, hazing and indoctrination of "shrill," "polarizing," "bitch," "inauthentic," etc., before "war-mongering" entered the picture.

When *Time* magazine published its two covers of Clinton, then Obama, the titles said it all. Hillary's was published on August 28, 2006: "Love Her. Hate Her. [check one] The Presidential Ambitions of Hillary Clinton." Obama's was published on October 23, 2008: "Why Obama Could Be The Next President. — Plus: An Exclusive Excerpt from the Senator's Book."

One thing Plouffe got right about the long election season: Time was a friend to the Obama campaign. As time went by, team Obama was able to make its case, with Hillary's campaign strategy falling apart the further we got into the primary season. That's because Mr. Plouffe's strategy was genius and it was executed nearly flawlessly. The only rub was Hillary's maturation as a candidate, growing into a formidable force, which even her adversaries recognized; while Barack Obama, when face to face with blue collar workers, looked like a candidate without a clue how to connect. Once she became the underdog, Hillary didn't have anything to lose. Her campaigning style became freer, stronger and more tenacious. A stunning transformation from where she began, sitting on a comfy couch in Chappaqua.

During the 2008 primaries the Obama campaign claimed it was the mean old Clintons who were doing all the dirty campaigning. Nice narrative that worked well for the newcomer against the Clinton machine, when in truth he was the establishment's choice that came with their backing, with the media acting as the Obama campaign's megaphone, a sweet gift.

Now fast-forward to the first term of President Obama's administration. With a Democratic majority in both houses when he began, Barack Obama found leadership a different ballgame. Candidate Obama called for "fundamental change." Everyone who had voted for Barack Obama, including me, starving for a new direction from the Bush-Cheney years and you didn't have to be a liberal to feel that way. By April, 2011, President Obama's approval was at 41% according to Gallup, tying his low, which was beat in early August in a Daily Gallup registering 40%. After compromise and capitulation time and again, on health care, on Gitmo, on secrecy and rendition, on military tribunals, extending the Bush tax cuts and starting another war in the Middle East, President Obama found the activist base and the "professional left" holding its collective nose as it readied for Obama's reelection campaign to begin.

In the spring of 2011, a Washington Examiner op-ed was entitled: "Mean Streak: Obama Is Not as Nice as He Looks." Oh, really, who knew? Flash back to this beauty from 2008 by Mayhill Fowler, who was at the Huffington Post at the time; it's part of a transcript of an April 2008 fundraiser in San Francisco, with Barack Obama speaking:

"But the truth is, is that, our challenge is to get people persuaded that we can make progress when there's not evidence of that in their daily lives. You go into some of these small towns in Pennsylvania, and like a lot of small towns in the Midwest, the jobs have been gone now for twenty-five years and nothing's replaced them. And they fell through the Clinton administration, and the Bush administration, and each successive administration has said that somehow these communities are gonna regenerate and they have not. So it's not surprising then that they get bitter, they cling to guns or religion or antipathy to people who aren't like them or anti-immigrant sentiment or anti-trade sentiment as a way to explain their frustrations."

Candidate Obama promised "fundamental change" and a "new kind of politics," while slamming Hillary as "Bush lite," then as president, candidate Obama was rarely seen until he began running for reelection.

As far as the people out there still "clinging to their guns and religion," in April 2011, Public Policy Polling released results showing President Obama was beginning with the same problems in Pennsylvania he suffered during the '08 primaries when Hillary cleaned his clock, with 42% of Pennsylvanians approving, 52% disapproving.

From Public Policy Polling on April 12, 2011: "...Numbers suggest that a lot of the voters who fueled Hillary Clinton's primary victory in the state and then sucked it up and voted for Obama in the general election the last time around haven't been real thrilled with what they've seen from him so far and could split their tickets next year — if the Republicans put up someone who's seen as a reasonable alternative."

Obama turned this around against McCain, so he can do it again, though now he's got his first term as a record, with his inability to sell a strong economic vision a real issue.

However, most voters don't begin to tune in until October before any general election, even if the rest of us are obsessed with the horse race, with a real unknown being whether Republicans can serve up someone who isn't batshit crazy. The good news for them is that Obama is weaker than he was in '08, but as of September 2011, President Obama still had an approval rating of 79% among liberal Democrats, 70% among moderate Democrats and 64% among those identifying as conservative Democrats, even if the most activist elements of the Democratic base, the die-hard, progressives, are demoralized. When people are faced with a dreadful Republican alternative, Democrats usually "come home" to vote for Democrats, though party affiliation continues to fracture. In close elections settled on the margins, the lack of political party loyalty and growing strength of independent voters makes things a lot more complicated, as does the spreading discontent with the two-party-only options.

Hillary Rodham Clinton's presidential run unleashed eighteen million voters, including a lot of feminist men, and a wave of relief, along with belief that a woman could actually crack the toughest glass ceiling. With Clinton's move to the State Department, the post-Hillary political era arrived, even if many of her supporters dream of a 2016 run that picks up where Fighting Hillary left off in 2008.

In the void left after Hillary's run for president the yearning for what might have been remains, with the energy around her candidacy morphing into something else as people continue to watch her as secretary of state.

By April 2011, Secretary Clinton's approval was at 66%, according to Gallup, whose records go back to 1993 when she came in as first lady, her highest since 1998 when it was 67%, at the height of her husband's impeachment.

Women who rise in her wake owe a debt of gratitude to the woman who came the closest to competing for the most prestigious political prize on earth, but had the toughest battles to wage amid a climb no other woman has successfully made.

Chapter 8: **The Hillary Effect**

When the Republicans picked the first woman ever to run on their national ticket, Sarah Palin, the Hillary Effect manifested in history, a journey which began the moment First Lady Hillary Rodham Clinton made her speech in Beijing, but whose impact was cemented once she lost the Democratic nomination.

As Gloria Steinem said to Charlie Rose, Hillary "changed the molecules."

The Hillary Effect gained ground when Clinton began to re-establish herself as a democratic diplomatic force through her appointment as President Obama's secretary of state, which vaulted her into a position as international stateswoman, above the political dog- and catfights for the first time in her life. Her absence in the political landscape left an incredible void in the domestic landscape after a presidential battle that proved a woman could win, with people wanting to see more from females who were making the case they could lead.

It solidified in January 2010 when twenty-five female ambassadors from around the world — the highest number ever — were representing their countries in Washington, D.C., out of 182 "accredited ambassadors" altogether. Only five women represented countries in the late 1990s. The *Washington Post*, in a January 11, 2010, article citing "the Hillary Effect" for the five-fold increase, interviewed Amelia Matos Sumbana, ambassador from Mozambique, who told the *Post* that "Hillary Clinton is so visible" as secretary of state, "she makes it easier for presidents to pick a woman for Washington."

In October 2011, three formidable female activists, Liberian President Ellen Johnson Sirleaf, Liberian peace activist Leymah Gbowee, and Tawakkul Karman of Yemen won the Nobel Peace Prize. These women stand on their own courage and their own actions leading to the changes still evolving in their countries. They certainly didn't need Secretary Clinton to tell them their own passions and purpose. However, as the *New York Times* reported October 7, 2011, when Thorbjorn Jagland, the former Norwegian prime minister who heads the Nobel committee, awarded the prize, this is part of what he said: "We cannot achieve democracy and lasting peace in the world unless women obtain the same opportunities as men to influence developments at all levels of society."

This is the Hillary Effect.

It is Hillary Rodham Clinton who has tirelessly trumpeted what women's contributions mean to their countries and to anyone wanting stability in still-developing, often troubled regions. From the same *New York Times* article mentioned above: "Most of the recipients in the award's 110-year history have been men and Friday's decision seemed designed to give impetus to the cause for women's rights around the world." By the Nobel committee acknowledging these women's efforts at changing their corners of the world, Hillary Rodham Clinton's chief intent in her work, going back to when she was first lady, was manifest.

The Hillary Effect is certainly seen through parts of President Obama's Afghanistan policy, which implements "women's rights are human rights" as a fundamental tenet of U.S. foreign policy, and is historic.

> I have consistently raised with all levels of the Afghan Government, with everyone else from the EU to ISAF and the UN, the absolute necessity of our standing firmly together in our demands that women not be marginalized in the process of reintegration and reconciliation. I have pushed hard for women to have, literally, seats at the table in the Loya Jirga and the London conference and the Kabul conference, et cetera.

— Secretary Clinton, Kabul Afghanistan, July 22, 2010

We saw the Hillary Effect when President Obama attacked Libya, her muscular, behind-the-scenes diplomacy part of how the Arab League and other nations joined in on the effort to condemn, then launch, the no-fly zone, along with efforts that helped oust Moammar Gadhafi.

The Hillary Effect was felt when President Obama appointed Melanne Verveer as the first-ever ambassador-at-large for global women's issues in U.S. history, to work with Secretary Clinton, elevating women higher in U.S. foreign policy prerogatives, with Hillary applying "human rights are women's rights" as a foundational tenet of the U.S. State Department.

The Hillary Effect for Clinton at the State Department has also proved important. Take when we all watched the reaction to Hillary when she gets into the fire on her trips overseas. When she bristled in Africa at a question she was asked about her husband's opinion, replying, "My husband is not the Secretary of State, I am."

This happened before *Washington Post* political reporter Anne Kornblut released her 2010 book, *Notes from the Cracked Ceiling*, her comments below, from a 2009 transcript from ABC's *This Week*:

> But these incidents are kind of bigger than that. It's sort of the perfect encapsulation of the burden of being Hillary Clinton. That you are seen in relation to your husband wherever you go, not just by the media, but by the world and asked questions about him.
>
> And it reminded me a lot of the campaign, when she was seen in relation to him and having to respond and trying to be her own person....
>
> Some people, when this whole incident happened said to me, "You know, she looks kind of like a first lady on this trip. She's out there. She's been gone for eleven days, seven countries. She's away from the center of action here."
>
> So I expect we may see some shorter trips from her, ones where she's not going to get as tired when she's on the road. But at the end of the day, I think her — again the underlining sentiment is one that certainly the White House and she defend that she had the right to say that.
>
> — Anne Kornblut on ABC's *This Week*, August 16, 2009

Hillary goes to the far ends of the African continent to visit areas where human rights are not yet women's rights, because of the violence against them, including a culture of rape. But instead of being hailed, she's diminished for looking first-ladylike but also tired for her grueling journey, though in the same breath Kornblut supports her having the right to say what she did.

Anne Kornblut's part in helping create the negative national narrative on the Clintons in the first place, belittling Hillary and the "burden" of being, well, Hillary, makes this section of her book particularly interesting. *Notes from a Cracked Ceiling* came with advice for female candidates, some of it below:

- Don't take women — especially young women — for granted.

- Prepare your family.
- Expect them to hate you because you're beautiful.
- Speak softly and carry a big statistic.
- Beat breast cancer? You may beat your opponent.... Once an awkward, taboo subject, breast cancer has become as familiar in politics as in the rest of society.... It is, some strategists believe, the equivalent of a man's war wound.
- Seize the moral high ground.

— Anne Kornblut, *Notes from the Cracked Ceiling*, 2010

Some of these are just silly, but the truth about the first one above is that women don't vote for women because they're women. Sisters are tough on each other. We sense what it takes to do the job and we expect a woman running for office to be able to explain herself as well as any man who made it, but we also expect her to do it differently. We want her to be a cut above, including on issues. Women also want women to lead like women — not how women think men would lead if they were women — and to sound like women while doing it.

Oh, and you really can't prepare your family, with even the Clintons having trouble. It's just too cruel and backbreaking a grind, so they'll never get it without living through it, which former President Bill Clinton proved as spouse in chief of Hillary, the presidential candidate.

As for the magic formula for winning, it includes timing, the "it" factor and whether you can come across on camera and in media, and a little bit of luck.

But Kornblut does get down to it eventually. The "share of women in office in the United States is smaller than in more than seventy countries in the world, from Cuba to Rwanda to Norway," she writes.

As to *why* women aren't poised to break through to the presidency as has already happened around the world, it's difficult to peg, but it began with our John Wayne – Phyllis Schlafly, B-movie corn culture, which ramped up in the Reagan years as a reaction to the 1960s and feminism, with the rest of us left with a hangover we're still trying to shake off.

But there is a sign of serious progress in what Kornblut wrote in her book. There was a time when Hillary would have had to be defensive about standing up for herself like she did in Africa. However, as even Kornblut admitted, Hillary had the right to say what she said and the White House backed her up.

Voilà, another Hillary Effect moment.

That's not close to how Hillary was treated in the '90s or during the '08 campaign. In defending herself, she did what any man would do and finally, at long last, got a pass from a good many, though there will always be those who criticize, saying "Clinton loses cool," etc., especially on the right. But there were also those who used to whack her giving her some grace, including Ms. Kornblut, and even Chris Matthews who, just to remind, after 2010 Ladies' Night said of Hillary's presidential run, "It could well be that her strong showing is what's inspired these other women to test their mettle in the ring this year." The Hillary Effect made manifest in the media among the most unlikely of suspects.

Secretary Clinton being asked what her president husband thought about something doesn't cut it, no matter where the question comes from or how it's meant. No woman having achieved what Hillary has, should be asked to defer to her husband. So, Hillary becomes a beneficiary of her own groundbreaking work and campaign that moved us all forward, with Kornblut finally giving her some space at a moment that was asking the professional diplomat to acquiesce to her globetrotting, "President of the World" husband.

From a column she did on the WowOWow website in January 2010:

> When I went back after the campaign was over, however, and read through all the transcripts, columns and stump speeches, interviewing dozens of campaign aides who advised the candidates and prominent women who watched the race from the sidelines, there was just too much evidence pointing to the influence gender had on the race to pretend that it had been otherwise. Clinton was often reluctant to talk about being a woman, and worked so hard to compensate for the perceived shortcoming of being female that she came off looking, to many, too tough. "She didn't get there on her own," was a refrain I

heard repeatedly, which although factually true failed to take into account the fact that she had, just a decade earlier, been criticized for not being enough of a housewife. Here she was taking heat for being too much of one.

Ms. Kornblut recognized what was obvious to people looking in, certainly to Hillary's die-hard supporters, as well as to fair minded individuals who saw it for themselves, including myself. The mind numbing cleavage-alert signaled media coverage that treated a woman differently from a man, simply because of who she was. That over sixteen years in public life and being hounded from one side, then the other and back again, Hillary had put together a presidential campaign that blew all doubts away that the woman was judged by a different standard, simply because she was a woman. The verdict catching people off guard on their own culpability, since they either denied what was happening or stood by silently as it did, even defending those who did it or giving a platform for others to weigh in on Hillary in a way that never happened to any man.

Ms. Kornblut reviewed the facts herself, coming to the obvious assessment that is unmistakable: "There was just too much evidence pointing to the influence gender had on the race to pretend that it had been otherwise."

As for what all this talk means for Hillary Rodham Clinton, she's come into stateswoman status and is utilizing her power at the State Department in dramatic fashion, with the 2008 election filed away until she's ready to write her side, though let's hope it's not one of those mindless and carefully censored tomes for posterity.

The post-Hillary political era comes with uplifting, sobering and even colliding dynamics that make up the Hillary Effect. Some don't believe it exists, but the rise of the consciousness of everyone to what Hillary endured, as well as what she accomplished, but also where she fell short, has opened people's eyes. Even people who once vilified Hillary are finally seeing her power and her place in political history, which isn't quite complete as far as her most ardent fans are concerned. You don't know what you've got until it's gone, though good riddance can be said to the sexism and misogyny we saw in 2008, the likes of which we'll never see again. Though we're not talking about the phenomenon of derogatory sexist language disappearing, because there will always be the lazy or disrespectful who prefer a cheap shot, but also those who believe women aren't equal.

However, utilizing sexist invective to damage a woman's reputation or career has lost its power and potency, because people are now wiser to look at the messenger first and judge what it says about him or her before allowing the smear to ruin a woman's potential. The influence that sexism and misogyny had to ruin a woman's potential at power, a force that's been around long before feminism hit, has finally petered out in politics, as long as the woman on the receiving end fights back.

It coincided with Clinton's run and a new generation of women who just don't see sexism as a problem, or fealty to feminism and a first female president their goal, with sisterhood, if it ever existed, a thing of the twentieth century. Many younger women laugh sexism off, rarely have to fight it, but will never see it as the impediment Clinton's generation had to endure. That's a great thing. However, unlike what the new generation of women face in their lives, the political landscape in this country isn't so enlightened. There's a reason the U.S. lags behind in female leadership, while countries like Liberia have already elected a female president. Our Jack Bauer culture, religious conservatism in politics, and the wide impact of our male-dominated media are impediments, as is the imbalance of males to females on the national political scene, no matter the role.

Hillary Rodham Clinton's life and rise to become the first female in history to win a presidential primary was the most visible and teachable moment for women in politics we've had in modern history. It was ugly, exhausting, triumphant, but ultimately disappointing, because she fell short of the Democratic nomination. However, the fight was unquestionably groundbreaking.

Susan Faludi writing in the *New York Times*, "The Fight Stuff," May 2008:

> If anyone has been guarding the rules this election, it's been the press, which has been primly thumbing the pages of Queensberry and scolding [Clinton] for being "ruthless" and "nasty," a "brawler" who fights "dirty."
>
> But while the commentators have been tut-tutting, Senator Clinton has been converting white males, assuring

them that she's come into their tavern not to smash the bottles, but to join the brawl.

Deep in the American grain, particularly in the grain of white male working-class voters, that is the more trusted archetype. Whether Senator Clinton's pugilism has elevated the current race for the nomination is debatable. But the strategy has certainly remade the political world for future female politicians, who may now cast off the assumption that when the going gets tough, the tough girl will resort to unilateral rectitude. When a woman does ascend through the glass ceiling into the White House, it will be, in part, because of the race of 2008, when Hillary Clinton broke through the glass floor and got down with the boys.

The Hillary Effect is so new to some that it's also causing confusion. Within a two-month period, the *Los Angeles Times* printed three separate articles that ran the spectrum on the possibilities for women, covering all the editorial bases. On June 10, 2010: "The Year of the Conservative Woman?" By July 24, the question mark turned pessimistic in, "For GOP Women, 2010 May Not Be Their Year." A month later, the *Times* went with "Women in Washington, Your Seats Are at Risk." Lisa Mascaro reporting:

"Women now hold ninety seats in Congress: Sixty-nine are Democrats and twenty-one are Republicans. After the November election, Congress could end up with as many as ten fewer female members, prognosticators now say, the first backslide in the uninterrupted march of women to Washington since 1978."

The reality is that as women make executive political moves to compete with men, they will also be subject to the same forces that male candidates face, which obviously can dwindle their numbers. Democrats faced a tough fight in 2010, so it makes sense women's seats would be on the block, too. Equanimity has its risks, but at least women are competing, with conservative females finally seriously in the game.

When the fight got tough for Democrats during the 2010 midterm, stories started popping up to counter the popular perception of 2010 as the "year of the woman." Hotline On Call's Reid Wilson, as well as Jamie Shufflebarger, and *The Atlantic's* Chris Good, all chimed in. *USA Today's* Susan Page went further, talking about how the year of the woman was actually a downer year. Her proof? Because there were a lot of femme Dems taking incoming from Republicans in a tough midterm year and some of them were going to lose, thus lowering the number of women in Congress.

"Overall," Page wrote in October 2010, "forty-seven Republican and ninety-one Democratic women are on the ballot for the House, along with six Republicans and nine Democratic women for the Senate. Both totals set records.... Many of the women who aren't incumbents are running in districts so dominated by the other party that they are all but certain to lose."

It was as if competitiveness in politics was all about invigorating the vagina vote, which we found out all too well never existed and really shouldn't. At the same time Ms. Page proved something else that actually bolstered why 2010 was indeed the year of the woman. Regardless of facing tough reality, women candidates set records in 2010. South Carolina's Nikki Haley, Oklahoma's Mary Fallin and New Mexico's Susana Martinez are the first female governors of their states, all conservatives elected in 2010.

Sarah Palin, the anti-Hillary, wasn't a fluke. Her selection happened because of the long shadow Hillary's candidacy cast and because McCain was hoping to capture disaffected Hillary voters from her historic presidential run and loss. Instead he launched a political phenomenon. No female in conservative politics has ever taken hold of the imagination of the right like Sarah Palin, or created a midterm juggernaut, multimillion-supporter base and media platform from Facebook to Fox News to the TLC/Discovery channel, her *Alaska* series taking a page from Reagan's playbook. Through it all, Palin's "new conservative feminist" contrivance is more an opportunistic gambit to exploit the Hillary Effect than it is an honest mining of it.

As Gloria Steinem told Katie Couric, in a June 2010 CBS interview, "We're free to call ourselves whatever we wish, but I think [Sarah Palin] calling herself a feminist has mostly to do with how many votes Hillary Clinton got in the presidential race."

Sarah Palin has taken what she started with and maximized it. Even after a humiliating national debut and being called a "quitter" when she *quit* her job as governor, and regardless of the 2010 Republican wins stoked by Palin and the Tea Party, however unaffiliated, all of these accomplishments still aren't seen by some as monumental on their face. Name a person of either party who ran against the party establishment and had such an impact as Sarah Palin had in 2010. You can't, because no other woman has led a revolt inside the conservative party and taken on the elite like Sarah Palin, let alone successfully, which has led to the Republican establishment being forced to embrace the Tea Party or fail. It's no way predictive of what will happen in the future for Palin, whose present revolves around her Fox News Channel contract and trying to stay relevant after announcing she won't run in 2012. We'll see if Sarah Palin can still pull in crowds and if her loyal fan base stays with her as she moves to help the Republicans beat Obama.

It took the Hillary Effect from 2008, after Clinton was defeated for the nomination, to even get the Republicans to join the twentieth century and nominate their first woman on the national ticket. Sarah Palin then took the power she was handed and ran with it, tripping, but getting up and regrouping, without any help from the men at GOP central — you could even say in spite of the establishment.

Sarah Palin began her national political career by admitting that Hillary Rodham Clinton got "more concentrated criticism" during the primary season. Then from the other side of her mouth she simultaneously argued that Hillary "does herself a disservice to even mention it."

> But when I hear a statement like that coming from a women [sic] candidate with any kind of perceived whine about that excess criticism or a sharper microscope put on her, I think, man, that doesn't do us any good. Women in politics, women in general wanting to progress this country, I don't think it bodes well for her, a statement like that. Because, again, fair or not fair it is there. I think it's reality and it's a given, people just accept that she's going to be under a sharper microscope. So be it. Work harder, prove to yourself to an even greater degree that you're capable, that you're going to be the best candidate. That's what she wants us to believe at this point. So it bothers me a little bit to hear her bring that attention to herself on that level.

> — Sarah Palin Q&A, by Karen Breslau, *Newsweek*,
> August 28, 2008

What Palin missed in this initial interview early on in her national exposure was that it's not about a "sharper microscope." It's about all the things I've written here, including that Hillary's ambition was seen for a woman far differently than Obama's ambition; her bare knuckle campaigning seen critically, while Obama's similar fighting was ignored; that standards for Hillary were not equally applied to Obama. Treating Hillary differently because she was a woman, because she was *Hillary*, while condemning her when she presented herself as equal to any man, which got her depicted as a "nutcracker" in airports across the country and much worse on the web, no matter the political party. That was the sexist double standard, misogyny in America.

By July 2009, after enduring withering national scrutiny that included unforced errors on her part, Sarah Palin was backtracking on her earlier critique of Clinton at warp speed.

> *TIME*: At one point during the campaign you said Hillary Clinton whines a little bit too much about being in the public eye. Do you now sort of sympathize with her? PALIN: What I said was, it doesn't do her or anybody else any good to whine about the criticism. And that's why I'm trying to make it clear that the criticism, I invite that. But freedom of speech and that invitation to constructively criticize a public servant is a lot different than the allowance to lie, to continually falsely accuse a public servant when they have proven over and over again that they have not done what the accuser is saying they did. It doesn't cost them a dime to continue to accuse. That's a whole different situation. But that's why when I talk about the political potshots that I take or my family takes, we can handle that. I can handle that. I expect it. But there has to be opportunity provided for truth to get out there, and truth isn't getting out there when the political game that's being played right now is going to continue, and it is. When you realize that it doesn't cost them a dime and it's a fun sport for some, you know it's going to continue. I love Alaska too much to put her through this in a lame-duck session.

> — Sarah Palin Q&A, by Jay Newton-Small, *Time*, July 8, 2009

When it happened to Hillary, it was whining, but when it happened to Sarah, it was "there has to be opportunity provided for truth to get out there."

Uh-huh, got that?

Eleanor Roosevelt said it a hell of a lot better than Sarah. Women in politics "have to grow skin as thick as a rhinoceros." Watching Hillary's fight for the nomination proved that much and more, with Palin not knowing what she didn't know, so she couldn't admit that her premature judgment of Hillary *whining* came from a place of naïveté.

Try walking a mile in Hillary's heels.

We've come a long way since Eleanor Roosevelt said, "It is certain that women do not want a woman for president, nor would they have the slightest confidence in her ability to fulfill the functions of that office. Every woman who fails in a public position confirms this, but every woman who succeeds creates confidence."

The Hillary Effect that came after 2008 proved that in the century after Eleanor Roosevelt women (*and* men) do want a female president, that we do have confidence she can do the job, and that even through Clinton's failing we are confident the time is near. Even after Palin's train wreck of a vice presidential run, while watching the woman of the 2012 primary season, Michele Bachmann, give back-to-back poised performances that helped her win the Ames straw poll, we all know we've gotten a step closer to the goal of an American female president.

The dynamic finish to Hillary's nomination bid left people on a high that opened the door for McCain to choose Palin over all others he'd been considering in the hope that Palin could offer the pizzazz to compete with Barack Obama's unprecedented popularity in the summer of '08. But the notion that Palin would bring in disaffected Hillary supporters was not only unlikely, but absurd on its merits. Hillary supporters were issue-centric, not gender-driven, so serving up a woman to get their vote was never going to be enough.

No matter where you stand on Sarah Palin, even with Bachmann's rise, she's remained the fairest queen on the right, which is why she once had a shot at the nomination, though her poll numbers reveal she simply can't beat Obama. But getting the GOP nomination would still have been a historic milestone, a first for the United States and both political parties. But in the spring of 2011 she was faced with a new obstacle, her "Darryl Strawberry-like playing career," according to John Podhoretz, who was among those on the right proclaiming her political career dead.

Palin remains like no other conservative female and made political history by doing it faster than anyone of her party, age and résumé. She is the only politician to quit a governorship, then go on to not only be a queen-maker but the life of a conservative movement inside the national Republican Party, a woman with her own political wing. So, whoever is the 2012 nominee will still need her Tea Party faction's nod. Sarah Palin's natural marketing gifts have elevated Republicans out of the pasty white male party faze and into a historic moment for Republicans, including Bachmann's candidacy, because they've been fifty years behind Democrats on empowering women, though considering Palin's and Bachmann's stance on issues, the right still doesn't have women's vital interests at heart.

Palin's politics and her foreign policy thinking are the same as George W. Bush's, and her domestic prescriptions, well, who knows? Her laughable Sunday show appearance with Chris Wallace in August 2010, when they both chuckled about the notes she had written on her palm was an embarrassment. Who can imagine Hillary, Liz Cheney or Nikki Haley going on a Sunday show using such antics? Michele Bachmann would never try such a stunt. Hillary would have been laughed out of politics. However, it's this persona that provides the other side of the political coin for Republicans, including the Tea Party wing, which has all the energy, a fact that alarms establishment conservatives, who have no juice on their own. "Mama grizzlies" — yet another Hillary Effect — cuts both ways too. The Tea Party will be a formidable force among the base that helps choose the next Republican nominee, but their views will run into a brick wall when independents are factored in come the general election, especially among the majority of voters who believe the government has no business in a woman's life.

Sarah hides her views in speechifying sound bites and never elaborates, forever refusing interviews outside the Fox cocoon after her Couric catastrophe. A wonk she is not. But contrary to her critics, Sarah is anything but "stupid" or a "moron," the customary smears used to demean her.

Sarah Palin even took a page from Obama's "different kind of politics" playbook in July 2010, because it's one hell of a marketing campaign, when the NAACP called the Tea Party racist, which pissed Palin off. She turned her response to them into a Facebook post and tweet, saying, "It's Time to Bury the Divisive Politics of the Past." Never mind that her "divisive politics of the past" shot came just weeks before she railed that President Obama didn't have "cojones" on immigration and hasn't stopped since.

Sarah's "drill, baby, drill," with Reaganism deregulation her guide for business, has been catnip to conservatives. It's not just anyone who can get ten thousand people to Searchlight, Nevada. It was also Sarah Palin who beat Obama and the Democrats on health care messaging in 2009, when she wrote on Facebook, no less, about the "death panel," igniting the Tea Party and giving political discontent a place to land, even if the actual roots of this group began in the Bush budget-busting era with Rep. Ron Paul. It took Obama to ignite them, then close to six months for him to get the momentum back from Sarah's "death panel" push, and even then he gave it to Rep. Bart Stupak, whose views on abortion are similar to Sarah Palin's.

This would never have happened under Hillary, someone who has fought for decades for women's individual freedoms. Now, the "ideological battles that we fought during the '90s that were really extensions of battles we fought since the '60s" wing of the Democratic Party has handed over our advances to people who quickly began reversing progress that women over five decades have fought to win. They've taken the Hyde Amendment from a budget item to health care law and given the right a victory without the Republicans lifting a finger.

Sarah Palin also inspired a reinvented Michele Bachmann, who went from frumpy back-bencher to front line "mama grizzly" fighter, complete with a makeover that had her looking like a new woman, as she became a presidential contender, even getting a mention in the September 2011 *Vogue*. In 2011, a *Rolling Stone* article that reported Bachmann spending $4,700 in the weeks since she'd announced her candidacy on hair and makeup went all out to accuse her of basically betraying economic conservatism. A post on the Feministing blog let fly:

> Remember Palin Sexism Watch and Hillary Sexism Watch
> during the last presidential election?

I guess it's time for the Bachmann version. *Mother Jones* of all places wrote yesterday about Michele Bachmann's hair and makeup bill....

Calling out Bachmann, still one of very few women ever with a shot at being a viable presidential candidate, in an increasingly visual culture, for her stylist bill is just tired sexism. And it really sucks when I'm joining Fox News in pointing this out."

— Posted by JOS, Feministing, July 27, 2011

Bachman raised a lot of cash for fellow conservatives in the midterms and has the advantage of being a formidable femme force for Tea Party conservatives inside the party, while Sarah does her work on the outside. Bachmann's leadership ambitions were first revealed when after the midterms she challenged the House boys club for Republican Conference chairmanship, which went nowhere. She then went on to get a primetime Tea Party Express response on CNN after President Obama's 2011 State of the Union speech, which pissed everyone off no matter their politics, especially Rep. Paul Ryan whom she upstaged while besting the right's media diva, Sarah Palin. The problem was her performance revealed very poor advance work, which showed her looking at the wrong camera when her time to shine rolled.

Watching Hillary included watching her fail, and by 2010, women and a lot of men realized what had been lost, especially as conservative women continued to rise. This isn't an aspersion on President Obama's win, because he fought hard and dirty and won. But by the 2010 midterms, President Obama's leadership represented all compromise and conservatism, no audacity to be found. After living with the puny Democratic messaging coming from President Obama in his first two years, there was an even greater sense we'd lost the first real moment to make our own history. The appetite among Hillary's progressive, independent and conservative supporters to see Hillary in the White House only heightened when President Obama didn't deliver Democratic change, but compromised to manifest a capitulation to conservatism.

As far as American groups sticking with their own, women didn't stand by Hillary, but African Americans rallied 'round Obama and continue to. The difference helped elect a president. It's still an exciting outcome for this country, but women remain waiting. It's why Sarah Palin's "mama grizzlies" began such a phenomenon, which is joined by Michele Bachmann's fans, something that isn't matched on the left, though the targeting of female freedoms, as well as Planned Parenthood, certainly should be enough to rile women up.

As I write this, there isn't a national Democratic female to take Clinton's place, though one of her strongest supporters, Debbie Wasserman Schultz, was appointed by President Obama to chair of the DNC with the job of helping him get reelected, which means reaching out to women, a group who split their vote with Republicans in the 2010 midterms.

Where's the left's Sarah Palin? And before you launch your bitch-wit at me, I'm not talking about a media wunderkind without policy prowess of her own making. I'm talking about a woman who is as tough as any man and as smart on policy, but who has a woman's heart and compassion that comes across in her own language. But I'd settle for a Fighting Hillary clone, circa the Pennsylvania primary 2008.

The most exciting female star, Elizabeth Warren, is challenging Scott Brown in Massachusetts for Senate. The brain-power behind the Consumer Financial Protection Bureau, Ms. Warren had warned of the coming mortgage crisis in 2007, with the attention she had garnered freaking out Tim Geithner so thoroughly, as recounted by Ron Suskind in *Confidence Men*, that Geithner reportedly concocted an "Elizabeth Warren strategy" to keep her from heading the agency that was her brainchild.

Once President Obama refused to put the full weight of his office behind Warren, she had two choices: remain a public voice for the people outside Congress, or run for elected office where she might be able to represent the people directly, which would give her renewed clout that counted. But no matter how promising she seems, Warren is yet untested, with it too soon to tell if she can weather the terrain of electoral politics to get her voice heard beyond the screaming.

Senator Kirsten Gillibrand now holds the Senate seat Hillary had. It looks like she's learned a lot from Hillary, especially when it comes to helping other females get elected. When Kathy Hochul was running in a special election in a Republican stronghold in upper New York, it was Gillibrand who came out to fight and help Hochul win. What made the difference? Hochul ran against the Republican Paul Ryan plan to privatize Medicare, and she won, with a lot of help from Kirsten Gillibrand.

"Like Bella Abzug and Shirley Chisolm, she doesn't hold her finger to the wind. She is the wind," Gloria Steinem said about Senator Gillibrand.

Senator Gillibrand put together a campaign aimed at getting women off the sidelines, which New York public radio station WNYC reported about on its website on July 7, 2011:

> "I want to try to help get more women engaged so that their voices can be better heard in electoral politics," Gillibrand explained last month. "I believe that enough women aren't off the sidelines fight[ing] for the things they care about. And it's not just about reproductive health and about women's rights. It's about every issue women care about."
>
> She readily admits there's room to lead here, where the momentum of Democratic women's groups has sputtered.
>
> "We have to take responsibility as a generation to do something about this, because the women's movement is stalled. They are not moving forward," Gillibrand said on MSNBC in May. "We are literally fighting the same battles as our mothers and our grandmothers. And if we don't wake up and we don't start engaging, we will not like what we find."

There has never been a better time for women to get involved. Senator Gillibrand launched a site to help do just that: www.offthesidelines.org.

"We are in an interesting, critical time, in crisis, but it's also a huge opportunity to engage and educate women that their voices have to be heard, if they stand up, get off the sidelines, whether by voting, running for office, [it's] time for women of all generations to get involved in politics," said Stephanie Schriock, president of Emily's List, in the same WNYC report.

The void created by Hillary's historic presidential run, as well as the effect of seeing Hillary come so close, came at a time when Sarah made her own history, however disastrous it ended and even if her future clout is now in question. The post-Hillary political era has been filled by an avalanche of women, the latest to make conservative history being Michele Bachmann, the first Republican female to win a straw poll, caucus or primary in American history.

Two career Clinton smear merchants finally awakened after Hillary lost and with Sarah Palin's rise. Andrew Sullivan, perpetual Hillary-hater and Palin conspiracy theorist, at least understands Palin's power and has led the charge against her. Unfortunately, as with many on the left, the unhinged nature of his attacks makes people defend Palin or turn away; the issue analysis goes missing since he doesn't find Palin worthy. Hillary-hater Chris Matthews gets what's possible for Sarah, too, with Matthews not beginning to say the things about Sarah he said about Hillary, but maybe it's got something to do with what turns him on.

> "This isn't just another electoral cycle 'mom' constituency," [Mary] Matalin said. "These moms are bringing their parents, husbands and children along...."
>
> Matalin, the longtime GOP strategist, said she was uncertain if Palin's Mama Grizzly image and recent foray into policy was enough to vault her to the presidency. "I don't think she's there," said Matalin, who has offered some advice to Palin. "But every time this conversation takes place she has advanced the ball in her favor."
>
> — Politico, July 8, 2010

No one could have been more of an underdog than Sarah Palin when she took to the podium at the Republican National Convention in the fall of 2008. She delivered the speech of her life, then promptly proceeded to make a fool of herself. It was bad enough Hillary lost, but now the second woman to make history, this time on the Republican national ticket, was tripping her way from stage to stage.

Then after the election season was over, Clinton now secretary of state, it didn't take Sarah long before she'd shucked the governor's office and ensconced herself as the head of the Tea Party. Rebecca Mansour, a top Palin aide, was quoted in *Vanity Fair*'s October 2010 issue saying, "We would literally walk across hot broken glass for this woman.... She's our family, and you protect your family; it's like the mafia." Wow! Not just broken glass, but "literally... hot broken glass," certainly a new devotional standard for fan politics. But considering the article also talks about Mrs. Palin demanding, "I want my straws! I want 'em bent!" one has to wonder what the hell else is required to be in Palin World. Notwithstanding the bendy straw demands, and remembering Hillary's legendary *and fictional* "lamp-throwing Delilah" tirade, one should be careful about what one chooses to believe about powerful women who make people nervous.

Michele Bachmann hasn't made Hillary's mistake of running a general election campaign in the primaries. The reality is she simply hasn't got one. Her way to do it was by beating the boys on the ground in Iowa, pulling in evangelicals, then taking on the men by staying on message about jobs and economics, hoping everyone will simply ignore that she has no record on these issues. Bachmann's also bringing conservative women into her campaign movement, taking a page from Palin, even if she's not convincing anyone outside her own choir she's ready to lead. Unfortunately, Rick Perry derailed her hopes, so that by the time September 2011 came, her former campaign manager went on CNN to pontificate the impossibility of a Bachmann victory.

"The Perry-Romney race is now the story, with us the third candidate," Ed Rollins said on CNN.

After the debate at the Reagan Presidential Library, this fact was incontrovertible, but then Herman Cain happened.

In mid-March 2011, a *Washington Post*/ABC News poll showed catastrophic numbers for Sarah, with "a new high" of 37% of Republican and independent-leaning Republicans having a negative view of her. In another first, less than 50% of Republican-leaning independents (47%) have a favorable view of her.

For the first time in *Post*/ABC News polling, fewer than six in ten Republicans and GOP-leaning independents see Palin in a favorable light, down from a stratospheric 88% in the days after the 2008 Republican National Convention and 70% as recently as October 2010.

Long after the Republican post mortem of 2008, no one could have imagined John McCain would fall into such desperate straits that he'd need Sarah Palin to campaign for his re-election. It doesn't matter that Palin can't reach independents, because McCain was having problems with his own yet again. So the fact that she talks to the conservative choir is all McCain needed.

Kathleen Parker, a columnist for the *Washington Post*, delivered the first and most deftly placed evisceration of Palin when she was on McCain's ticket, way back on September 28, 2008:

"If BS were currency, Palin could bail out Wall Street herself. If Palin were a man, we'd all be guffawing, just as we do every time Joe Biden tickles the back of his throat with his toes. But because she's a woman — and the first ever on a Republican presidential ticket — we are reluctant to say what is painfully true."

A Democrat pulling Sarah's stunts would be an instant laughingstock.

Called the Republican Party's bullshit artist by a leading conservative woman, Palin remained the brightest conservative star in the klieg lights, with everyone taking potshots at her, while forgetting the fact that she's still standing and making waves. It proves how volatile the conservative movement is today, while foreshadowing the maneuvering ahead between the Republican establishment and Tea Party conservatives that helped them take back the House.

By August 2011, a Fox News poll no less showed 71% of registered Republicans didn't want Palin to run for president. Among Tea Partiers, 66% didn't want her to run for president, with another conservative favorite, Rick Perry, making his play for the nomination, starting out by tripping his way from one debate to another.

On Labor Day weekend 2011, in a speech in Iowa, Palin revived a theme that was foundational to her rise in Alaska. Invoking "crony capitalism" in a speech that took on Republicans, too, and had her fans hoping for a presidential announcement, Palin touched a nerve that hits home to everyone, regardless of party affiliation. Saying that when candidates raise "mammoth amounts of cash... we need to ask them, too, 'What if anything do their donors expect in return for their investments?'"

This led Laura Ingraham, subbing for Bill O'Reilly, talking with her guest Ann Coulter, to challenge Palin to "fish or cut bait here." Red State's Erick Erickson simply said "enough is enough," everyone tiring of Palin's political tease act.

So, Sarah Palin made the only choice she had, announcing on Mark Levin's October 5, 2011, radio program that she was bowing out of the 2012 presidential contest. The clout she'd amassed during the 2010 midterm season was long gone. There was simply no way for her to win. It's also hard to be considered presidential when you have the power-king of the Republican Party and Fox News Channel Roger Ailes saying, "I hired Sarah Palin because she was hot and got ratings."

An Eleanor Roosevelt image does not come to mind.

But it's always good when the patriarchal power brokers on the right are honest about their feelings about women, our value and how seriously they take us — as if the blonde brigade on Fox News Channel didn't send that message already.

The end of Sarah-for-2012 began after the Tucson tragedy. Not listening to Roger Ailes is not only a cardinal Republican sin, but stupid considering his success rate with Republicans. Her subsequent video message addressing Loughner and the Tucson shootings proved that even if Sarah has the fan base, she doesn't have the judgment for the serious times of today.

But you can never take the Tea Party queen's 2010 crown away.

Sarah Palin was instrumental in the right's Tea Party army, giving them cachet and clout from the moment her "death panel" squeal went up. From there it was a short hike to "mama grizzly"-world and super-celebrity on the way to her million-dollar spokesperson career. Now she's fielding calls from GOP wannabes who want the Sarah Palin seal of approval.

The what-ifs abound. What if she'd been the one to hire Ed Rollins right after the 2010 November midterms, instead of Michele Bachmann, deciding to dig in and do as much due diligence as possible to gear up for a presidential run? What if Sarah had decided it was time to go back to her roots in Alaska, when she was taking down Republican insiders and exposing their dirty deeds?

The Sarah Palin who started out taking on "crony capitalism" might even have joined the Occupy Wall Street protesters, representing the right, making common cause where she actually once would have had one. If any moment is an opportunity for *all* Americans to join together it's these protests.

Sarah Palin is not the first person to be seduced by bright lights and the big league, ignoring what got her into politics in the first place. She won't be the last.

No matter what I write and know, there are many Hillary supporters who still await her run in 2012. Supporters who want her to take Peggy Noonan and Sally Quinn's advice to challenge President Obama. Recycling the scorched earth, '08 Democratic convention nonsense into an Obama primary challenge fantasy, which would only help the right and tarnish what Hillary's achieved, never mind that there isn't a chance in hell Hillary Rodham Clinton would ever play a part in damaging the Democratic Party brand. However, the Hillary Effect has hit conservative women too, though in their case, they simply see her as a tool.

Take, for example, Peggy Noonan, who in the midterms of the conservatives' discontent, started opining that Hillary should prepare to rise again now, that she was needed. From her June 18, 2010 *Wall Street Journal* column entitled "A Snakebit President":

"But it's also true that among Democrats — and others — when the talk turns to the presidency it turns more and more to Hillary Clinton. 'We may have made a mistake. She would have been better.' Sooner or later the secretary of state is going to come under fairly consistent pressure to begin to consider 2012. A hunch: She won't really want to. Because she has enjoyed being loyal. She didn't only prove to others she could be loyal, a team player. She proved it to herself. And it has only added to her luster."

This is pure fantasy, because Hillary Clinton would never play spoiler, though that's not to say President Obama hasn't earned a challenge. There is also what Secretary Clinton has said herself, stating emphatically when asked by NBC's Ann Curry in October, 2009:

CURRY: I can't help but think nine months into this administration, having campaigned so fiercely to be president yourself, that there can't be moments for you where you wish you could make the decisions yourself.

SECRETARY CLINTON: I have to tell you it never crosses my mind.

CURRY: Never?

SECRETARY CLINTON: No, not at all. I am part of the team that makes the decisions.

CURRY: Will you ever run for president again?

SECRETARY CLINTON: (Laughter.) No. No, I mean, this is a great job. It is a 24/7 job, and I'm looking forward to retirement at some point.

Of course, Noonan's real job was to put the proper stink on President Obama by declaring, "He's starting to look unlucky, like Jimmy Carter." What Noonan is fantasizing is that Hillary will play Ted Kennedy, resurrecting 1980, in 2012, which is a non-starter.

The other message Noonan is sending with "we may have made a mistake," is to sow more discontent. Though Ms. Noonan certainly remembers Republicans like retired Gen. Colin Powell, who also came out for Obama. Even with Hillary's rising stature, people like Ms. Noonan have another agenda if praise is dripping off their lips for Clinton. Noonan remembers 1980 all too well.

Even champion Hillary-hater Sally Quinn got into the act. Never one to miss an opportunity — President Obama's difficulties and his sinking status with independents, not to mention the disgruntlement of movement progressives — Quinn perhaps saw an opening to get herself out and back up to the *Washington Post* op-ed page. Her June 2010, *Post* piece went the full 180, not only to endorse Hillary for vice president, but beginning her Clinton-in-2016 campaign, too, which is the only time Quinn has ever hit a right note on Hillary in her writing career.

> Clinton is also young enough to be the Democratic nominee at the end of an Obama second term; she will be in her late '60s in 2016, but still younger than Ronald Reagan was when he was inaugurated in 1981 (just shy of 70) and younger than John McCain, who was 72 when he ran in 2008. Most important, were she vice president and Obama were for some reason not able to fulfill his term, she would be ready to step in....
>
> Another scenario is that Obama could wait and choose Hillary as his running mate for 2012 and then have her step down as secretary of state so she could start campaigning. The catch with that plan, however, is that it would make Biden a lame duck and Obama would

probably have to appoint an interim secretary of state.
Take it seriously.

Take Sally Quinn seriously when she's trumpeting Clinton's praises? *Ha.* It's all about what's good for Sally, which always means getting attention, which Hillary got for her by the mere mention of a 2016 run.

We've come a long way from when the youngest and first female press secretary, Dee Dee Myers, was appointed by President Bill Clinton. She didn't have it easy back in the '90s, because Washington has always been a boys' club. In a February 2008 *Time* magazine interview with Ms. Myers, Lisa Takeuchi Cullen recognized the unfairness in a question to Myers:

"You were appointed the country's first female White House press secretary. Yet you were stiffed when it came to proper pay, authority and even the press secretary's rightful office. When you went to argue for a raise, [then-chief-of-staff] Leon Panetta told you you didn't deserve what a male colleague of lower rank made because you weren't a man supporting a family. Would that have happened if a woman was your boss?"

Democrats standing up against conservatives who were against the Lilly Ledbetter Fair Pay Act have put women equal with men on pay. When comparing Democrats and Republicans on policy, it's another point against the vagina vote where Republicans are concerned. They don't support women's equality from the start. At least with Democrats, women have a chance, because they wait until they're elected to use our issues as a trump card.

Clinton has had time at State to also decompress from the political-arena fighting and backbiting, with her status and favorable numbers rising as a global stateswoman. She left the political scene in 2008 a heroine, fighting her heart out, so she's got many reasons to be satisfied with her historic place in U.S. politics. Dee Dee Myers in another part of that *Time* magazine interview, reminds us all what it took:

"I think what I've been struck by in this campaign is that it's still more difficult for women to be taken seriously. Hillary has had to prove she was tough enough to be commander in chief. That's one reason her campaign made her thirty years of experience its foundation. Then again, if you're too tough, then people think you're too hard, you're not feminine enough. The B-word comes up. It's a whole other set of obstacles. There's still a double standard.... I hope we will have a conversation, looking back, on how it in some ways exposed obstacles. Maybe we thought we were further along. You can still say some things about women that are pretty shocking, and there's no penalty for saying it."

The Hillary Effect also impacted the media, which is still playing out. The misogyny on cable is likely to be called out faster and harder, and to receive a quicker backlash, because the lightning rod, or heroine, Hillary Clinton, and her candidacy exposed the depths to which men would stoop to keep her down. As for the right, their Rush Limbaugh talking points are centered in another century, as is his medium. The far right never sees sexism and misogyny, because they're centered in patriarchal fundamentalism that reconfirms their insecurity that men were meant to rule women.

America and the world need a lot more "bitch is the new black," and a lot less twentieth century subservient expectations.

Next time simply won't be anything like the last. Nobody will feel about the next female contender like the usual suspects felt about Hillary and who she was, the time she represented, and the politics out of the '60s and the '90s that stuck to her in good ways and in bad, the worst of both concocted by her adversaries. Hillary Clinton's presidential candidacy was the first and last of its kind and the next woman will be accepted differently on different standards, with different coverage, coming in with a different background. However, it will still be a fight.

Even Clinton has benefited from the Hillary Effect with her perpetual haters now even making nice about her. They like her, they really like her, as long as she's at State. She's made history there, not only because of her continuing the call she began in 1995 — human rights are women's rights — but because of what she unleashed in the Congo as well as in other countries that look at female leaders differently, and also because she's invigorated the importance of diplomacy and soft power being an important partner with U.S. might, which took an almost-fatal blow during the Bush-Cheney era, even if the Pentagon still always wins.

The fight to elect Hillary president ended up manifesting an integral shift in American politics where sexism and misogyny are concerned. People are now unafraid to call it out. Hillary made a difference and moved everything forward. It now makes it much harder for sexism to be delivered unchecked like it was against her without outrage pouring forth from women and men, unless the female target simply says nothing. Because of Hillary's rising tide at the end of the primaries, in the post-Hillary political era things are different. This is another Hillary Effect to add to Clinton's résumé, with the most exciting chapters yet to be written. That says something on its own.

As for the fight over feminism, it's over and we all won. Women can do anything a man can. A woman can stand up against a man to be commander in chief and be just as viable, even if we haven't learned to channel our own language and policy prescriptions, instead of the militaristic macho cadence they use to *show* toughness. That will come.

It's also hard to rock the cradle and run the world if your husband won't help or even play second fiddle so you can conduct the orchestra. Women have their hands full with children, when that act alone often precludes rising in politics. Sacrifices can be made, including not having children, but then if you don't have a husband and family you're judged politically unfit, not a real woman, or rumored to be gay, which contrary to fundamentalist notions, isn't a curse, but in national politics is seen as an albatross. That, too, is shifting, depending on where you live.

Look at what happened to Supreme Court Justice Elena Kagan when she was nominated. Politico ran a story entitled, "Elena Kagan's Friends: She's Not Gay," with quotes abounding on "friends of Elena Kagan," who all attested to her heterosexuality. The Obama administration rushing out to assuage the public and Republican senators that Ms. Kagan, who is single, wasn't a lesbian — God forbid — because we all know what a mess those dykes can make of our courts. The entire conversation was embarrassing, including those who demanded that she come forward and confess, telepathically sensing she was holding back for fear of being hurt if she declared it true. The whole sorry spectacle was made complete when Kagan was pictured on the front page of the *Wall Street Journal* in a softball stance that would impress any athlete. Hint: if she's playing softball... well, you know... she's batting for the Other Team.

Whatever happened to the so-what defense? In all of the noise, the most important conversation was whiffed, an opportunity missed by the Obama White House to simply say: You think Elena Kagan is gay? We have no idea. But so what if she is?

If it weren't for movement progressives, that much-maligned group of activists who were instrumental in fighting against the corporatization of health care against President Obama and the massive health insurance complex, a battle they lost, things would be even worse. They fought for strengthening financial regulation, saving Social Security, Medicare and Medicaid, which most believe could be changed after 2012, including by President Obama, to name just a couple of policy fights they waged for progressive reform. These same progressive movement activists were also instrumental in working for justice on don't ask, don't tell, on behalf of soldiers serving and dying for our country at a time when President Obama was incomprehensible on the subject.

Two years after Barack Obama was elected, the Obama coalition shattered with 56% of independents and 59% of seniors voting for Republican House candidates, according to exit-poll results cited by *the Washington Post*. Women stunned the Dems by tilting slightly Republican, a study by the nonpartisan group Project Vote showed. The vote gave the Republicans and the Tea Party-right control of the House with the biggest victory since Harry Truman; unified control — meaning both houses — of twenty-six state legislatures; power in Wisconsin, Ohio, Pennsylvania, Florida and beyond, which extended Republican strength from the industrial Midwest and through the old confederacy.

Hillary came a long way from where the 2008 primaries began, with her image, prestige and power stronger in the post-Hillary political era than ever before. Being secretary of state has made even her harshest critics soften on her. That she's long past needing their approval goes without saying. But there can be no doubt she's enjoying her prowess, which out of the political food-fights is a much more placid road, even if her job at State is grueling.

It's not fair to Clinton, but the talk of "buyer's remorse" has risen in President Obama's third year, with Hillary 2016 percolating, because of the state of the economy at home, but mainly because Obama's answers to problems haven't cut it, with his political message missing beat after beat. It's also because the legend of candidate Obama never was going to match the mere political mortal. Reality seldom cooperates with marketing. Now Hillary Clinton's positives are soaring, and President Obama's challenges and missteps have caused his to sink. There's plenty of opportunity for that to change, however, because the voting populace is fickle, and Republicans could end up revealing their political ugly through a hard right nominee.

The Hillary Effect is unique where President Obama is concerned. In the wake of her loss and move to State, he's been left to prove himself as president as opposed to candidate Obama, with no one to blame but himself for the difference in what he marketed versus what he delivered. His reaction to the 2010 midterms gave the distinct impression that he thought the presidency wouldn't be about actually having to promote Democratic policies and being judged on what he was actually delivering, as opposed to a perpetual campaign and adulation from fans.

Hillary's not there to beat up politically anymore either, with media stories dramatically shifting from where they were during the campaign, as is the country's mood. Stories about the Clintons' popularity abounded before the 2010 midterms, while many Democratic candidates openly walked away from President Obama in their campaigns. The white working-class exodus in 2010 proved electorally dangerous for Democrats, with women tilting Republican for the first time since 1982.

What a difference two years make.

Now it's President Obama and his team, not Hillary, continually taking the media to the White House woodshed for delivering harsh critiques on the president and his administration; there's been much administration hand-wringing about the left not giving him enough credit, or expecting "ideological purity." It seemed unbelievable that in the second year of Obama's presidency he was complaining about the media. As the midterm verdict proved, most Americans just don't think President Obama knows what the hell he's doing. He's got time to change minds, which with his talent, helped along by the Republican batshit crazy that has been on parade during the primary GOP debate season, is more than doable.

Hillary has now graduated to the Al Gore echelon of politics, only in a category all by herself. Her presidential loss washed away her perceived sins, but it also forgave her enemy status that the right hung onto for close to two decades.

Nobody in traditional or new-media circles, or the Clinton camp for that matter, ever considered that the impact of Hillary's losing presidential campaign would be so nationally altering of the gender dynamic in politics. And after the right wing creatively caricatured Hillary Clinton for sixteen years, the same stereotyping many on both sides of the aisle utilized in 2008, it's a great irony that even in her defeat, Hillary has succeeded in changing the political game.

Through Clinton's candidacy, women broke a barrier and blasted a hole through the ultimate glass ceiling with eighteen million cracks that allowed the Hillary Effect to squeeze through. It came because she was at the exact moment, time and place to make it happen and because the time had come for women to arrive. It was one historic election, Hillary Rodham Clinton being the first woman to have a real shot at the nomination, which has coincided with many other women breaking out as well. Now that women have seen a champion that looks like them vanquished, even if she finally rose at the end to take a higher place than when she started, the stage is set for her successor.

There isn't a woman I talk to or hear from who doesn't want a female president *now*. Both parties should be looking for that candidate, because the one who drafts the best one first will win.

The Hillary Effect makes it easier for women coming after her. They simply couldn't have it any harder. None will have been in the limelight as long or as high, or have a husband as powerful politically. All will have come after a time when misogyny and sexism had one target, Hillary, with everyone loading up and letting loose.

But don't get too comfortable, because we've still got a long, long way to go.

Women are still marginalized in areas where we should be leading. According to Businessweek's Barbara Kellerman in June 2010: "Three percent of Fortune 500 companies were headed by women as of 2009; 15% of members of Fortune 500 boards were women as of 2009; 6% of the one hundred top information-technology companies had female chief executives in 2007; 16.8%

of seats in the U.S. Congress are held by women; 14.5% of 249 mayors of U.S. cities with populations over one hundred thousand are women; 21% of nonprofits with budgets of more than $25 million are headed by women; 5% of generals in the U.S. Army were women as of 2008; 8% of admirals in the U.S. Navy were women as of 2009; 19% of senior faculty at the Harvard Business School are women in the 2009-2010 academic year."

And we still haven't elected a female president. Hillary Rodham Clinton's candidacy taught us why.

It's why Tina Fey's "bitch is the new black" resonated and loving Betty White is so easy. Women will not be victimized by the bitch syndrome anymore, because the caricature before Fey intoned it and after Hillary Rodham Clinton was victimized by it no longer reigns. As the saying goes, you say "bitch" like it's a bad thing. It took Tina Fey to help Hillary and her supporters embrace it, because being tough and getting shit done is what women do and we all know it. But as Hillary also proved in New Hampshire, we do these things because it matters and we're passionate about it. Hiding competence, toughness and intelligence is just too twentieth century, though Sarah Palin's popularity and babe factor prove that being great-looking can be utilized too. Sex appeal matters in national politics, and in the era of celebrity, it can even defy the importance of policy prowess at any given moment.

Hillary ran the gauntlet of first lady wonk, delving into policy, and ended up with baggage for her efforts. In the Senate, she was first thought not to have the right stuff, but she kept her head down, worked harder than anyone else and gained respect. Her battle for the Democratic nomination lit the final fires of our political gender wars, with the media stoking the flames that eventually burned themselves out in the primaries. Fighting Hillary stood up, a different woman from where Inevitable Hillary began, because humiliating losses, stumbles, climbs and victories over your accusers change a person, and if we're lucky, a generation of women and eventually a nation.

After Hillary's concession speech where she invoked eighteen million cracks, it was over. The battle that had the accomplished, seasoned, wonky woman place second had left its mark on everyone fortunate enough to see it happen.

When the next woman rises, we'll remember Hillary's run and know that the Hillary Effect will render the next woman's battle less bruising. By virtue of not being Hillary it almost has to be — that is, of course, unless it's former Secretary of State Hillary Clinton who walks into the room, greeted by cheers, because they've been earned on her own. The first failure has been digested. It was no fault of her performance, though the destiny of her loss came through her generation and its language that paved the way for another. The baggage was built around her that no presidential campaign could crack, especially when that baggage is built up by the self-righteous right and sucked up by the self-loathing Democratic elite, then regurgitated by mostly men in the media who have already picked a side.

Looking back to 2008 from today, when it was all done, the most emotional moment for me came when I was standing inside the Democratic National Convention in Denver after an interview I'd done in the sky-booth that Al Jazeera shared with NBC. Looking down from the rafters, I watched as Hillary Rodham Clinton walked out to give her speech. The auditorium erupted, with the sound ricocheting off the ceiling above. "Hillary" signs were everywhere, the applause deafening and never-ending. There had been so many emotional moments during the campaign season, including during the convention, but hearing Hillary that night was something I'll never forget. After "thirty-five years in the trenches," Hillary reminded everyone, it would be one last, big campaign, then it would all be over. It was thrilling to hear her give the most important speech of the campaign season after her flawless concession speech. A woman who had come into her own after a grueling presidential campaign, learning lessons on how to find your own voice, reveal your heart, and give it all you've got until there was no more left to give.

We'd come so close to electing our first female president, but missed our chance for so many reasons, yet knowing there was definitely going to be a next time and it would be easier. But I couldn't help thinking it could never be like this again.

Hillary Rodham Clinton would make a great president. Watching her as Secretary of State proves that beyond a doubt. That's the happy ending to Hillary's history-making political story as currently written.

As for the American odyssey in securing the presidency for a woman, I can't name a potential viable female candidate today who will stand up for a woman's individual freedoms and the working class, and who talks like a woman on national security, instead of like a man would talk if he were a woman. A woman who is qualified to be president beyond Hillary, but I know she's out there. Who knows when she'll surface? I'll be ready when she appears, and so should you, because next time she simply *has* to win.

Epilogue

Gloria Steinem said in an interview with Christiane Amanpour in August 2011 that she believed Hillary was the "ideal candidate" but that it "was too soon." Clinton's conundrum manifested in the destiny of loss *and* the Hillary Effect, because as heartbreaking as her defeat was, Hillary's fate was she *had* to run to affect what happened next.

In January 2011, Tavis Smiley asked Secretary Clinton if she would serve as President Obama's secretary of state in a second term. "No, I really can't," was her reply, though she did go on to clarify her own bluntness stating, "the whole eight, I mean, that that would be very challenging...." Clinton doubled down in March 2011, when she gave a short and sweet "no" to every question CNN's Wolf Blitzer asked on being vice president, secretary of defense, serving another term as secretary of state, as well as whether she'd run for president again.

CLINTON: You know, I had a wonderful experience running, and I am very proud of the support I had and very grateful for the opportunity, but I'm going to be, you know, moving on.

BLITZER: I asked my viewers and followers on Twitter to send questions, and a lot of them said, "Ask her if she'll run in 2016 for the presidency." A lot of folks would like you to do that.

CLINTON: Well that's very kind, but I am doing what I want to do right now, and I have no intention or any idea even of running again. I'm going to do the best I can at this job for the next two years.

So, what's next for Hillary Rodham Clinton?

Some sleep and a long vacation, no doubt some writing as well, possibly including a follow-up to her *Living History*, the book she wrote while in the Senate, in preparation for her presidential run. The next book is likely to focus on her time as President Obama's secretary of state, even if many would also like to see her weigh in on the campaign brawl of 2008.

However, her most anticipated move is Hillary's international women's foundation, which if fully manifested will take her "human rights are women's rights" platform around the globe and beyond the constraints of American politics and domestic policy. It will jump over the barrier of funding to tap private reserves of the powerful that won't depend on government scrutiny or restraints. She's certainly got a template for it in her husband's Clinton Global Initiative, with the power Hillary Rodham Clinton has amassed formidable energy to unleash in countries struggling to stabilize, while the men in power marginalize their only hope for this to happen, the women.

Whatever she does, nobody I talked to believes Hillary's done changing the world. That's great news for the multitudes of supporters who still follow her every move.

For the longest time, no one would acknowledge or admit the sexism Hillary was subjected to during the 2008 primaries. By the end, the over-the-top sexist coverage she received was no longer in doubt. It had set her supporters on fire, with some leaving the Democratic Party forever because of it. But no one could say they didn't know how sexism was utilized against the first viable female candidate for president anymore, because they'd witnessed it. Winks and nods were tabled.

When Sarah Palin entered the scene on the coattails of the Hillary Effect, her babe factor up against John McCain's octogenarian frailty made her even more attractive. However, well beyond the insulting "idiot" calls from the haters or real policy differences from her Democratic detractors, Republicans began putting up a serious public front against her, because as good as her instincts were leading up to the 2010 midterms, the gravitas question hovers over her like a vulture, a preemptive strike required if she's ever going to run for office again.

Rep. Michele Bachmann doesn't have the Palin gravitas problem, or Sarah's cowering in the corner over the "lamestream" media, though she is "prone to gaffes and non-answer answers," as Mark McKinnon wrote in the Daily Beast, just like her Tea Party sister. From his Aril 7, 2011, post, "How Michele Bachmann Can Win": "Her 'positive intensity' among Republicans and right-leaning independents, as measured by Gallup, is higher than Palin's, even though her name-recognition is far lower. Though political pundits pounce on her every misspeak and mangled factoid, while being far more forgiving of the president's mispronunciations, and historical inaccuracies, she electrifies crowds and displays unnerving message discipline."

But that was before Rick Perry dropped in and blew Bachmann out of the race.

As of August 2011, the only place Rep. Bachmann showed strength is in her home state of Iowa, so the evidence points to her becoming a political player rather than a presidential nominee, but she's accomplished enough to remain a force.

There was a reason *Saturday Night Live* did a skit in February 2008 that eviscerated the pro-Obama media. It focused on CNN, asking Fred Armisen, playing Obama, if he was comfortable or needed another pillow. CNN's John King called it "a wake-up call." The network's political analyst Gloria Borger told a roomful of television critics in August 2008, "I think the skit on Saturday Night Live made us take a look at ourselves."

Not everyone felt the same as Ms. Borger, denial still running deep.

Phil Griffin, MSNBC president, charged that the Clinton campaign wanted to "rally a certain demographic, and women were behind it," as he was quoted in the *New York Times*, but the evidence proved it was a much bigger issue than a campaign tactic.

"Like her or not, one of the great lessons of that campaign is the continued — and accepted — role of sexism in American life, particularly in the media," CBS' Katie Couric told the *New York Times*.

Nicholas Lemann, dean of the Columbia University Graduate School of Journalism, didn't see the media learning a damn thing. From the *New York Times*, June 13, 2008:

"'I have not had a lot of regretful conversations with high-ranking media types and political reporters about how unfair their coverage of the Hillary Clinton campaign was.' Among journalists, he added, the coverage "'does not register as a mistake that must not be allowed to happen again.'"

In the same *Times* article, Howard Dean said plainly that "the media took a very sexist approach to Senator Clinton's campaign," which is undeniable. Hillary Rodham Clinton, Dean continued, "got treated the way a lot of women got treated their whole lives." Many women related to this, while the new generations did not.

The Hillary Effect manifest, people at least recognize it now. So when I talk about Ken Rudin, an editor at National Public Radio, who went on CNN to compare Clinton to Glenn Close in *Fatal Attraction*, what he's saying doesn't require an explanation anymore. Nor does Alex Castellanos' remark on CNN at the opening of the 2008 Democratic convention in Denver: "I think the specter of Hillary Clinton hangs over this convention like Glenn Close with a knife in *'Fatal Attraction.'*"

As for Tucker Carlson, his "When she comes on television, I involuntarily cross my legs" analysis and the Hillary nutcracker appliance fetish won't cut it next time.

At the end of it all, Keith Olbermann remained in denial like his former MSNBC boss Phil Griffin, saying there were "individual sexist, mistakes," but no overall sexism, according to a quote in the *New York Times*. Oh, the irony, because if you have enough individual sexist remarks — er... *mistakes,* which there most certainly were, you've got sexism.

People got away with this crap, because when no one wanted to admit sexism was running rampant and the only female in the race is the recipient, the silence acted as tacit approval to continue the pile-on or look the other way. If she takes it on herself, she's called a whiner.

The Hillary Effect proved that's no longer the case as Nikki Haley stood up against her attackers, as did Christine O'Donnell, as did a little-known Virginia candidate, the twenty-eight-year-old Krystal Ball, her response one of the best examples of the impact of the Hillary Effect. Provocative photos of Ball and her ex-husband appeared online; he played Rudolph to her sexy Mrs. Claus, complete with "his nose adorned with a Rudolph-red plastic penis," to quote NPR. It happened during her long shot 2010 midterm candidacy to unseat a Republican in a Virginia district the GOP had controlled for three decades. Ms. Ball made national news when she refused to sit by quietly during attacks. From the NPR story, October 2010:

> In recent days, Ball has relied on advice from Siobhan "Sam" Bennett of the Women's Campaign Forum, which in August, along with the groups Political Parity and the Women's Media Center, launched the "Name It, Change It" campaign. The effort is designed to target instances of

sexism against female candidates — whether in the media, or coming from political opponents.

MS. BALL: The first thing that my mother said to me when all of this happened was, "Isn't this what they always do to women?"

One of the campaign's mantras: Silence about sexism, perceived or otherwise, is no longer an option.

Amen, sister.

Gloria Steinem, in an unintentionally amusing analysis, deduced that the reduction of all the media and political men to little boys by such a powerful force as Hillary Rodham Clinton was just too much for them to handle.

"We associate female authority with childhood," Steinem told CBS' Katie Couric in a June 2010 interview. "We think it's appropriate to childhood and not to adult life and politics because we really haven't seen it that much. And some people, especially men as we saw during this last election, men on camera felt regressed when they saw Hillary Clinton, a powerful woman, because the last time they saw a powerful woman they were eight."

So, I wonder, does that make the men who fawn over Sarah Palin hostage to their smaller brain?

After the midterms, Chris Matthews gave a moving monologue on the working class, bemoaning the loss of real jobs "from Scranton to Oshkosh," part of what caused great leaders like Joe Sestak and others to lose, because Dems split the union vote with Republicans in the rust belt states. It reminded me why *Hardball* was once a must-see show, before Matthews was stricken with sexist outbursts, terminal Clinton derangement, and man-crushes. It was a beautiful homage to the working man and woman, an important coalition of voters that Obama and the Democrats lost in 2010.

"Why'd they lose? Because the American manufacturing heart has been cut out of this country. We used to build trains and subways and airplanes for the world. Now we read about trains running three hundred miles an hour in France and China, and we piddle along ourselves on Amtrak like we're on a buckboard....

"Why don't we build America anymore?" Matthews asked. "We need to build."

It's ironic that the very candidate who roused the working class in Pennsylvania was the candidate Chris Matthews did his most to deride and defeat, Hillary Rodham Clinton.

In mid-April 2011, David Brooks likely got President Obama's attention when he weighed in on vanity presidential candidate and birther king, Donald Trump, in "Why Trump Soars" for the *New York Times*: "He is riding something else," Brooks wrote, "the strongest and most subversive ideology in America today. Donald Trump is the living, walking personification of the Gospel of Success."

It's more about the gospel of greed. But it's that perceived "Gospel of Success" in the midst of economic insecurity and unemployment that Mitt Romney is also riding, damn the details of his vulture capitalism, but also his record on jobs in Massachusetts. Rick Perry hopes to do the same with his Texas jobs marketing, even if the truth is murkier and filled with low-wage jobs, an oil-rich state and more than a dozen military bases.

Hillary's line from her speech at the Democratic convention in 2008 still reverberates and encompasses what Brooks was writing about: "This is the story of America. Of women and men who defy the odds and never give up. How do we give this country back to them?"

The energy behind Occupy Wall Street, which sprang up in the early fall of 2011, is at the heart of this question.

But the second the Occupy Wall Street protests manifested, conservatives and Tea Party types immediately began disparaging what was happening on the ground in Manhattan. That's because they didn't get it. The Tea Party might have begun with some of this type of energy, represented best through Rep. Ron Paul's supporters, but as Jane Mayer reported in her August 2010 article for *The New Yorker*, "Covert Operations: The Billionaire Brothers Who Are Waging a War against Obama," David and Charles Koch were backing the Tea Party movement. So was Dick Armey's FreedomWorks organization, as well as Move America Forward, to name just a few of the entrenched Republican political power-brokers and corporate backers who make the Tea Party "movement" financially viable. The big-buck funding efforts resulted in mostly astroturf theatricalities, rather than a foundational, people's uprising that existed beyond political party lines.

In contrast, Occupy Wall Street is pure grass roots, with no political party ownership of it whatsoever. This is one reason it scares Republicans, but also Democrats.

What fueled Occupy Wall Street protests is the frustration and anger over the concentrated wealth in the United States. It's this top 1% ownership of America that finally inspired the "I am the 99%" chant of the people in downtown Manhattan. American voices were delivering a message that so resonated that on October 15, 2011, it broke out into a global event that went from New York City to Rome and Berlin, from Geneva, Amsterdam, Athens, Brussels, Paris, Zurich and beyond, to Tokyo, Manila, Taipei, Seoul, Hong Kong and cities of South Africa.

In America, there is no longer anywhere to go to be heard. Democrats and Republicans alike have been bought off by corporations, with senators, representatives and our presidents now spending the majority of their time fund-raising for reelection or for their party's apparatus. It's why independent Senator Bernie Sanders has become a folk hero; he's stood alone innumerable times against the moneyed interests. Unfortunately, politicians from both political parties today sell out their constituents regularly for the corporations that fund their campaigns. They rightfully fear that if they don't, the corporate interests and lobbying entities will jump sides and throw their millions behind the other guy. There's a reason most of the American public has no respect for Congress; the people's disdain has been well earned.

Former Senator Russ Feingold, founder of Progressives United, in an interview with Keith Olbermann on Current TV in October 2011, spoke eloquently about the problem: "The crimes against the working people in this country have mounted up and people have finally realized they have to actually deal with it. They can't just take it." But it's the specifics of why average people can't take what's going on that get to the heart of why Occupy Wall Street and the passion that is at its foundation could linger and even end up impacting the 2012 elections, perhaps even fueling an outside, independent candidacy to challenge the two-party American system.

It begins with the wealthiest Americans, and corporations, who have lived in a protected economic bubble for decades, going back to their primary patron, Ronald Reagan. The subsequent generations of entitled wealth were made possible by Republicans *and* Democrats. This was proven when President Obama extended the Bush tax cuts for the wealthy after the 2010 midterms, something he campaigned against.

The Occupy Wall Street protesters have now popped the bubble of the 1%, with average Americans in cities across the country joining the uprising, because they've lost either their jobs, their homes, both, or have seen their wages slide, while watching the rich get richer and richer, while corporations take jobs and their profits offshore. Students have joined in because, while they are loaded down with student loan debt, too-big-to-fail banks get bailed out.

Mr. Feingold pegs what's fueling the rage and frustration: "The complete domination of the political process by unlimited, secret contributions, the shipping of our jobs overseas, the lousy trade agreements while at the same time taking away the collective bargaining rights of the public employees unions. You know, it's finally reached a point where people are saying, that's it. We are tired of being ripped off."

However, the political tone deafness that helped start Occupy Wall Street continues. At the very moment when Occupy Wall Street protests raged, President Obama flip-flopped on his campaign pledges, sending "NAFTA-style job-killing trade bills," as Lori Wallach, director, Public Citizen's Global Trade Watch, called them in the Huffington Post, to Congress for passage. "A larger share of House Democrats voted against a Democratic president on trade than ever before," Wallach reported. But the "NAFTA-style job-killing trade bills" passed anyway, because of President Obama and the Republicans, with Democrats joining in.

That is the foundation of American disgust with both Democrats and Republicans. The question Hillary asked back in 2008 is at the heart of why anyone worth his or her salt makes a run at the presidency today: "How do we give this country back to them?"

Whoever figures the best way to market and sell their answer to this question wins the White House.

With only 37% of Americans approving of President Obama's stewardship of the economy, he's about to face the challenge of his life, with a *Wall Street Journal*/NBC poll after Labor Day 2011 showing a job approval at 44%, the lowest of his presidency, with a dueling *Washington Post*/ABC poll revealing 43% on job approval, with 53% disapproving, an all-time low record for President Obama.

So, yes, President Obama is beatable in 2012. However, as of November 2011, the latest right wing front-runner du jour was Herman Cain, a man facing multiple allegations of serial womanizing, making a mediocre Republican field look even worse, which was proven when Cain handed his frontrunner status over to Newt Gingrich in December. With the only candidate capable of giving President Obama a serious challenge, Mitt Romney, still unable to convince the right he's real.

The trends continue to reveal people have lost their loyalty to political party. This is another element for President Obama in 2012, because it wipes out the traditional lesser-of-two-evils reaction voters have had at the polls going back to at least the 1980s. More and more voters now see all establishment politicians as part of the problem.

Independents got what they wanted in the polls in November 2010, which wasn't sending a message that they wanted Republicans, but that they wanted anything other than what was going on at the time. I believe this feeling continues to grow among everyone interested in politics and solving this country's challenges. The two-party voter drone syndrome is slowly diminishing, with independents the most fickle component of American politics today.

The stark view of Hillary amid all the men on stage in primaries, but also in media events and interviews, showed the imbalance as it never had been seen before. Sexism in the work place we'd all heard about, even witnessed or experienced, but seeing it in action on our television set and through news reports and new-media stories was an education. Watching the talking-head honchos take out after a female running for president in ways we'd never seen a man experience was jolting.

American women liked seeing themselves represented on the national party tickets. Why shouldn't we? We're a majority of the voting public and without us our politics would be even sicker. But instead of political parties trying to find messages to inspire women to vote, they should find female candidates who represent and speak to our issues. It's a no-brainer.

After running a presidential campaign that Lois Romano in the *Washington Post* called "notoriously insular and unhappy, managing a group of egos and backstabbers whose dysfunction may have cost her the White House," many wondered what would be the reviews on Secretary Hillary Clinton as steward of the State Department. But her invigoration of the State Department could end up being her defining tribute, because State was left demoralized after Bush-Cheney. It's ironic that Hillary may succeed at State where she failed through her presidential campaign team. Reviews of Clinton at the State Department prove what she's learned, how she's stepped beyond the past and into the future and never looked back. From Lois Romano's March 2010 piece in the *Post*:

> She became a heroine to the Foreign Service when she went to bat to get funding for three thousand new Foreign Service positions for State operations and the U.S. Agency for International Development — the first boost of this magnitude in two decades.
>
> Jeffrey Feltman, assistant secretary for the Near East and a Foreign Service officer, is one of those whom Clinton surprised — and won over. He was already looking for a new job when she tracked him down at his barbershop twenty-four hours after she was sworn in to seek his advice. A few weeks later, she asked him to stay on.
>
> "We've heard it before: Yes, diplomacy matters. Yawn. Sounds great, but we tend to be cynical about such language in comparison to the actual resources devoted to DOD versus State," Feltman said. "She has tried to demonstrate that it's more than lip service by fighting for resources ... and listening to us."

But not even Secretary Clinton could change the Pentagon's money advantage, which over many years has squeezed the State Department dry.

Clinton's prowess on national security and diplomacy was seen most vividly when President Obama decided to launch attacks against Libya, with news reports out of the *New York Times*, which were quickly picked up, that it was Secretary Clinton, human rights expert and Obama confidante Samantha Power, and U.N. Ambassador Dr. Susan Rice, who guided Obama to act. No one is saying President Obama didn't make his own decision, but the emotional humanitarian policy the administration adopted is still regime-change, though by another name. But at the center of the decision-making were women, at the hub of a national security decision that in the U.S. is usually made only by men. That their answer was militarism is revealing and hardly inspiring when hoping women will govern differently than men.

During the protests in Egypt, Secretary Clinton was the first out front and ended up taking one for the team. "Our assessment is that the Egyptian government is stable and is looking for ways to respond to the legitimate needs and interests of the Egyptian people," she told reporters at a January 25, 2011 news conference.

Coming in the midst of Al Jazeera English's coverage that showed the opposite developing in a country that didn't allow challenges to the regime, Clinton's "stable" comment sounded tone-deaf, though it's always hard throwing a "war on terror" and rendition ally under the bus. So, I wasn't surprised to see her comment eventually picked up. The *Washington Post*'s Glenn Kessler highlighted it a week later.

> The history of the Egyptian uprising has not been written. But depending on how events turn out, *Clinton's "stable" statement may enter a diplomatic hall of infamy* that includes Jimmy Carter's Dec. 31, 1977 toast in Tehran in which he said that the Shah of Iran, then a key U.S. ally, was "an island of stability" in the troubled Middle East.
>
> — *Washington Post*, February 2, 2011; emphasis added

Eight days after Clinton's "stable" remark, she convened a meeting with most U.S. ambassadors present, where she addressed the shifting diplomatic reality she had witnessed on her watch, which first showed itself in the Green Revolution in Iran in 2009. During that uprising, State's official blog, Dipnote, never noted it was happening, driving me crazy and inspiring me to do a short series about it, ending with a post called, "While Dipnote Slept." Of course, State was following Obama administration policy.

Part of Secretary Clinton's learning curve had to do with the use of rapidly changing technology and its possible effects on the world stage. She showed she was up to the task when she interceded with Twitter, Inc., getting the company to shift the timing of a planned tech upgrade to 1:30 a.m. in Iran, so as not to interfere with the steady stream of information pouring out of the region in conflict.

At the time Clinton said, "I wouldn't know a Twitter from a tweeter." But clearly, she did now. Speaking to U.S. ambassadors in February 2011, after Egypt's uprising, as reported by Josh Rogin for *Foreign Policy*'s The Cable blog:

"'It goes without saying — but I will say it anyway — that this is a critical time for America's global leadership,' Clinton told the ambassadors. 'From the theft of confidential cables to twenty-first-century protest movements to development breakthroughs that have the potential to change millions of lives, we are all in uncharted territory, and that requires us to be more nimble, more innovative, and more accountable than ever before.'"

Secretary Clinton's job-approval ratings top President Obama's, and when he needed help with Benjamin Netanyahu, after a squabble erupted when more settlements were announced during a trip to Israel by Vice President Biden, it was Hillary who picked up the phone to give a widely reported forty-three-minute "tongue-lashing" to the Israeli prime minister.

President Obama has not only empowered his former adversary, they've made a formidable alliance, which along with former Secretary of Defense Robert Gates, enabled President Obama to risk everything to send SEAL Team Six in to Pakistan, leading to the killing of the most wanted terrorist in the world, Osama Bin Ladin.

The Hillary Effect makes it better for women in politics, but they still have it a lot tougher than men. They can't be afraid to smile, have fun and show their sex appeal, no matter their age, while running for office as a woman, not as a woman thinks a man should if he were a woman. Doing it her own way, while never allowing a man to fight harder or blame her for fighting dirtier, which can always be defused with a laugh and a shot like, "Well, if I'm being too tough on the poor guy...."

Women can win if we stand up, own our freedoms, responsibilities, choices and relationships, as well as our own job of running our lives and not expect men with experience to have our answers. We've never ruled the world before, so we won't be able to make the same mistakes as men and get away with it. But considering women are inherently more flexible, emotionally adept, humble, adaptable and resilient, there's no reason we can't run the show while utilizing what men have to offer, too.

Hillary Rodham Clinton paved the way, and her presidential candidacy ended the gender discussion while destroying sexism's power by taking the lengths people would go to take her down and exposing the tactics for what they were. It's up to women to let go of the fear of failing, take the risks, and ride our dreams, talent and intentions the rest of the way, because there is now a template on how to put down the gender issue if it arises; following the Hillary Effect reaction of Krystal Ball's aggressive offense, or Michele Bachmann, who ignored the media goading, and other women who take sexism on directly by confronting it honestly, openly and in their own way. Hillary's presidential candidacy forever destroyed the power of sexism in politics, because it can no longer be wielded without a backlash. That's the Hillary Effect.

It's not that people won't try to sling sexist smears and use double-standards against women. It helps that the new generation doesn't play that game; they don't play race games either. But there are too many people who saw what misogynistic sexism and piling-on look like for the first time. Hillary's candidacy showed them. We're better than that now, and next time we have to prove it.

So, when the words "Madam President" are finally uttered, she will have many women who came before to thank. None more so than Hillary Rodham Clinton, who worked for decades learning, raising a daughter, then serving her country, as well as presidents, while championing Democratic policies that benefit ordinary people and the middle class, but most of all women, wherever they reside in the world.

Hillary Rodham Clinton's "human rights are women's rights" started as an emphatic challenge to China, as well as the rest of the world. It has grown into a global mission to make women's lives and choices equal to those of men, no matter where they live. It's the chant she took into her presidential campaign in 2008, which began as nothing remarkable, but evolved into a fighting cry that ignited a nation and set into motion the final wave that will one day deliver a woman to the White House, though I'll be damned if I can tell you when.

The talk of Hillary beyond State has proved her longevity, as well as the newfound respect and popularity she's garnered since leaving the political arena. In May 2010, after Secretary Robert Gates announced he was leaving the Defense Department, it didn't take long for rumors to zoom around Washington that Hillary was allegedly on the short list to replace him. When I emailed a knowledgeable source inside Hillaryland, teasing, "When do I start calling her SecDef?" the response was short: "Um, never?"

At the height of the 2010 midterms, Bob Woodward was hawking his book *Obama Wars*, going on CNN October 6 to proclaim that Joe Biden and Hillary Clinton switching jobs for 2012 was "on the table," according to "some of Hillary Clinton's advisers." For all we know, that could mean a guard who *advises* people on how to follow map directions to get around State. The story exploded.

When Woodward belches in a book, the media runs with it.

The fact that President Obama's popularity had fallen, especially among working-class white voters and "waitress moms," helped stoke the story. The right ate it up, with Fox News having already commissioned a poll propping up the notion based on Hillary's popularity, 55% among voters, versus Biden's 25%, which among Democrats swung to 67% to 25%. Republicans would love to see any Democratic chaos for 2012, but Obama firing Biden for Hillary would be particularly sweet, however preposterous the notion.

Woodward let everyone run amok without talking about what he wrote specifically in his book, which came from a perfect source for scuttlebutt, none other than Mark Penn:

> Penn always had his eye on the prize — the White House. If she did the job for four years, Obama might be in trouble and have to dump Biden and pick her to run with

him as vice president. She had nearly beaten Obama and had won substantial margins in the primary among four important constituencies — women, Latinos, the working class and seniors — voting blocs Obama would need in 2012. Her addition to the ticket might be a necessity.

— *Obama's Wars*, Bob Woodward, 2010

The only job left *in politics* for Secretary Clinton to tackle is another run at the presidency.

On that subject, according to Woodward, back when President Obama was lobbying Hillary to become his secretary of state, Mark Penn's advice to her on the subject came through the prism of a future presidential run.

"In terms of 2016, Penn noted, if she served eight years at State, she could not be better positioned to run for president again," Woodward wrote. "She would be only 69 — the age Reagan had been when he took office. And statistically, women lived longer and generally stayed in better health during their later years."

No doubt Mr. Penn knows polling, but why Hillary would still be listening to him on political strategy is a mystery, though it does tease of long-term thinking about a possible future run her strongest supporters hope will manifest, even as she denies interest repeatedly in the press.

The question of what's next for Hillary includes whether she will run in 2016. Most think no, and no one can be sure, but I can tell you this: She's earned another shot. It would also be terrific to see a woman at age 69 competing for the toughest, most rigorous and prestigious job in the world.

"She told one interviewer that the United States 'should be' ready to have a woman as commander in chief," the AP reported in November 2010. "Yet, when asked if that could be her, she answered: 'Well not me, but it will be someone.' Asked by another interviewer if she would rule out a White House run in 2016 or before, she replied: 'Oh yes, yes.'"

But remember what James Carville said about the presidency: "Running for president is like sex. You don't do it once and forget about it."

Still, at the end of 2010, she speculated to CBS News' Political Hotsheet online that, "I think I will serve as secretary of state as my last public position." Clinton went on to say she'd like to "continue working to improve lives for others," with a focus on advocacy for women and children around the world. It was the first time she'd ruminated publicly about her life after being President Obama's top diplomat.

The reality that Hillary Clinton will not serve a second term and the likely possibility of a Hillary Clinton foundation for women and girls in no way changes how so many people now feel about her and the kind of president she would be, which this country still needs.

The only certainty for Hillary Rodham Clinton is that her secretary of state tenure is coming to a close and the world awaits what she chooses next, with Hillary having more fans and supporters today than she's had in her entire public career. She really can do anything she wants, though many still feel there's only one job Hillary is destined to hold.

In mid-August 2011, former Pennsylvania Gov. Ed Rendell told the *New York Post,* "It's going to be Hillary Clinton in 2016."

He then had a separate conversation with Politico, in which he said, "I think, and this is just my thinking, that if she leaves after the president's first term is over and she leaves and she teaches, does something like that, and rests, I think the possibility of being president and being the first woman president in history would probably be too much for her to resist. Her life is public service, that's all she cares about, and I don't think she's ready to retire."

Hillary's already made history and she's had a long, hard haul from the '08 primary season to President Obama's globetrotting secretary of state, so it's no wonder she's ready for a break. But I don't think anyone, including Hillary, can say for sure what she'll do once 2016 comes into view.

So, *if* by some serendipitous call, Hillary changes her mind about running for the presidency again in 2016, her supporters will come out in droves to help her, with many who didn't support her in '08 ready to stand by her side next time. And you can bet I'll be there to cover it. I wouldn't miss that party for the world.

Because if anyone knows the meaning of "never give in, never give up on your dreams, we're going to keep on going," it's me.

Acknowledgements

Every writer should be so blessed as to have a creative tour de force like Judith Proffer in her corner.

Thanks to Hugh Syme who took the cover and made it extraordinary.

...A nod to Spencer Proffer for all he does when someone wants to manifest magic.

I'm grateful to Premier Digital Publishing for knowing the story I was telling could be of interest to a lot of people.

Eric Estrin, my copy editor and fact checker, made a real difference, and I'm grateful to him for it.

Along the way, as I quietly researched and wrote, while continuing my daily political analysis on my site (www.taylormarsh.com), talented bloggers took over on the weekends, giving me some time, unbeknownst to them, to concentrate on excavating this political tale. Now maybe they'll know how important their contributions have been to me over the two years it took to get this book written and published. As for my readers, I'm forever indebted to them for sticking around in happy times and through rougher ones, but always coming back because they trusted the political analysis I offered. This book is because of them, too.

Lorie Miller, V.P. of Web Services at Agora Net, is the tech guru behind my new-media blog who makes it sing. It has been a never-ending retooling enterprise for her, and I'm extremely lucky to have Lorie's generous patience.

I've met a lot of people along my "Hillary Effect" journey and have communicated with even more, from insiders to regular voters — individuals who shared their stories that helped me get the full picture. The outpouring of information and passion that came my way over several years enlightened my efforts and kept me on the trail, reconfirming time and again just how important Hillary Rodham Clinton's presidential candidacy was to American politics and women's history.

As for my beloved sister Susie, who forgave my unintended sins that are too numerous to list, as well as my brother Larry, the only father I've ever known, they always supported the hell-bent nature of my artistic soul.